The Foundations of Justice

The Foundations of
Justice: WHY THE RETARDED AND THE REST OF US HAVE CLAIMS TO EQUALITY

Robert M. Veatch
Kennedy Institute of Ethics
Georgetown University

New York   Oxford
Oxford University Press
1986

Oxford University Press

Oxford NewYork Toronto
Delhi Bombay Calcutta Madras Karachi
Petaling Jaya Singapore Hong Kong Tokyo
Nairobi Dar es Salaam Cape Town
Melbourne Auckland

and associated companies in
Beirut Berlin Ibadan Nicosia

Published by Oxford University Press, Inc.,
200 Madison Avenue, New York, New York 10016

Oxford is a registered trademark of Oxford University Press

Library of Congress Cataloging-in-Publication Data
Veatch, Robert M.
The foundations of justice.
Includes index.
1. Mentally handicapped—Care and treatment
—Moral and ethical aspects. I. Title.
HV3004.V43 1986 362.3'8 86-12641
ISBN 0-19-504076-7 (alk. paper)

2 4 6 8 10 9 7 5 3 1

Printed in the United States of America
on acid-free paper

For
Eunice and Sargent Shriver
Whose passion for justice has meant so much for
the retarded and the rest of us.

Preface

Some members of our moral community are in the tragic position of having physical or mental handicaps that are both severe and uncorrectable. All of the world's resources would not be enough to make these persons normal, and although these resources could make their lives much better, those resources would never be enough to compensate for the burdens these individuals have borne.

There is wide variety of opinion and intuition about how much we ought to do in trying to improve the lot of the most burdened among us. Some people would favor devoting great amounts of our medical, economic, and intellectual resources to helping them, while others appear to feel no moral obligation toward them at all. They see those who have lost in the natural lottery of life as unfortunate, but do not conclude that anything need be done about it.

The issues raised by such cases of severe, uncorrectable handicap pose some of the most fundamental, most difficult questions a society can face. They require a basic exploration of what counts as a just or fair allocation of a society's resources and, beyond that, what the ground or foundation of a theory of justice is.

In *A Theory of Medical Ethics* I argued that the basic ethics of society can be conceptualized by the use of the metaphor of a social contract in which persons taking the moral point of view would be imagined to come together to either discover or invent the basic moral principles of the society. I suggested that both secular and more theologically inclined persons could come together around such a model, agreeing on some basic principles even if they could not agree on what the source of those principles was.

This left me with several problems, however, and they are posed most dramatically by the claims of the severely handicapped. While secular persons and the more religiously inclined can agree on many of the basic moral principles, when it comes to questions of a just distribution of resources the consensus seems to fall apart. Moreover, to some extent the division seems to follow the secular/religious split. Those within the major Western religious traditions who think they are discovering moral truths tend to support a more egalitarian theory of justice in which the least well off have special claims on the rest of the society. Those working in more strictly secular frameworks, on the other hand, seem to hold a wide range of views on the principle of justice, from the most egalitarian to the most libertarian.

We are left with a series of perplexing questions. Do the severely afflicted among us have any moral claims at all? Assuming they do, are these claims to be ''normal'' (or at least as normal as current science can provide)? Are there limits on such claims when the resources would do more good elsewhere? When other people ''own'' the resources? Are there at least limits when extraordinarily large resources will produce benefits that are very small? If there are such claims, where do they come from? From God? From the will of the community? From the individuals who control the resources? From some moral ''laws of nature''?

This volume is an exploration of these issues posed by the existence of persons within our society who have needs that are virtually infinite. It attempts to identify the basic premises of the egalitarian and non-egalitarian responses and to examine the ways religious and secular people ground those premises. In the end, the book reaches egalitarian conclusions, but it attempts to provide a way in which both religious and secular people may accept those conclusions. It also attempts to argue that there are realistic limits on what at first appear to be infinite demands generated by those with severe, uncorrectable handicap.

A large number of people have been of great help to me over the years that this manuscript has been in preparation. All of my faculty colleagues at the Kennedy Institute of Ethics have contributed by reading portions of the manuscript and offering provocative, enriching conversation. Warren Reich, in particular, has read and commented upon the entire text. My former Kennedy Institute colleague, H. Tristram Engelhardt, has, over the years, often been my adversary in debates over the egalitarian premises of a theory of justice. Stephen Mott of Gordon-Conwell Theological Seminary and Shannon Jordan of George Mason University have been extremely helpful, as have the two anonymous reviewers at Oxford University Press. Many people have helped in research and administrative assistance including Kathleen Buckley, Carol Colgan, Emilie Dolge, David DeGrazia, Caren Kieswetter, and Marcia Sichol as well as the professional staff at the Kennedy Institute of Ethics library. Finally, I want to express my appreciation to Eunice and Sargent Shriver and to the Joseph P. Kennedy Jr. Foundation for support, moral and intellectual as well as financial, for the writing of this volume.

Washington, D.C.   R.M.V.
January 1986

Contents

The Foundations of Justice

1

The Retarded and Our Problem of Equality

Eddie Conrad is a ten-year-old boy born with multiple deformities; his mental retardation is considered to have preceded birth. He has a hearing impairment probably related to chronic ear infection in early childhood, visual impairment possibly resulting from too high a concentration of oxygen administered at birth, and a speech impairment apparently inexplicable either in terms of his hearing or palate difficulties.

The immediate problem for his parents is that Eddie is to be transferred from a private to a public school and will be placed in a classroom for multi-handicapped children. In the private school, he had been receiving twenty minutes of speech therapy three times a week from the speech therapist and twice a week from a graduate intern. The therapist recommends that an intensive program be continued, and independent evaluations by the public school therapist indicate that such a rate of intensive therapy would be of benefit to the child—although both evaluators concur in the opinion that Eddie's speech will never be normal. The benefit to the child will be to improve articulation, which is now sufficiently clear that others can, with some effort, understand him. No one believes that the therapy will eradicate the problems, however.

The public school system in the county where Eddie lives provides one speech therapist whose decision as to which children she will see is based on (a) need and (b) the possibility of benefit from the service. The therapist has selected this child as one she will see, but she can schedule him for only one twenty-minute session per week.

3

The parents have obtained from the division of special education the following facts: there is only one speech therapist for the school system; there are no funds for hiring another; P.L. 94-142 assures that "all handicapped children have available to them . . . a free appropriate public education that emphasizes special education and related services designed to meet their unique needs. The term 'special education' includes classroom instruction, instruction in physical education, home instruction, and instruction in hospitals and institutions. 'Related services' includes corrective and other supportive services including speech pathology and audiology, psychological services, physical and occupational therapy, recreation, and medical and counseling services (for diagnostic and evaluation purposes").[1] Legal counsel has advised the family that grounds exist for filing suit against the school system.

The parents have also learned that because of funding difficulties the county school board has cut both art and music from the elementary school curriculum. If these cuts do not resolve the budget difficulties, the school board's next step will be to eliminate physical education in the elementary schools followed by elimination of art, music, and—as a last resort—physical education from the high school curriculum. The parents believe that they would win a case on behalf of their handicapped child. They also realize that winning the suit would result in the hiring of a second speech therapist, but would also entail the sacrifice of the physical education teacher for the elementary schools. Eddie's parents believe their primary obligation is to their child, yet they also feel they have an obligation to support art, music, and physical education in the elementary school curriculum.

The Moral Claims of the Retarded

The image of the tragic dilemma posed by Eddie Conrad's need for intensive speech therapy leaves one haunted by the fundamental moral problems raised for the parents, for the school officials, and, indirectly, for the rest of us. Our civil religion as well as our more traditional religions all acclaim the equality of human beings. "We hold these truths to be self-evident that all men are created equal," begins the original declaration of that civil religion. Thomas Jefferson, in his First Inaugural Address, stresses the theme of "equal rights, which equal laws must protect." And Abraham Lincoln returns to the original language, speaking of a nation "conceived in liberty and dedicated to the proposition that all men are created equal." Alexis de Tocqueville, in comparing the human taste for liberty and equality, insists that the distinguishing characteristic of democratic ages is not the emphasis on liberty. The "preponderant fact that marks those men in those periods," he says, "is the love of this equality."

But this love of equality is by no means limited to democratic ages; concern for equality, or at least justice, is a dominant theme in history. It is a vision shared by both the Greek and Judeo-Christian heritages that make up the roots of Western culture, whether in Aristotle's plea that equals must be treated equally or in the Judeo-Christian doctrine of creation leading to the affirmation that a loving act done "to the least of these thy brethren" equals one done to a god. Nothing cuts more quickly through the centuries of platitudes about all being created equal than Eddie Conrad standing before us in need of speech therapy and his parents realizing that demanding that therapy will deprive others of important elements of their education.

Despite its surface clarity, equality is a difficult term that means many things to many people. It is sometimes equated with the broader, even more confusing term, justice. In fact, sometimes it is held that justice means equality. Such a view is controversial and denied by many, but that view will be defended in this volume. A claim of justice for Eddie Conrad or for any one of the rest of us is first and foremost a claim for equality. To understand precisely what that means and why it is so will take some digging.

Aristotle makes clear that there are two totally different meanings of the term *justice*. One is very broad: "complete virtue or excellence."[2] Others have used the term equally broadly, meaning roughly "the right action" or the right course, all things considered. Still another broad use of the term is the traditional notion of justice as rectitude, as in Amos's pairing of justice (that rolls down like waters) with the synonymous righteousness (that is like an everflowing stream).

Aristotle contrasts that broad or complete justice with a narrower, more precise meaning of justice as fairness in distribution. This narrower or "partial justice," as Aristotle calls it, is what he analyzes in Book Five of the *Nichomachean Ethics* and what modern philosophers and policy analysts are concerned with when they debate theories of justice.

Justice as fairness in distribution is not always taken to imply equality. There is substantial agreement on a formal definition of justice (in this narrower sense) that equals are to be treated equally (and, as Aristotle points out, the corollary is that unequals are to be treated unequally). Aristotle takes it as obvious that this can be converted to the principle, "To each according to his deserts,"[3] although he concedes that not everyone agrees on the criterion of deserving. "Democrats say it is free birth, oligarchs that it is wealth or noble birth, and aristocrats that it is excellence." Others do not identify desert at all but need, effort, usefulness, ability, or some other characteristic thought to be morally relevant to know how goods are fairly distributed.

Even among those who emphasize equality, there is no consensus on what that might mean. The case of Eddie Conrad makes clear to us that equal distribution of resources (health and educational resources, let us say) would surely make outcomes very unequal. On the other hand, striving for equality of outcomes may produce very strange results as well. If we wanted to make people equally happy, we would be forced to distribute goods in a way biased in favor of those who have expensive tastes or who are simply hard to please. Thus, asking what is fair for one youngster who has suffered more than his share of handicaps and who could benefit from an intense concentration of resources may force us to be more specific about what it means to be fair or just or equal. What is striking about the debate over justice in contemporary society is the lack of willingness to reach all the way back to fundamental principles— not only to examine the alternative claims for the retarded and otherwise disadvantaged and to cite the surface reasons given for or against such claims, but to reach as far back as possible to the most basic premises of moral discourse about the equality of human beings, the notions of personal private possessions, and the nature of the moral community.

Cases like that of Eddie Conrad press us to the limits of possible claims about what is fair. One group in our society may be so crass as to suggest that the retarded, perhaps just because of their retardation, have no claim at all. The retarded one's fate, according to this view, is surely unfortunate. From this point of view there exists bad luck to which there is no direct social obligation to respond. On the other hand, virtually all of us do respond, or at least we feel we ought to respond, to need where it exists. Even if, as is certainly not the case here, an individual through carelessness or foolishness gets himself into trouble requiring someone or some institution to rescue him, most people feel compelled at least to extend a hand.

In this case, however, something more than a hand is called for; it will require individual tutoring by a professional with highly specialized skills. Everyone involved in the case acknowledges that therapy will help. It will not make Eddie a statistically average child, whatever that term may mean, but it will help. Twenty minutes of private therapy a week is offered, but why that amount? Why should the school system decide it can afford that much rather than ten minutes or the hour and forty minutes a week available in the private school? If, as may well be the case, after twenty or thirty *hours* of individualized therapy a week more would still be marginally beneficial, why should not a boy who has suffered so much deficit obviously through no fault of his own be entitled to that therapy?

The retarded and others with handicaps press us to deal with these fundamental questions. Do they have any claim at all upon us? Assuming that they do, what is the basis of that claim? Where, ultimately, does it come from? If in some sense equality will be an essential element in understanding the claim of the retarded, what does equality mean morally? Again assuming that the retarded do have a claim and that it is related to some idea of equality, are there any limits on the claims made against society to provide equality or as close to it as we can get for Eddie Conrad and others similarly situated? If the goal has to do with equality for everyone and some members of our moral community are so desperately handicapped that equality of outcome may be an impossibility, will our concern for them generate impossible demands eventually leading to either social or moral collapse? And, finally, still assuming that the retarded have some rigorous claim on the rest of us and that that claim has something to do with moral community, what is the nature of the special obligations faced by certain members of that community who occupy special roles? Is it fair, for example, to ask Eddie Conrad's parents to meet their moral obligation to serve the interests of their child and to expect them simultaneously to wrestle with the problem of fairness to other children who could benefit from physical education? Do people in special roles have special commitments—the speech therapist in Eddie Conrad's case, or health care professionals more generally—so that they may respond to the demands of justice in a manner different from those who fill no such special roles?

Before we can have any insight into how parents or care-giving professionals in such situations might respond appropriately and how the rest of us in society ought to respond, a great deal of work is ahead of us. It is my hope and conviction, however, that one boy's plight and the anguish of his parents might shed some light on what it means to treat people fairly.

Equality and the Rest of Us

This, then, is a book about the claims of the retarded and others suffering serious handicaps. It is an exploration of what it means to treat them fairly. Its fundamental premise is that the handicapped will never be treated justly until there is frank and open discussion, and finally understanding, of the basis of their claims and our response.

But it is really more than that. We are all, in some sense, handicapped. Given the richness of human pursuits, the value we place not only on mental ability but physical skill, beauty, artistic talent, psychological stability, graciousness, warmth, capacity to love, and spiritual wholeness, who among us can say, "I am without handicap"? Unless we understand the moral foundations of the claims of the retarded, none of us can feel confident that we will be treated fairly in areas where we are inevitably deficient.

I have chosen the case of a young boy with mental and physical handicaps as a way of pressing a question of crucial relevance to all of us. The problem of the claim of the retarded is a specific example, a "pure case," of the question of whether members of a moral community ought to be treated as equals. This study might have been conducted by exploring the claims of the alcoholic, the lung cancer victim, or of the adult suffering from mental illness. These cases are, it turns out, more complicated, however. All of them raise the problem of whether the disadvantaged individual might in some way have been at least partially responsible for his or her condition. Whether that is so raises complicated medical, psychological, sociological, and moral questions. We shall eventually have to confront those questions when we try to understand what it means to treat people equally. That will come late in the analysis. The problem of how to treat fairly those who may be partially responsible for their disadvantaged positions is appropriately viewed as a footnote to the fundamental moral principle that justice means treating people equally. We will face that footnote in due course, but the major theme must be justice as equality.

By exploring the claim of the retarded we shall really be exploring our own status as human, moral agents, our own rights and obligations as members of the moral community. If all of us in the end are finite, human creatures sadly deficient in some way, mentally, physically, socially, or spiritually, then the problem of the claim of equality for the retarded is really a problem for all members of the human community. Unless we understand the moral foundations of the claims of the retarded, then, neither the retarded nor the rest of us will be treated fairly.

Pluralism and the Problem of Ethical Method

The project before us is one of seeing whether we can make sense of the claim that justice as fairness in distribution requires that people be treated equally. Defense of that interpretation of the principle of justice, explication of a common meaning for it, and the application of it to the retarded and others with handicaps may seem like an impossibility in a world as overwhelmed with pluralism as the contemporary, secular, liberal, individualistic West. Beliefs about what is fair or just, let alone who counts as a member of the moral community, are widely divergent. Religious and secular communities divide not only between each other, but also within their own ranks; it may seem utopian to hope for establishment of some commonly agreed-upon interpretation of the principle of justice or any other fundamental principle of ethics.

We should probably admit from the beginning that if we are searching for irrefutable proofs that all of the human moral community must be treated equally, we will probably be disappointed. Were there such proofs or refutations of them, they probably would have been articulated long ago. To use the metaphor of the courtroom, we will have to be satisfied with something less than clear and convincing evidence, perhaps evidence that reasonable people should find convincing beyond a reasonable doubt.

In *A Theory of Medical Ethics* I dealt at length with the problem of an ethical method that would bridge the seemingly unbridgeable gulf between secular and religious ethics.[4] I argued that a contractual or convenantal ethic was common to both traditions and, although secular and religious thinkers might have different assumptions underlying their particular notions of contract or covenant, they would in the end arrive at the same substantive normative ethic.

Secular social contract thinkers would determine what the fundamental principles of ethics ought to be by asking what people actually agree to or, more appropriately, what they would agree to if they made certain assumptions and had certain relevant characteristics. Among the characteristics most often insisted upon are a willingness to respect the liberty of others[5] and to take "the moral point of view," that is, to let the welfare of others count equally to one's own or to pretend one is blind as to what position one will occupy in the social system (which amounts to the same thing as counting the welfare of others as equal to one's own).[6] John Rawls is often viewed as the dominant example of this kind of secular, hypothetical contractarianism. Its historical roots are in John Locke[7], Thomas Hobbes[8], Rousseau[9], and, to a lesser extent, the Kantian tradition. Under such a theoretical model, a principle such as utility or justice is a right-making characteristic of actions if the contractors did or would agree to it.

Such contractors are sometimes seen as "inventing" morality. Those who hold that an actual social contract at some point in history is the source of morality normally see humans as generating or creating moral obligations where none previously existed. By contrast, religiously grounded ethicists have sometimes seen human moral obligation rooted in covenant, the original covenant between Yahweh and his people and subsequent covenants that spell out religious and ethical duties. Ethical principles are, according to the religious version of covenant ethics, no more the invention of humans than the law of gravity.

Although these two perspectives may seem far apart, it is critical that covenanting and contracting are essential to both. In fact, secular notions of social contract in modern society surely have historical links to religious notions of covenant and, in turn, ancient Hebrew notions of covenant are widely believed to have historical links to the suzerainty treaties binding powerful political leaders to vassal states in the Ancient Near East.[10]

What is more immediately relevant to the problem at hand is how those committed to a religious view of the world go about determining the specific response to modern problems (such as how much ought to be spent on speech therapy for a child with multiple handicaps) and how they might put into modern language the moral principles underlying the vision of preexisting moral order. Protestants and, increasingly in the post-Vatican II era, Catholics as well reject the idea that there is any one individual with authoritative knowledge of what is morally required. The theory that posits esoteric, mysterious knowledge of a Logos transmitted to individuals with special powers to know the Word and receive mystically transmitted spiritual truths is playing less and less of a role in religious ethics. Moreover, there is increasing reluctance to accept the idea that certain individuals possess priestly wisdom that must be accepted by others on the authority of the priestly one.

Instead, we are turning to more communitarian methods for discerning ethical wisdom. Members of the community gather together, try to equip themselves with the relevant knowledge, adopt an attitude of compassionate empathy for the feelings of others, and attempt to come to some agreement about what the basic principles of ethics are and even what is required in specific situations. That agreement, when combined with a pledge to abide by the agreement, is functionally the equivalent of a covenant or contract. Members of the community come to an understanding of what they *discover* to be the moral law. They pledge one to another to live by the moral principles they discover. The contract is an epistemological device for discovering the moral order and articulating what has been discovered.

The process and the result may be strikingly similar to those obtained by secular social contractarians who envision people coming together to invent a moral order. That should not be surprising. Those who think contractors might invent a set of ethical principles *de novo* could reasonably expect that the more religiously inclined, fooled into thinking that they are gathering to discern a preexisting order, would in fact invent one to their liking, based on their innate beliefs, values, and preferences.

On the other hand, from the point of view of those convenanting together to describe what they take to be a preexisting moral order, it would be perfectly understandable that those who mistakenly think they are inventing a moral order would, because of beliefs, values, preferences, and moral laws inherent in the universe, in fact come close to "inventing" the moral order that actually exists.

As long as both groups draw on their knowledge of the world and the beliefs, values, and preferences existing in it, and view with empathy all involved, one would expect the two groups to end up espousing similar positions—which, in fact, they do. This conclusion is not particularly radical. It merely reflects the long-standing epistemological conviction that what is known about morality through revelation to those within the Church is also known to the secular world through reason. To be sure (and both religious and secular contractors agree on this), the human being is a finite animal so that knowledge will not be perfect either through revelation or reason. It is human fallibility that requires the contract method in the first place. But, at least in general terms, secular contractors who come together to try to invent a morality are likely to come up with the same answers as religious contractors (or covenantors, if you like) who come together to try to discover the preexisting moral order. The latter group has additional sources of knowledge: the Bible, tradition, and perhaps mystical knowledge as well, but the two groups ought to find the same thing, whether one believes that they are really inventing or discovering.

Justice and the Problems for Contract Ethics

In developing the contract method as a bridge between secular and religious ethics—as a way to have common discourse about the principles of ethics—I have generally been comfortable with the conclusion that both the inventors and the discoverers would, if they used contract theory, come up with the same ethical principles. Empirically, a good case can be made that that is in fact what happens. Among secular philosophers, those believing they invent the ethical principles agree rather closely with those who think they are discovering them. If there is a controversy over some principle, over major schools of normative ethics (say between teleological and deontological systems), or over a specific ethical problem such as slavery, or the rights of women, or abortion, it is certain the conflict will divide both those taking the "inventing" perspective and those taking the "discovering" one. The religious account of the foundations of a particular position may be quite different from the secular one, but the normative positions have, for the most part, been replicated in both perspectives.

In *A Theory of Medical Ethics* I concluded that reasonable people would agree to the principles of beneficence, autonomy, promise keeping, truth telling, and even the avoiding of killing whether they were working from secular or religious contractarian frameworks. When the principle of justice was considered, however, the problem became somewhat more difficult. It is clear that there is little agreement today, especially in the secular world, over what the content of the principle of justice would be. Religious ethicists working on problems of justice either at the most abstract level or, as is more often the case, at the level of applied ethics, tend to emphasize some version of an ethic of justice based on need, striving toward greater equality of outcome. Secular ethicists, on the other hand, seem to range from egalitarian to extremely inegalitarian interpretations. More important for our purposes, there may be a reason closely related to the difference between secular and religious thinkers to account for this pattern. Religious thinkers, at least in the major religious traditions of the modern West, all share a belief in an infinite God who transcends finite human beings. In comparison with an infinite, all finites are equal in their finitude as well as in their relationship with a Creator. If this is part of the basis of the religious belief in justice as equality, then clearly secular thinkers would not have access to the same insight. The religious thinker can solve the problem of why Eddie Conrad should be treated equally with other humans by saying, in effect, all are equal in the eyes of God. If the secular thinker arrives at that conclusion, he or she will have to arrive by some other path.

Diverging Secular Interpretations of Justice

In fact, secular thinkers who have struggled with the problem of justice hold very diverse views. If asked what contractors would agree to as a fair distribution of resources, say between the retarded and other students in a school system, they seem to offer every imaginable answer that might have happened regarding the other basic principles: beneficence, promise keeping, autonomy, and truth telling, but in practice it really has not, at least at the level of basic principle. Even on the more controversial ethical issue of whether life is sacred—whether humans may purposefully be killed for good reason (such as self-defense or mercy)—there is relatively little disagreement among secular thinkers and even between secular and religious thinkers. The question of the principle of justice, however, is another matter.

First, some secular thinkers, recognizing the impossibility of proving beyond a shadow of a doubt the superiority of one formulation over any other of what it means to be just, simply abandon the project. They analyze, catalogue the possible positions, show the implications, strengths, and weaknesses of each position, and then leave it to their readers to choose among the alternatives.[11]

The bolder among them trumpet a cacophony of positions. Libertarians argue, without foundation or justification, that people are entitled to what they possess provided it was appropriated justly from goods not previously possessed, or by just transfer through gift or exchange.[12] Utilitarians argue that the principle of justice is nothing more than a summary of the empirical fact that the usual way to maximize the good in aggregate is to distribute resources more equally so that, because of decreasing marginal utility, more good can be produced with the resources.[13] Marxists say "to each according to his need," though their reason for saying this is unclear.[14]

Secular contract theorists have argued, at one time or another, that reasonable people gathered to articulate a social compact would choose any of these arrangements. Cunningham, for example, has claimed that the reasonable person would opt for the utilitarian distribution scheme.[15] Nozick, for the libertarian scheme. John Rawls, probably the most sophisticated of the contributors to this genre, has claimed, again without any clear justification, that reasonable people would opt for none of those distributional principles, but for one that first distributes liberty equally to all and then one that distributes social goods such as income and wealth according to the "difference principle," a principle whereby inequalities are justified only when they provide benefit to the least advantaged.[16]

Egalitarians have claimed that even Rawls sacrifices equality too much, that he would permit wide-ranging disparities provided only that they benefit the least well-off groups.[17]

Brian Barry, in *The Liberal Theory of Justice,* reverting to the analytical mode of the philosophers, argues quite persuasively that at least on the basis of secular rational argument, it is not clear why people in Rawls's original position or some other contractarian posture would necessarily opt for any one of these interpretations of the principle of justice.[18]

At this point one seems forced back to the despair of liberal pluralism. Many options are available; no good reason is forthcoming to choose any one of them beyond the mere personal whim or preference of the individual. On that basis, groups of like-minded individuals should band together and create their societal islands, one full of libertarians where the misfortune of retardation is never to be confused with the unfairness of appropriating some fortunate soul's goods in order to help the unfortunate ones; the next where the distribution of benefits and harms counts for nothing except insofar as it contributes to the greatest good for the greatest number; still another where social institutions are structured so that there are only inequalities in institutions and practices when they redound to the benefit of the least well off (meaning enormous wealth can be concentrated in the hands of the elite provided the benefits trickle down to the masses); and, finally, another that strives for greater equality even at the expense of liberty, aggregate utility, maybe, even at the expense of improving the lot of the least well off.

The Project

There are good reasons not to retreat to that kind of radical pluralism. The project for this volume is to attempt to find out why those who have struggled with the question of what justice means have arrived at their conclusions. The question is virtually never approached by religious or by secular thinkers. One author starts his monumental and influential treatise by positing individual rights: ''Individuals have rights, and there are things no person or group may do to them (without violating their rights).''[19] From that he derives a theory of private property that justifies withholding needed resources from the retarded and others. On the other side, one of the most profound philosophers ever to have addressed the subject rests analysis of equality on the claim that equality is ''popular'' and worth defining more carefully even though it is not to be defended against critics advocating other positions.[20]

While we are all in debt to these authors who have made enormous contributions to our understanding of what justice might mean, this volume is written on the premise that we must go further. It is worth trying to find the fundamental premises that lead us to make the claims for justice that are being made.

It is crucial to examine the premises of both the religious and secular thinkers to see if we can identify what leads one author to posit equality as an obvious starting point for a morality of just distribution of resources and another to assume that private property or some other fundamental commitment requires us to separate the misfortune of the retarded one from any claim he or she might have on the rest of us for resources needed to become more equal.

It seems more and more clear that the key to understanding the fundamentals of the principles of justice is to be found in the long tradition of Jewish and Christian religious thought that so permeates both explicitly religious and presumably secular thought of modern persons. We must, therefore, in the next chapter examine some of the major elements in the Judeo-Christian tradition that so strongly emphasizes equality as a moral foundation for justice. The mission will be not only to review the history of that tradition, but to identify its basic premises (what I shall later call "faith moves") in order to justify the moral core of that tradition.

The following chapter is more systematic in summarizing what can be found. I shall attempt to show that there are three premises upon which the Judeo-Christian understanding of justice rests, premises that are at once part of the main core of Judeo-Christian theology and beliefs that have by now penetrated far beyond explicit religious belief systems. First, God is absolute, the ultimate center of value in comparison to which all humans are equal in their finitude. Second, the earth and all that is in it was created and given as a gift to the community such that there never was a time when there were unowned resources in the state of nature waiting to be appropriated by anyone clever, ambitious, or powerful enough to take them. Then, finally, because the resources of the world are in some critical sense a common possession of the community and because all are bound together as equals in that community, people individually and collectively bear within limits a responsibility to see that those resources are used to recreate or maintain the equality that is the appropriate relation among humans.

Once that core of underlying premises is identified, I shall move to secular philosophical thought in Chapter 4 to see if the premises underlying its interpretations of the principle of justice can be identified. The critical element of this chapter will be the argument that secular thinkers who deal with the problem of justice must also take a stand on precisely the same fundamental questions that have been addressed by the more theologically inclined. They must, if you like, make faith moves, just the way the religious person does. In some cases they will move in the opposite direction, denying the premises of the religious tradition and affirming their opposites. In other cases they will accept "on faith" precisely the premises of the theological tradition, in effect disguising their theology in secular garb. The critical element of this analysis will be the argument that whichever way the secular thinker moves, he or she must make a commitment on these key premises; he or she must make faith statements. There may well be no logically compelling reason why one set of faith moves ought to be made rather than another—that we will concede. But some faith move becomes necessary. It is necessary because we must move on to take a stand on critical questions: what it means to be just or fair, what our public policies ought to be regarding the rights of the retarded, the physically handicapped, and other oppressed and less well-off groups of our society. Moreover, we will discover that the choice of basic premises, though not *logically* compelling, is nevertheless not arbitrary. Scientists can finally not avoid taking a particular stand on fundamental premises—on the existence of an external reality and a belief in the laws of causation, for example. We will find, too, that those engaged in debate over ethics and public policy—whether working from religious or secular versions of the basic premises—will be forced to a particular set of conclusions upon which their views of justice must be based.

Once the relationship between secular and religious foundations for the principle of justice has been explored, I will turn to the more practical, applied, public policy implications. Chapter 5 explores precisely what the basic premises—the faith moves—mean for the notion of equality. Is the goal to provide equality of opportunity or actual equality of outcome? What adjustments, if any, must be made for the fact that some people will surely choose freely not to take advantage of their opportunities for equality? Is equality of welfare the objective or equality of resource commitment? If resource commitment equality is the goal, is adjustment to be made for the fact that some of us start off very unequal in mental or physical ability? Is the objective of the principle of equality to produce equality at any one time or does each individual have a claim of equality considered over a lifetime? And, finally, is overall equality among lives the goal or must we go beyond that to have equality in each area of our lives, in education, health care, standard of living, and the like?

Chapter 6 begins with an exploration of the implications of the policy of equality, first for the retarded, and then for the rest of us who, I have argued, are essentially in the same position as finite, human beings handicapped in one way or another. That chapter will conclude with an examination of the special problem suggested by the unique role of Eddie Conrad's parents. The question will be what special duties exist for those in special roles as parents, educators, health professionals, and so forth.

With this background before us we turn to the question of stigma.

One of the most profound moral problems with a theory of justice as
equality is that social redistributions based on need may well have a
tendency to stigmatize those who receive them. This last chapter asks
the question "Is it possible to give special priority for resources to the
retarded and the rest of us who are physically, socially, and culturally
imperfect without stigmatizing?" Before we can address these practical
public policy question, however, we first have to see if we can identify
the foundations of the principle of justice as it has emerged throughout
our religious and secular history.

Notes

1. U.S., *Statutes at Large,* Vol. 89, 94th Congress, 1st session, 1975, 773–96.

2. Aristotle, *Nichomachean Ethics,* trans. Martin Ostwald (Indianapolis: Library of
Liberal Arts, subsidiary of Bobbs-Merrill Co., Inc., 1962), Book V, Chap. 1, p. 114.

3. *Ibid.,* Book V, Chap. 3, p. 118.

4. Robert M. Veatch, *A Theory of Medical Ethics* (New York: Basic Books, 1981).

5. Robert Nozick, *Anarchy, State and Utopia* (New York: Basic Books, 1974), pp.
150–153.

6. Kurt Baier, *The Moral Point of View: A Rational Basis of Ethics* (New York:
Random House, 1965); John Rawls, *A Theory of Justice* (Cambridge, Mass.: Harvard
University Press, 1971).

7. John Locke, *The Second Treatise of Government,* edited, with an introduction by
Thomas P. Peardon (New York: The Liberal Arts Press, 1952 [1690]).

8. Thomas Hobbes, *Leviathan* (New York: E.P. Dutton, 1953 [1651]).

9. Jean Jaques Rousseau, *The Social Contract* (London: Everyman's Library, 1947
[1762]).

10. George E. Mendenhall, "Law and Covenant in Israel and the Ancient Near
East," *The Biblical Archaeologist* 17 (May 1954): 26–46, and (September 1954): 49–76.

11. Allen Buchanan, "Justice: A Philosophical Review," in *Justice and Health
Care,* ed. Earl E. Shelp (Dordrecht, Holland: D. Reidel Publishing Co., 1981), pp. 3–21.

12. Robert Nozick, *Anarchy,* pp. 150–53. H. Tristram Engelhardt, Jr., "Health Care
Allocations: A Response to the Unjust, the Unfortunate, and the Undesirable," in *Justice
and Health Care,* pp. 121–37.

13. John Stuart Mill, *Utilitarianism.* 1863, ed. Oskar Priest (New York: Bobbs-
Merrill, 1957), Chap. 5.

14. Karl Marx, *Critique of the Goltha Programme* (New York: International
Publishers, 1966), p. 10.

15. Robert L. Cunninghan, "Justice: Efficiency or Fairness?" *Personalist* 52 (1971):
423–82.

16. John Rawls, *Theory,* p. 302.

17. Robert M. Veatch, *A Theory,* p. 263; Robert Paul Wolff, "A Refutation of
Rawls' Theorem on Justice," *Journal of Philosophy* 63 (1966): 179–90; Norman

Daniels, "Equal Liberty and Unequal Worth of Liberty," in *Reading Rawls: Critical Studies of "A Theory of Justice,"* ed., Norman Daniels (New York: Basic Books, Inc., 1975), pp. 253–81, esp. p. 254; Christopher Ake, "Justice as Equality," *Philosophy and Public Affairs* 5 (Fall 1975): 69–89, esp. pp. 76–77.

18. Brian Barry, *The Liberal Theory of Justice: A Critical Examination of the Principal Doctrines in "A Theory of Justice" by John Rawls* (Oxford: Clarendon Press, 1973), p. 109.

19. Robert Nozick, *Anarchy,* p. ix.

20. Ronald Dworkin, "What is Equality? Part I: Equality of Welfare," *Philosophy and Public Affairs* 10 (Summer 1981): 185, and "What is Equality? Part II: Equality of Resources," *Philosophy and Public Affairs* 10 (Fall 1981): 283.

2

The Religious Basis for Equality: Its History

The problem of why a retarded adolescent has a claim on the community forces us to consider a much more basic question: why does anyone in need, disadvantaged through physical or mental handicap, have a claim? It is really the question of why any of us has a right to expect fair treatment from fellow members of the moral community. Thus what starts as a very specific, narrow problem turns quickly to a quest for the premises that justify a moral stance that says justice means treating people fairly. As a way of gaining insight into these basic premises, this chapter will examine the history of Judeo-Christian thought, a tradition that without doubt has contributed heavily to our contemporary political philosophy. Looking for attitudes toward the mentally retarded, however, will not take us very far; on this the tradition is relatively silent. More important, as an approach to the problem, it misses the point. What is critical is a more general attitude toward the disadvantaged and the kinds of claims they might have against the rest of the community. After seeing what has happened in the religious traditions, then we shift our attention to the more secular understandings of justice to see what the basic premises are of modern secular political philosophy.

Biblical Roots of Equality

The Judeo-Christian tradition can only be comprehended as the history of a people who understand themselves as a once-oppressed group of slaves who were rescued by their god, bound together as a community with common loyalty and obligations, and given a place in history. In exchange, they were forever to see themselves as a people linked in covenant with a radically transcendent power, the source of all that is.

In the context of that self-conception, it will take some work to discern the attitude toward the retarded or any other handicapped group. The Bible, as the written record of the history of Yahweh's relation with this people, says virtually nothing about the retarded.

Although several commentators maintain otherwise,[1] a close scrutiny of Biblical writings uncovers only passages related to the poor and needy, the blind, and the lame. While all these disadvantages represent losses, they fail to illustrate the handicaps specific to the retarded.

The absence of a specific moral stance toward the mentally handicapped in the Biblical history should not necessarily be taken as the end of the matter. In the light of widely expressed attitudes in many cultures about children thought to be defective, the very silence is significant. In contrast to Biblical writers, the Greeks were more obvious in expressing their dissatisfaction with those they considered defective. In Plato's *Republic,* strong and healthy offspring were to be well cared for so as to ensure the future flourishing of the ideal city. On the other hand, those children born inferior or defective would be "put away as is proper in some mysterious, unknown place."[2] There is evidence to indicate that in Rome, the Tiber River was the "mysterious place" which served as repository for defective infants.[3] Such attitudes are not surprising when viewed within the context of a culture in which even the infanticide of mentally healthy infants was condoned as an acceptable means of population control.[4]

The real argument for a more positive attitude toward the handicapped, however, should not rest primarily on the relative silence of the Judeo-Christian tradition on the specific issue. For one thing, the language and categories used today did not exist then. A medico-genetic understanding of mental handicap could emerge only in a much later period. For better or worse, the retarded as a group did not exist then as they do today.

The key to understanding how the tradition might approach the problem has to be gleaned from the much more general attitude about the oppressed, the needy, the sick, and the poor. At this level the Judeo-Christian tradition is unequivocal.

The Old Testament Period

Again and again, the Biblical authors tell the story of an oppressed people brought out of bondage and given a chosen status in return for which they were forever bound by the laws of a covenant with their god. A dominant theme of that story and the law to which it refers is the obligation to those in need. As the Israelites were once in need and had their needs met, so they also must respond to need as it exists within their community. Moses, stating the law as recorded by the Deuteronomic historian, says it repeatedly:

> You shall not pervert the justice due to the sojourner or to the fatherless, or take the widow's garment in pledge [for a loan]; but you shall remember that you were a slave in Egypt and the Lord your God redeemed you from there.[5]

It is striking that the Hebrew scriptures see Yahweh as identified with the poor and needy in almost every type of text—in all the strands of the early historical accounts of the Torah, to the later lyrical literature of the Psalms and Proverbs, as well, of course, as in the prophets from Amos[6] dating from the eighth century through to Ezekiel in the sixth[7] and on to Third Isaiah after the rebuilding of the temple in the fifth century, in which it is claimed that the Lord anointed Isaiah:

> to bring good tidings to the afflicted;
> he has sent me to bind up the brokenhearted,
> to proclaim liberty to the captives,
> and the opening of the prison to those who are bound.[8]

Ronald Sider, a professor of theology at Eastern Baptist Theological Seminary, set out to collect Biblical passages dealing with the themes of justice, hunger, and poverty, and amassed over two hundred pages of them drawn from forty-nine of the Bible's sixty-six books.[9] In the Old Testament twenty-eight of the thirty-nine books are represented, with only such obscurities as Nahum and Haggai missing.[10] The resulting impact is an overpowering cry for identification with the poor and needy that can be overlooked only by those whose cultural biases turn their heads in other directions.

Some of the most powerful and beautiful testimonies to this passion for justice for the needy occur in the Psalms. The 72nd Psalm, apparently singing the praises of Solomon,[11] portrays him as compassionate friend of those in need:

> For he delivers the needy when he calls,
> the poor and him who has no helper.
> He has pity on the weak and the needy,
> and saves the lives of the needy.
> From oppression and violence he redeems their life;
> and precious is their blood in his sight.[12]

THE SABBATICAL AND JUBILEE YEARS

The texts showing Israel's belief that Yahweh identified with the poor are too numerous to cite. However, a pair of remarkable institutions, the Sabbatical Year and the Year of the Jubilee, deserve special mention. The Sabbatical Year occurs every seven years. It contains two main strictures, one pertaining to the use of land, the other to the treatment of creditors. The versions reported in Exodus and Leviticus emphasize letting the land rest every seventh year.[13] This is done to honor the Lord who is giving the land to the Israelites, a theme that will later on prove vital. Even here, however, there is a direct link to the poor: "The poor may eat what grows there, and the wild animals can have what is left."[14]

The radical implications for the needy become even clearer in the Deuteronomic writer's version, in which the second provision gets emphasis.

> At the end of every seven years you shall grant a release. And this is the manner of the release: every creditor shall release what he has lent to his neighbor; he shall not exact it of his neighbor, his brother, because the Lord's release has been proclaimed. Of a foreigner you may exact it; but whatever of yours is with your brother your hand shall release. But there will be no poor among you (for the Lord will bless you in the land which the Lord your God gives you for an inheritance to possess).[15]

As part of the Sabbatical Year release, if a Hebrew has been sold to a fellow Hebrew as a slave, in the seventh year he or she should be set free, but not only that: "when you let him go free from you, you shall not let him go empty-handed; you shall furnish him liberally out of your flock, out of your thrashing floor, and out of your wine press.''[16] Again, the direct tie to Israel's history explains this. ''As the Lord your God has blessed you, you shall give to him. You shall remember that you were a slave in the land of Egypt and the Lord your God redeemed you.''[17]

The pragmatist would argue that a seventh-year sabbatical with a required forgiveness of debts would be a disaster for commerce. No one would lend, knowing they would lose everything in the seventh year. The Deuteronomic writer reports that Moses anticipates this and warns against anyone who eyes his brother hostilely because the seventh year is near. Even in the face of the sabbatical:

> If there is among you a poor man, one of your brethren, in any of your towns within your land which the Lord your God gives you, you shall not harden your heart or shut your hand against your poor brother, but you shall open your hand to him, and lend him sufficient for his need, whatever it may be.[18]

The Sabbatical Year was not the only institution of this kind in Hebrew culture. Leviticus also provides an account of ''the year of restoration'' or the ''Year of Jubilee,'' which occurs after forty-nine years.[19] During that year freedom will be proclaimed for all the inhabitants. Moreover, property will be restored to its original owner. This means that land is essentially transferred on a rental basis. The text points out that it makes sense, therefore, that the price for land should be set by the number of years remaining before the next Jubilee. In what some scholars have taken as evidence of an historical confusion between the Sabbatical and Jubilee Years,[20] some provisions of the Sabbatical Year also apply to the Jubilee. Fields shall not be planted, and slaves shall be freed. The most significant provision, however, is the restoration of the land. Commentators have pointed out that ''the Jubilee was a marvellous safeguard against deadening poverty. By it, houses and lands were kept from accumulating in the hands of the few, pauperism was prevented, and a race of independent freeholders assured.''[21]

There is marked dispute about how faithfully the Sabbatical and Jubilee years were observed. With regard to the Sabbatical Year, Jeremiah transmits the condemnation of the God of Israel for the Israelites for their failure to free the slaves as called for.[22] The

Chronicler explains the attack of the King of Babylonia as being punishment for failure to keep the sabbatical prohibitions.[23] After the return from exile, Nehemiah reports an assembly of the people that is exactly the image of the affirmation of a set of moral obligations by covenant suggested in Chapter 1 as the appropriate way of articulating moral principles. Nehemiah puts in the mouths of the masses the pledge of the post-exilic Israelites. The leaders join with them almost parenthetically in taking an oath to live according to God's law. Among the short list of commandments enumerated is a pledge to ''forego the crops of the seventh year and the exaction of every debt.''[24]

These texts have been interpreted by some as evidence that the Sabbatical Year was not observed faithfully.[25] On the other hand, some scholars are convinced that the practice was an important part of Hebrew life.[26] A similar controversy arises in determining whether the Jubilee Year laws were actually observed. Some commentators find it difficult to accept the idea that land redemption and freedom of all slaves could be accomplished in a society as well developed as that of Israel.[27] Despite the lack of direct reference to the Jubilee in later Biblical writings, other scholars contend that incidental legislation, such as that relating to kinsman's right and the duty of property redemption, imply that Jubilee Year laws were in fact observed.[28] The failure to document fully the Jubilee in either Biblical or historical texts prompts many other commentators to hold that while the Sabbatical and Jubilee Years may have been practiced only infrequently, their major purpose was to serve as an ideal for rectifying economic and social inequalities.[29]

From the point of view of someone attempting to understand the historical foundations of the premises that underlie a contemporary sense of justice as a commitment to the needy, it does not really make much difference whether the Sabbatical and Jubilee years were actively practiced. The norm is present, at least as an ideal. For Jeremiah it is sufficient to explain why Israel would be punished; for the Chronicler it explains why the King of Babylon could succeed in devastating Israel.

THE GROUNDS FOR COMMITMENT TO THE NEEDY

Whether or not the provisions of the Sabbatical and Jubilee Years were actually followed by the Hebrews, there is ample evidence that the normative ideals included a radical concern for the poor, the needy, and oppressed. More must be said, however, on what underlies these commitments. Overwhelming everything else in the history of Israel is the belief in the radical transcendence of their God, Yahweh: creator of all that is; rescuer of the Israelites from bondage; one who intervened to make a gift of land and to create a people by covenant with them, and who continues to protect the oppressed and punish those who fail to join in that mission.[30]

The Sabbatical and Jubilee Year commandments are premised on the belief that ''the earth is the Lord's.'' the Deuteronomic text, which is so critical for the Hebrew understanding of the Sabbatical Year, includes within it an explanation based on the belief that the resources of the land are a gift. ''The Lord will bless you in the land which the Lord your God gives you for an inheritance to possess.''[31] All the earth, all natural resources, are viewed as God's;[32] it is understandable that people with such a conviction would perceive certain residual obligations to use those resources, on loan, as it were, according to the plan and desires of their all powerful, transcendent donor. Thus the writer of Leviticus explains the obligation to restore the land to its original owner in the Jubilee Year by quoting God as saying:

> The land shall not be sold in perpetuity, for the land is mine; for you are strangers and sojourners with me. And in all the country you possess, you shall grant a redemption of the land.[33]

The belief in an all-powerful, transcendent creator god accounts for much more than a sense of obligation in the use of natural resources. It also begins to give us some sense of why the law would call for the use of the resources in the way it does—to care for the poor, needy, and oppressed. The Hebrews viewed their god not only as the creator and original owner of the land and its resources, but also as the creator of man and woman; in fact, he created them in his own image. Yet if all are seen as created in the image of God, all descendents of a common mythical ancestor, there is a fundamental unity in their relationship to that creator. The late apocryphal wisdom literature makes the link in a particularly poignant way when King Solomon says:

> I too am a mortal man like all the rest, descended from the first man. . . . When I was born, I breathed the common air and was laid on the earth that all men tread; and the first sound that I uttered, as all do, was a cry. . . . No king begins life in any other way; for all come into life by a single path, and by a single path go out again.[34]

Again in Proverbs, "Rich and poor have this in common: the Lord made them both,"[35] and "Poor man and oppressor have this in common: what happiness each has comes from the Lord."[36] The common heritage and the unity and even-handedness it implies are seen in the Book of Numbers when Moses transmits the principle upon which the new land is to be apportioned:

> The land shall be apportioned among these tribes according to the number of names recorded. To the larger you shall give a larger property and to the smaller a smaller; a property shall be given to each in proportion to its size as shown in the detailed lists. The land, however, shall be apportioned by lot; the lots shall be cast for the properties by families in the father's line. Properties shall be apportioned by lot between the larger families and the smaller.[37]

The great equalizing principle of distribution by lottery thus has its roots in an ancient Biblical story. The resources are the possession of the divinity who created not only them, but the people who use them. Those people, rich and poor, have a common heritage, and began life with land given as a gift and distributed by lot. In case that distribution should become rearranged, a restoration to the original owners every fifty years is provided for. As part of the obligation of the covenant, complex laws for the protection of all manner of poor—the fatherless, the widow, the oppressed—are provided. It is easy to understand how anyone with that view of the world would be pushed in the direction of some notion of equality. In fact, it may be hard to account for any limits on it.

LIMITS ON THE COMMITMENT TO THE NEEDY

In spite of these powerful beliefs pushing the Israelites in the direction of a commitment to care for the needy, there were such limits. The inequalities of ancient Hebrew culture can hardly be overlooked. All of this literature presumes without question that certain inequalities will persist, will be present to be corrected by the institutions promoting greater equality or, even worse, will be so deeply ingrained that they escape the levelling implications of a belief in Israel's god. A sensitized world of the twentieth century cannot help noting that in the text just quoted land will be distributed along the father's line. No provision is made for the fact that some families will be larger than others. More dramatically, in the discussion of the Sabbatical and Jubilee Years the institution of slavery is presumed, even among the children of Israel. On a larger scale the hurbis of the notion that one particular ethnic group could be the elect of God favored among all peoples is perhaps the most glaring of the counter-themes with which anyone defending a Hebrew origin of the principle of equality will have to cope.

The only honest response is to acknowledge that historical Israel, though perhaps radically different from its neighbors in its self-conceptualization as people of a transcendent, equalizing sovereign, and in its commitment to the needy, would not be expected to escape entirely the influence of the culture and times.[38] What is remarkable is that even in these areas where certain inequalities were perpetuated by institutions, they were attenuated by institutional protections. In the face of the obvious sense of pride of election, Israel is warned over and over again to treat the alien fairly. ''You shall not wrong an alien, or be hard on him; you were yourselves aliens in Egypt.''[39]

The tolerance of slavery calls for a special accounting. It is clear that both Hebrew and foreigner were subject to becoming what is often referred to in English as slaves.[40] Moreover, reflecting the particularism of Israel's sense of being a special chosen people, different laws applied to the Hebrew and the alien slave. No Israelite could become a permanent slave to any earthly master as he was already a servant of the Lord who had rescued him from the bondage of Egypt. Israelites could voluntarily choose to become slaves temporarily, usually because of default on a debt. Since they were subject to release after six years,[41] their situation has been compared to one of a person with a work obligation with a six-year limit. Such slaves were not to be treated as bondsmen, but as members of the household, wage earners, or guests. Upon release, Hebrew slaves were to be provided with food, clothes, and money to reestablish themselves.

Alien slaves, on the other hand, were not afforded all of the same protections. They were subject to sale as bondsmen; and not subject to the six-year time limit. They were considered property to the extent that they could be passed on as inheritance to succeeding generations.[42]

In spite of the existence of the institution of a servitude that had many of the characteristics of slavery and the differential treatment of Hebrew and alien slave, slavery in Israel is clearly something vastly different from our traditional images of the institution in Greece, Rome, and antebellum United States.[43] Although there was in some sense a deprivation of freedom and even a notion of the slave as the master's property, slaves were treated as persons with significant protections. They lived as members of the master's household. According to de Vaux, the slave was at least assured of the necessities of life. He was part of the family, joined in the family worship, rested on the sabbath, shared in sacrificial meals, and celebrated religious feasts. The slave could even share in the master's inheritance and succeeded in the absence of heirs.[44] The role is so different from the modern stereotype of a slave that some modern exegetes even maintain that there was no true slavery in ancient Israel.[45] While it is now generally acknowledged that a true slavery did exist in Israel as well as in other societies of the ancient Near East, there was undeniably a disposition in Israelite law and culture to acknowledge the claims of slaves to substantial consideration, whether they be Hebrew or alien. There are broad hints that slavery was severely limited. Robert North, the Jesuit scholar who has studied the relation of slavery to the Jubilee Year, concludes that the Pentateuch recognizes even humane slavery as essentially evil.[46] Some unusual limits were indeed placed on *Israelite* slavery. In contrast to the common practice of ancient Near Eastern laws penalizing the aiding and abetting of runaway slaves, for example, Israelite law forbade anyone from handing over an escaped slave who had sought refuge.[47] Rather than denying the existence of slavery at all in ancient Israel, however, it seems more honest to admit that Israel, too, was culture-bound. Like its neighbors, it did not resist the common social institution of the time, but it did go to unusual—and indeed unprecedented—lengths to limit its most devastating and inegalitarian effects.[48]

The culture-bound constraint on commitment to equality is perhaps best seen in the subordination of women by the ancient Hebrews.[49] So oblivious to the issues are they that the eighth-century prophet Hosea, when looking for a metaphor to describe God's continuing fidelity to a faithless people, tells a story of Gomer, his wife, who played the harlot and abandoned her family. She had strayed so far that she was being sold as a prostitute. At that point, Hosea, the god-figure, buys her back ''even as the Lord loves the people of Israel, though they turn to other gods and love cakes of raisins.''[50] As an image of continued devotion to a faithless subordinate, it is a rather beautiful metaphor, and perhaps it was meant for nothing more than that. But the fact that a market in women could be used even as a metaphor without self-conscious awkwardness is embarrassing to lovers of human equality of a modern era. Even here, however, while the text is blatantly oblivious to the status of women, it retains, as with the Hebrews' treatment of the slave, a certain dignity and respect. Gomer is to be redeemed not out of a sense of moral superiority, but through love—not sexual love, but love "as the Lord loves the Israelites."

We are left with a remarkable, abundant testimony of a people, not perfect in their manifestation of a commitment to the equality of moral worth whose historical and philosophical roots we are seeking, but nevertheless unique in their sense of identification with the poor, needy, and oppressed. Their unique sense of commitment grows out of a unique self-understanding of a people who were once slaves and who were rescued by an all-powerful, transcendent force who was not only their creator, but the creator of all, that is, a divinity that bound them together as a people with obligations to use the resources of the land in a manner that would witness to the special status of each member of the community, rich or poor, slave or free, king or widow. It is a self-understanding that expresses itself in hard-nosed, concrete financial arrangements whereby every few years debts are forgiven, those who have fallen on hard times are restored to an equal starting point, and property is restored to its original owner. It is that self-understanding, that myth of common origin and destiny, that informs the rest of Judeo-Christian history and, as we shall see, much of modern secular philosophy of the West as well.

The New Testament

The Old Testament provides important egalitarian themes that grow and develop in the history of the Judeo-Christian tradition. However, if we are to continue our quest to understand how one interpretation of that tradition might justify a commitment to the goal of equality for the retarded, the handicapped, and others who are disadvantaged, it is critical to explore the heightening of this concern in the New Testament literature.

Several critical shifts take place. While the Old Testament is rigorous in its commitment to the poor and the oppressed, it is operating on a long and leisurely time track. With the New Testament, a new sense of urgency dominates, stemming from the belief that the messianic age has dawned or at least is coming soon. From this new, more urgent perspective, there is a continuing and heightening of the concern for the poor and the forgiveness of debts. In contrast to the Old Testament, the possession of wealth itself is condemned. Moreover, there is an expansion of concern from the financially poor to the weak in general. Finally, there is an important shift in the significance of the land and, at least in certain texts, the necessity of sharing possessions among the community of believers.

THE HEIGHTENING OF CONCERN FOR THE POOR

The New Testament, especially the synoptic gospels, makes life very hard, perhaps impossible, for the rich. The concern over wealth is so dominant that some have argued that certain texts, such as Luke and Acts, are addressed to members of the early church who are particularly well off.[51]

Luke unloads on the rich.[51] He concurs with Mark and Matthew in chastising the rich, apparently taking all the references that are available to him from Mark and from Q, the common source he shares with Matthew. Mark is presumably the source of the synoptic parallels in Luke as well as in Matthew condemning accumulation of riches, including the marvelous parable of the sower whose seeds that fall among the thorns symbolize the people who hear the Word but are choked by the cares and riches and pleasures of this life.[53] The rich ruler who has followed all the rules of moral conduct since his youth is told that he has to sell all he has and distribute it to the poor. Jesus, with what is taken by scholars as hyperbole, says it is easier for a camel to go through the eye of a needle than for a rich man to enter the kingdom of God.[54] For Luke (as well as the parallel in Mark) the two copper coins contributed by a poor widow were valued more highly that the gifts of the rich contributed out of abundance.[55]

One of the most fascinating developments of recent scholarship is the research that links the forgiveness of debts in the Lord's Prayer to the Jubilee debt forgiveness of the Old Testament. The prayer, common to Matthew and Luke, was first in mid-twentieth century Biblical scholarship linked in its Matthean version to the Sabbatical Year debt forgiveness.[56] Andre Tocme, and following him John Yoder, expanded this link to argue that all of the ministry of Jesus can be understood as proclaiming the inauguration of the Year of Jubilee.[57] More recently, Robert B. Sloan has developed the same thesis with regard to Luke in his doctoral dissertation entitled *The Favorable Year of the Lord: A*

Study of Jubilary Theology in the Gospel of Luke.[58] According to these scholars, when Jesus proposes that the debts of individuals are to be forgiven in the same manner that individuals forgive the debts of others, he is consciously referring back to the Sabbatical and Jubilee Years. The prayer links God's forgiveness to a tough-minded, revolutionary economic and moral reform appropriate for an eschatological age.

The stories unique to Luke are particularly devastating for the wealthy. The story of the unfaithful servant is told to get to the punchline, "You cannot serve both God and material wealth."[59] Zacchaeus, the rich tax collector, is saved when he gives half his goods to the poor.[60] The parable of the rich fool, who decides to eat, drink, and be merry and then loses his soul, is a story told to illustrate Jesus' saying that "a man's life does not consist in the abundance of his possessions."[61] John the Baptist, preaching at the Jordan to the multitudes, preaches equalizing by sharing: "He who has two coats, let him share with him who has none; and he who has food, let him do likewise."[62] Sometimes Luke warns that the rich will get theirs in due course as when the rich man clothed in purple and fine linen dies and ends up in the anguish of Hell. He longs to have Lazarus, a poor begger full of sores who used to lie at his gate waiting for the rich man's scraps, sent to warn his five brothers of the torment to come. Lazarus is now, however, resting comfortably in the bosom of Abraham.[63]

This condemnation of wealth extends beyond the Old Testament concern for the poor and needy. In the Old Testament, wealth was a mark of divine favor, although it carried with it responsibility for charity. According to commentators, that is why the disciples are puzzled when Jesus says the rich man's chances of getting into the kingdom are worse than those of the camel trying to negotiate the eye of the needle.[64]

The heightening of the concern of the poor and this newly introduced direct condemnation of wealth are by no means limited to Luke and the related synoptic parallels. Passages unique to Matthew praise giving alms quietly (so your left hand doesn't know what your right hand is doing),[65] and warn against laying up treasures on earth.[66] The Pauline letters, though generally not known for the radical critique of wealth as in the Gospels, strike their own telling blows. Paul needles the Romans by pointing out that the people of Macedonia and Achaia have made a contribution to the poor at Jerusalem.[67] The contributions are on his mind when he writes his letter to Corinth.[68] The goal is redistribution in order to achieve equality: "as a matter of equality your abundance at the present time should supply their want, so that their abundance may supply your want, that there may be equality."[69] The same themes appear in the letters associated with Paul, but almost surely not written by him[70]—I Timothy says that the love of money is the root of all evils—and in the letters that do not even purport to be Pauline.[71] In James, for example, the reversal theme occurs once again. The day will come when the lowly will be exalted and the rich will be humiliated and fade away.[72]

THE GLORIFYING OF THE WEAK

This reversal theme, which occurs over and over again in the New Testament, is often applied to the weak generally, not just those who are poor financially. Luke has Mary, when initially touched by the Holy Spirit, testify to the great reversal in her poem of praise to the Lord:

> he has scattered the proud in
> the imagination of their hearts,
> he has put down the mighty from their thrones,
> and exalted those of low degree;
> he has filled the hungry with good things,
> and the rich he has sent empty away.[73]

One of the important shifts in the New Testament that will help us understand how those standing within the Judeo-Christian tradition come to identify with the retarded, the weak, and the handicapped and to interpret justice to require equality of some sort is this expansion of the concern for the poor to include the weak in general. In fact, at places there is a rather striking glorification of weakness.[74] The parable of the laborers at the vineyard ends with the reversal line, "So the last will be first, and the first last."[75] In the last judgment when the Son of Man comes, those who have fed the hungry, given drink to the thirsty, welcomed the stranger, clothed the naked, visited the sick, and come to the prisoner will be counted as having done these things to the Messiah because "as you did it to one of the least of these my brethren, you did it to me."[76] Those who are blessed or the recipients of true happiness are the poor, but not really the financially poor, rather the poor in spirit, as well as those who mourn, who are meek, who are hungry and thirsty for righteousness and who are merciful.

The very choice of the savior-figure conveys the remarkable place of weakness in the myth structure of the tradition. Of all the images that could have been selected, we are given a son of a proletarian, born out of wedlock in the most demeaning of circumstances, a man who befriended peasants, chose prostitutes and outcasts as his heroes. When he did identify with those of more stature they were pariahs, tax collectors, and prodigal brats. He stoops to choose every symbol of weakness, taking on the role of servant, foot-washer. His final and most important symbol of triumph is the most painful, humiliating, and demeaning form of execution yet devised, reserved in the Roman world for the most despicable of criminals. When we come to construct the argument that might be given within this tradition for equality of treatment to the handicapped, it is easy to see how the stage is set by its basic symbols and myth system.

The texts give us a good picture of just who is referred to in the identification with the weak. The image is directly relevant to our concern about the claims of justice of the handicapped. Over and over again we are given lists of those who are to be singled out for special favor. They are invariably the handicapped: the maimed, the lame, the blind, the deaf, and the leprous.[77] Those who are less than perfect hold a special place in the tradition.

THE LAND AND PROPERTY

The heightening of the concern for the poor, the condemnation of wealth, and the expansion of that concern into a generalized glorification of weakness are all important themes in helping us understand how the Judeo-Christian tradition has provided an important cultural source for modern egalitarian theories of justice and a commitment to the handi-capped. One final theme in the New Testament, however, needs to be identified before we go on to see the playing out of this world view in post-Biblical Christianity, and before we attempt to construct more systematically the rational argument of that tradition for egalitarianism and see what implications that argument has for the secular modern world. The New Testament provides important growth in the tradition's understanding of the role of land and property. We have already seen that the Hebrew doctrine of creation is one in which the land and all that is in it are viewed as God's property, on loan as a gift to the people of Israel.

Abandoning Jewish Particularism. One of the embarrassments to anyone attempting to defend the thesis that the Judeo-Christian tradition has within it the seeds of a modern egalitarian theory of justice is the particularism of the Hebrew notion that they are an elect people chosen by God and given a special gift of the land. The New Testament ameliorates that embarrassment. The universalizing of salvation and equalizing of Jew and Gentile is particularly dramatic in the Pauline letters.[78] Paul simply is not interested in the land. Salvation is now grounded in faith rather than the promise of the land. Abraham is father to all.[79] Paul's extensive effort to raise money from the Gentiles to help the needy in the church in Jerusalem is interpreted by scholars as an effort to cement together the Jewish and Gentile churches.[80] According to Paul, "There is neither Jew nor Greek, there is neither slave nor free, there is neither male nor female; for you are all one in Christ Jesus."[81] The emphasis on sharing of property in common is not as fully developed in Paul as elsewhere in the New Testament, but Paul's emphasis on salvation by faith makes possible what some moderns have called equal rights for all God's children.[82] The result is a universalism cutting through the Hebrew particularism of the linking of election to the land.

In the Gospels the role of the land is considerably more ambiguous and controversial. Davies, after tracing a tortuous course of debate, concludes that it is unlikely that local geographical loyalties played any central role in Mark and Matthew.[83] John has as little interest in the land of the Old Testament as Paul. Debate continues over the Hellenistic and spiritualizing tendencies of John, but, regardless of the result of those debates, John's dominant theological imagery was vertical rather than horizontal. The election of the Jews and the promise of the land have been superseded.[84] In tracing the debate in Luke-Acts, Davies speaks of Jerusalem being "honorably demoted."[85] Luke was a Gentile concerned above all with the Gentile mission of the Church. He was aware of the mystical, symbolic importance of Jerusalem, but in the end his concern is universal, not geographic.[86]

Property and Possession. The most important contribution of Luke-Acts to the evolution of the Judeo-Christian commitment to equality is not his demoting of the significance of the Israelite land, but his radical critique of private property within the Christian community. The fixation on concern for the poor and the weak seen already in the gospel pales in comparison to the communalism Luke expects of the early church described in Acts:

> All who believed were together and had all things in common; and they sold their possessions and goods and distributed them to all, as any had need.[87]

The theme is repeated two chapters later:

> Now the company of those who believed were of one heart and soul, and no one said that any of the things which he possessed was his own, but they had everything in common. . . . There was not a needy person among them, for as many as were possessors of lands or houses sold them, and brought the proceeds of what was sold and laid it at the apostles' feet; and distribution was made to each as any had need.[88]

The result is what a great early twentieth-century social historian has called a "Communism of Love."[89] Enormous controversy continues to rage over how the author understood its context and the real extent of this communalism in the early church. The original purpose of the Book of Acts has generated endless controversy.[90] Summarizing the concept of the ideal community and communicating that vision to the Gentiles are widely taken to be central. Many scholars have noted the linguistic and conceptual links to Pythagorean communal ownership and to images of Greek utopianism in Plato and Aristotle.[91] It is also widely noted that there are similarities to the communal sharing of possessions in the Qumran community.[92] What the primitive church in Acts shares with Qumran is the eschatological excitement of a community that believes the messianic age is at hand. The context is not only one in which a community is suffering deprivation occasioned by persecution,[93] but one where communal sharing is a way of life particularly suited to an eschatological community.[94] It does not make much sense to be worried about providing for the future if the end is at hand.

The extent of the practice of communal sharing is at least as controversial as the question of historical context. There is considerable doubt that the practices were fully developed and practiced even in the community the author of Acts was describing, much less in the churches addressed by Paul.[95] The communal sharing texts in Acts are isolated. A great deal is made in modern scholarship of the references to individual Apostles such as Barnabas, who sold possessions to help the church, noting either that they may have been singled out as unique examples or that such incidents at least reveal that they still had possessions to sell.[96] We know that there were those who held out some of their private possessions. Ananias and his wife Sapphira were caught at this, but they were condemned to death for it, implying that the violation (or at least the dishonesty) was taken very seriously.

The New Testament provides an alternative view on possessions and the community's obligation to the needy to the communalism of Luke-Acts. The Pauline churches apparently accepted private property and the retaining of personal possessions. The mode of sharing for Paul was almsgiving—acts of charity presumably from one's private possessions. The expectation of an imminent end was relaxed in comparison to the church in Acts, and the utopianism of a small community is replaced with the beginnings of a world-wide mission.[97]

What is striking, however, is that all of the argument within Christian circles—ancient and modern—appears to be between the "love communism" of Acts and the mode of almsgiving charity of Paul. The obligation of the community to the poor and weak is taken for granted; it is beyond debate. The communal sharing of Acts has been taken seriously at least as an ideal. Although it was not universal even within the early church, it is an ideal that expressed one form of community responsibility for the weak—an ideal that recurs repeatedly throughout the millennia of the history of the church.[98]

NEW TESTAMENT COUNTER-THEMES

If there is some debate over the extent to which the communal sharing was actually practiced in the Luke-Acts vision of the early church and the relation of that communalism to Pauline almsgiving, that tension is even greater when other New Testament texts are examined. As in the Old Testament, there are occasionally themes that run counter to the egalitarian tendencies that so dominate the New Testament identification with the poor and the weak. It has been argued, for instance, that the Gospel accounts of the life of Jesus, while they unambiguously demonstrate his concern for the poor, identification with the weak, and his condemnation for wealth, do not show him directly attacking the system of private property as might be implied in the Luke-Acts summaries. He accepted hospitality of well-to-do sisters and the support of women of property.[99] He was upon occasion the guest of a rich man although, to be sure, the story is told to make an unfavorable comparison between him and a woman who, though a sinner, anointed his feet.[100] In the other story of a woman anointing Jesus—the one in Mark—Jesus defends her against the criticism that she wasted the ointment that could have been sold to help the poor, by saying that ''you will always have the poor with you.''

Although this is probably the text most often cited to attack the social egalitarian interpretation of the Christian tradition, the story was probably told not to make any economic point at all, but rather to show Jesus prophesying his impending death and final victory.[101]

Thus in spite of these occasional themes, which, upon inspection turn out really not to be significant counter-examples, the Biblical identification with the poor, the weak, and the deprived is overwhelming. To the extent that there is tension at all, it is between the communalism of Luke-Acts and the almsgiving of the Pauline letters. These two variants on the Judeo-Christian commitment to the needy set the stage for a long history of such commitment in the Christian era.

The Early Church

The ancient church kept the ideal of commitment to the weak, the sick, and the poor alive even if the tension remained between the more communitarian vision and the notion of the church as a community voluntarily giving alms for the needy. From the first century up to the emergence of modern Christianity, the radical egalitarianism of the earliest church constantly surfaces as an ideal that will not disappear. There were also those who accommodated to the comforts and conveniences of privilege, but over and over again the transcendence of the Christian God is interpreted as requiring an equality of all humans with special concern and compassion for the weak. Property is either communal or, if held privately, viewed as a gift requiring stewardship leading to the care of the weakest members of the community.

The Ancient Church

We have already seen that the first-century Near East was rife with communities of apocalyptic excitement and communal utopianism. Luke may have patterned his ideas or language from the Pythagorean notion of "one soul" with its communal holding of property and its requirement that trainees had to relinquish their possessions. The Qumran community demanded, according to its Manual of Discipline, that full members turn over everything to the community while those less fully integrated had to turn over wages of at least two days a month.[102] Another group of Jewish ascetics, the Therapeutae, described by Philo and apparently taken by Eusebius as an early Christian sect, gave away their money when joining and held that "inequality was injustice and equality justice."[103] An early Christian sect, the Ebionites, sometimes associated with Luke,[104] cultivated the ideal of religious poverty.

The Didache, a manual of church discipline from an isolated Christian community, possibly of second-century Syria, says "Do not turn away from the needy, but share all with your brother and do not claim that it is your own. For, if you are sharers in immortal things, how much more in mortal."[105] Lucian of Samosata, a pagan satirist writing at the end of the second century, depicts the Palestinian Christian church as kindly, but credulous for the communal holding of property and their generous support of Penegrinus, a purported Christian convert whom Lucian takes to be defrauding the Christians with his appeals for support.[106]

Early Gnostic Christianity also reflected this commitment to communal sharing. An extreme example is reported by Clement of Alexandria when he provides excerpts from the book *On Justice* authored by a young philosopher, Epiphanes. In contrast with the Platonic and Aristotelian view that equality should be interpreted proportionally (that equals should be treated equally and unequals unequally), Epiphanes pressed with some admittedly dubious analogies toward fuller "arithmetical" equality, and that for him meant communal holding of property. According to him, "God made all things for man to be common property." Human law, rather than divine plan, has taught man to long for privately held goods. Thus Epiphanes ridicules the Old Testament commandment against coveting since no one should possess private property in the first place.[107]

By contrast, Clement himself had a more modest interpretation of the requirements of justice. Troubled by the Markan story of the rich man who is told to sell what he has and give it to the poor, Clement interprets it allegorically. He could not believe wealth literally had to be renounced in all circumstances.[108] Here he differed from Irenaeus who saw private possessions as coming from avarice and injustice. For Clement they were a gift of God.[109] This did not mean, however, that Clement is anything like a precursor of the modern libertarian doctrine of private property. God, as creator of all, expects sharing. In fact, certain necessities—air and water, for example—are supplied in a way that they will be held in common and shared. Moreover, Clement's doctrine of property carries with it a more extensive obligation to share through almsgiving. ''All possessions are by nature unrighteous,'' he says, ''when a man possesses them for personal advantage as being entirely his own, and does not bring them into the common stock for those in need.''[110] And this from a defender of private property.

Clement's pupil, Origen, is much less ambivalent about the Christian's duties to the weak and the poor. He criticizes anyone who allegorizes the Biblical commandment to sell one's possessions and give to the poor. In a sermon based on Luke, Origen says ''Christ denies that that man whom he has seen possessing anything and that man who 'renounces' not 'all which he possesses' is his disciple.''[111] As in the New Testament period, there is a tension between two ways of bringing about equality. One group acknowledge God's requirement of equity by insisting on the duty of stewardship expressed by giving alms voluntarily to those in need. The other is far more radical, rejecting private property and insisting that God's equality cuts through any notion of one person being better off than another. In either case, the needy, as members of God's created community, have a fundamental claim on the resources of the community and its more prosperous members. The weaker members of the community stand in a special status.

As the church matures at the beginning of the third century and begins to accommodate to a less apocalyptic, more stable political reality, the less radical vision of man's responsibility for his fellow through voluntary almsgiving emerges as more dominant. For Tertullian riches are helpful for philanthropy. He advocates building of an ongoing voluntary community chest:

> Though we have our treasure chest, it is not made up of purchase-money as of a religion that has its price. On the monthly day, if he likes, each puts in a small donation; but only if it be his pleasure, and only if he be able: for there is no compulsion; all is voluntary.[112]

The community chest is to be used for all manner of the weakest members of the community: orphans, slaves grown old, shipwrecked mariners, and prisoners. They are drawn together as a community "united in mind and soul" and thus having "no hesitation about sharing property."[113]

This trend continues in the middle of the third century. Cyprian, Bishop at Carthage, did not question the legitimacy of private property.[114] Still, property was a trust to be used to support the prisoner, the widow, the sick, and even an actor converted to Christianity who could no longer act because it was forbidden of Christians.[115]

By the time of Constantine, at the beginning of the fourth century, Lactantius, the tutor of Constantine's son, captures the dialectic between these two positions as well as the emerging dominance of the more voluntarist acceptance of private property and almsgiving. "The ownership of property," he says, "contains the material both of vices and of virtues, but a community of goods contains nothing else than the licentiousness of vices."[116] Even so, he concedes the widely held view that in the golden age land was held in common. His conclusion is the duty of Christian charity: wealth is not for personal enjoyment, but for service to others.[117]

Later in the fourth century the church fathers attacked the overaccumulation of wealth among the rich. Influenced by Christian monastic asceticism, Basil, Theodoret, Gregory of Nyssa, Gregory of Nazianzus, and Chrysostom all attacked the evils of private property.[118] Gregory of Nazianzus spoke of an "original equality" and urged all to imitate God's equity. Chrysostom, Archbishop of Constantinople by the turn of the century, was ruined by his attacks on wealth. He recognized a right to private property, but insisted on sharing, as a duty of stewardship:

> All this about "mine," and "thine," is bare words only, and doth not stand for things. For if thou do but say the house is thine, it is a word without a reality: since the very air, earth matter are the Creator's: and so art thou too thyself, who has framed it; and all other things also.[119]

This notion of stewardship grows out of the early church fathers' identification of Christ with the poor producing that Walsh and Langan call "the patristic principle of equality."[120] Even Augustine, hardly known for his radical political and economic doctrine (he did not question the right of private property), condemns the desire for riches.

He was a supporter of the monastic life and on occasion criticized the rich. He was a proponent of the Christian duty of almsgiving, rapidly becoming the dominant Christian expression of the duty to the weaker members of the Church.[121] What is striking is not the increasing dominance of this more modest interpretation of the sense of obligation to charity over the more radical, communalist version, but that the debate should take place between these two versions of the sense of responsibility for the weak, leaving aside the Greek and Roman views with their more aristocratic, alienating, geometrical sense of justice, their status preserving inheritance laws, and willingness to abandon the weak, the deformed, and the unwanted.

The Late Middle Ages

During the early middle ages this tension remained between a charitable commitment to care for the weaker members of the Church community and the more communitarian vision. The state of scholarship on the social history of the church during this period gives us very little information, but what we have supports this conclusion.[122] While some Christians managed to accumulate great wealth and some of that wealth even found its way into the church coffers, the ideal of commitment to the poor and weak remained alive. We see it in the reformist spirit surfacing time and time again when the church began to revive in the thirteenth century.

THE FRANCISCANS

These themes are most apparent in the religious orders with their institutionalization of the vow of poverty and their mission to the needy of the community. The result is what Ernst Troeltsch has called a ''kind of communism [that] has its permanent living example in the Religious Orders.''[123] From its earliest manifestation, monasticism struggles with poverty, communalism, and the obligation of the Church to the weak of the community. From Antony in the late third century and repeatedly among the Benedictines, the call for poverty is central to monastic reform.[124] It is seen most dramatically, however, in the Franciscans with their repeated, almost yearly, anti-materialistic reform and renewal.

During the twelfth century, kings, merchants, and the Church had vastly increased their wealth. In fact, David Knowles, the great medievalist, describes them as "ostentatiously wealthy."[125] The task of restoring the ancient vision fell to Francis. From him that vision was of Christ-like poverty, simplicity, and a renunciation of possessions. Francis is unique, however, in capturing the spririt of poverty, an identification with the most wretched of the earth. First moved out of compassion for the beggars he saw on a pilgrimage to Rome, he exchanged clothes with one of them and spent the day begging for alms. Returning to Assisi he adopted a life serving the poor and ministering to lepers. In his spirit "the Church, not the government," as Barbara Tuchman has pointed out, "sponsored the care of society's helpless— the indigent, and sick, orphan and cripple, the leper, the blind, the idiot."[126]

Thus, the Franciscans captured the essence of the Christian commitment to the weakest of the community, but in what has been regarded as the supreme paradox, their simple, pure, pious life-style attracted substantial gifts and financial support so that wealth became an almost inevitable, if unintended consequence.[127] Moreover, the life of the saintly founder could not be successfully imitated by more ordinary members of the order. Various rationalizations for modest (and sometimes not so modest) accumulations emerged. They adopted the *usus pauper,* the "sparing" use of material necessities, they chose friends to hold their money, and they rationalized that the friars owned nothing since it was held in papal ownership.[128] This in turn gave rise to countless reforms. Soon after the founding of the order, the Spirituals, a branch insisting on literal application of the Christ-like ideal, began an endless effort at purification. The dispute was temporarily resolved by papal bulls from John XXII permitting the order to own goods corporately, and acknowledging that the more modest version of the Christian almsgiving vision was an acceptable form of the Christian life. Soon thereafter, however, the radical critics surfaced again, now as a schismatic group called the Fraticelli. A few years later the order was once again ready for an internal radical reform movement.

By the mid-fourteenth century the conflict declined, but has surfaced again continually throughout the history of the order in a fifteenth-century feud between Observants and Conventualists, a sixteenth-century movement of Capuchins led by Latteo di Bassi, and groups in the following centuries known as the Reformati, the Recollects, and the Discalced. It seems safe to say that the tension is an inevitable and perpetual one of any group built on the Christian commitment to renunciation of special status and wealth in favor of service to the weakest, sickest, and poorest members of the community.

JOHN BALL AND LEVELLING LOLLARD PRIESTS OF THE
FOURTEENTH CENTURY
Social reforms affirming a bond of equality among the members of the Church community were not limited to the religious orders. The late fourteenth century saw a much more widespread discontent among the masses.[129] While this infected most of Europe, it was particularly dramatic in England, where, in June 1381, a revolt of peasants erupted.[130] They were provoked by a series of poll taxes, but more fundamentally disturbed by the bonds of villenage (feudal servitude) and a lack of legal and political rights. They perceived no way of breaking the bonds of servitude except by open revolt. Stimulated by Lollard priests, they liberated the radical priest, John Ball, from prison to lead their revolt. He offered them a radical version of the Christian egalitarian vision. ''Matters cannot go well in England,'' he preached, ''until all things shall be held in common; when there shall be neither vassals nor lords, when the lords shall be no more masters than ourselves. . . . Are we not all descended from the same parents, Adam and Eve?''[131]

This was Wycliffe's doctrine attacking property and privilege in its most radical form. In classical Christian rhetoric the preachers denounced the ''evil princes,'' ''false executors who increase the sorrows of widows,'' ''wicked ecclesiastics who show the worst example to the people,'' and the nobles who ''empty the purses of the poor with their extravagances.''[132] The familiar Biblical theme of a great reversal on the day of judgment becomes a justification for a radical levelling revolt this side of the final days. ''The 'righteous poor' will stand up against the cruel rich at the Day of Judgment and will accuse them of their works and severity on earth.'' As Tuchman summarizes the religious roots of the mood of the levelling revolt, ''If the meek were the sons of God . . . , why should they wait for their rights until the Day of Judgment? If all men had a common origin in Adam and Eve, how should some be held in hereditary servitude? If all were equalized by death as the medieval idea constantly emphasized, was it not possible that inequalities on earth were contrary to the will of God?''[133]

Once again the more radical version of the Judeo-Christian egalitarian vision has surfaced. It is not, of course, that these were the only theological ideas competing in the cultural marketplace of ideas. As we saw in the earliest Biblical strands, themes counter to the view of humans as equal in some fundamental sense before God have always been present. At points in the Middle Ages, these counter-themes dominate, at least in the elite leadership of both Church and state. Rather, it is that in Judeo-Christian history the egalitarian themes are so central and so overpowering that they rise continually to the surface whenever the texts and stories of the tradition are applied to the local setting. They arise particularly to come to the aid of the oppressed, the disadvantaged, and the weak.

THOMAS MORE'S *UTOPIA*

Throughout Christian history the peasant classes have always turned to that egalitarian vision from early Judeo-Christianity for solace as well as inspiration in the quest for fair treatment. The lower classes, however, are not by any means the only ones captured by it. In the highest reaches of England's aristocracy not many years after John Ball led the English peasants in revolt, Thomas More, Catholic martyr and saint destined to become Lord Chancellor of England, advisor to Henry VIII, and finally defender of Rome by his life-and-death refusal to affirm the Oath of Succession, translated that vision into his famous, hilarious, charming *Utopia*. Written in 1516 as an imagined account of one Raphael Hythlodaeus, it reveals how the more radical communalism of Acts has left its lasting cultural impression on the imagination of this scholar and political leader of England.

As translator Paul Turner points out in his introduction to the Penguin edition, a feud persists between those who hold that More's work is essentially a Catholic tract whose communism should be interpreted as mere moral allegory and those who see it as a political manifesto whose references to religion should be ignored.[134] Neither view considers the possibility that both perspectives are to be taken seriously, that communal egalitarianism is an essential playing out of one version of the Christian vision.

More's Utopia surely is communalist. He has Raphael describe it by saying, ''I'm quite convinced that you'll never get a fair distribution of goods, or a satisfactory organization of human life, until you abolish private property altogether.''[135] Then, especially in the concluding summation, he waxes eloquent about the glories of his egalitarian Utopia in comparison to the injustices of the world of Thomas More's own day:

> Now, will anyone venture to compare these fair arrangements in Utopia with the so-called justice of other countries—in which I'm damned if I can see the slightest trace of justice or fairness. For what sort of justice do you call this? People like aristocrats, goldsmiths, or money-lenders, who either do no work at all, or do work that's really not essential, are rewarded for their laziness or their unnecessary activities by a splendid life of luxury. But labourers, coachmen, carpenters, and farm-hands, who never stop working like cart-horses, at jobs so essential that, if they did stop working, they'd bring any country to a standstill within twelve months—what happens to them? They get so little to eat, and have such a wretched time, that they'd be almost better off if they *were* cart-horses.[136]

It is not simply that More believes that hard work should be rewarded in order to make sure it continues. The traditional Christian compassion for the weak emerges in the next paragraph. Speaking of the unfair treatment of these laborers and working-class people he says:

> And the climax of ingratitude comes when they're old and ill and completely destitute. Having taken advantage of them throughout the best years of their lives, society now forgets all the sleepless hours they've spent in its service, and repays them for all the vital work they've done by letting them die in misery.[137]

More's plan is redistribution in order to meet the needs of the destitute by means of common ownership:

> Just think back to one of the years when the harvest was bad, and thousands of people died of starvation. Well, I bet if you'd inspected every rich man's barn at the end of that lean period, you'd have found enough corn to have saved all the lives that were lost through malnutrition and disease, and prevented anyone from suffering any ill effects whatever from the meanness of the weather and the soil. . . . I've no doubt that either self-interest, or the authority of our Savior Christ—Who was far too wise not to know what was best for us, and far too kind to recommend anything else—would have led the whole world to adopt the Utopian system long ago, if it weren't for that beastly root of all evils, pride.[138]

Once again, the surplus held by some would provide enough to meet the needs of others. The authority for this is both prudence (self-interest) and the Christian vision.

Modern Egalitarianism

By this time, of course, things were happening on the continent that, through religious, political, and cultural change, would usher in the modern era. Reform within the Church let loose the Biblical vision. Many were not content to dream of an egalitarian Utopia. They were ready to build the Kingdom on the spot. This same tension between a modest charitable concern for the underclasses and a more radical, militant building of a new egalitarian community remained. Even the more conservative forces, however, operated within this part of the spectrum in which justice is seen as pushing toward greater equality. John Calvin, despite his anti-egalitarian doctrine of predestination with its throwback to Jewish particularism, was, for instance, a proponent of Christian charity. He held that God wills equality so each member of the Christian community should provide for the needy according to one's means.[139]

The Continental Radical Reformation

On the continent, beginning about 1520, a fury of social and political activity paralleled the more orthodox reformation giving rise to what has been called the radical or left wing of the reformation.[140] Although the movements were small, fragmented, often short-lived, and were very diverse among themselves, they took the task of community-building seriously and along with it inevitably expressed their commitment to greater social equality among the brethren.

Sometimes that radical reforming spirit took the form of militant revolt. In 1525, Thomas Munzer stimulated German peasants to an ill-fated uprising. Their original demands, spelled out in the Twelve Articles drawn up in Memmingen in March of that year, were actually modest enough to claim Martin Luther's approval. They included certain property rights for peasants, justice in the courts, abolition of the *Todfall* (a practice whereby landlords appropriated property of the peasant at the peasant's death), and the abolition of serfdom. The mood, however, soon turned to mob violence with the burning of castles and monasteries and political efforts to destroy all authority. This led to Luther's intemperate tract, "Against the Robbing and Murdering Hordes of Peasants,"[141] and the ruthless extermination of the movement by the Schwabischer Bund, a confederation of Protestant princes.[142]

An equally militant community attempted to establish a "New Jerusalem" in Munster a decade later. Under the leadership of Jan van Leiden, agitators made up of "immigrants, shoemakers, tailors, furriers, and other artisans" attempted to set up a new regime by force. In it the more radical version of the Biblical vision of communalism was to be practiced. According to a contemporary chronicler, "After the prophets and preachers had reached an agreement with the council in this matter, it was announced in the sermons that all things should be held in common. Thus they said in the sermon, 'Dear brothers and sisters one to another, it is God's will that we should bring our money, silver, and gold together. Each one of us should have as much as any other.' "[143] The goal was communal equality. Their radical excesses and violence led to the same fate as that of the peasants of the previous decade.

By no means were all the reformers on the left of the reformation aggressive and violent. Some sectarians chose instead to withdraw from the world and build communities of the brethren more peacefully. Balthasar Hubmaier, who may have been one of the writers of the Twelve Articles,[144] went on to attempt to build such a community at Nikolsburg in Moravia. Some years later, Hutterites gathering outside of Nikolsburg reconstituted a group attempting to recapture the apostolic communalism. The Anabaptist Chronicle describes the scene: "At this time these men spread a coat before the people and everybody laid down his possessions, voluntarily and uncoerced, so that the needy might be supported according to the teaching of the prophets and the apostles."[145]

The Levellers and Diggers

The spirit of the radicals in sixteenth-century Europe was carried by groups such as the Mennonites to the Netherlands and then by Dutch emigrants into England where it joined forces with the remnants of the Lollard movement. By the time of Cromwell's England the spirit of the

New Testament expansion was captured once again by a gentrified urban movement which, despite its protests, became known as the Levellers. The Levellers were a movement for political and religious reform led by John Lilburne, William Walwyn, Thomas Prince, and Richard Overton. They pressed for economic reforms, for progressive taxation[146] and against poverty,[147] but they were not committed primarily or fully to compulsory communal sharing and economic equality.[148] Rather, theirs was a far more radical vision of equality of social and political standing. They urged a radical democracy by drawing up a series of agreements or covenants harkening back to the Old Testament covenants, especially that found in Nehemiah. One of them, "An Agreement of the Free People of England Tendered as a Peace Offering to the Distressed Nation," dates from the first of May, 1649, anticipating a later day celebrating people's revolutions.[149] These agreements press for full equality before the law, regardless of birth, wealth, or influence, individual consent of the governed, and what was taken as full freedom of belief. These were rooted in what Troeltsch described as the Levellers' belief in "the facts of Christian equality."[150] Of the explicit Biblical foundations of their image of a community of equals there can be no doubt.[151] In fact, they defended themselves against charges of economic levelling by pointing back to "the Community amongst the primitive Christians," noting that it was a voluntary community with sharing "occasioned by the abundant measure of faith that was in those Christians and Apostles."[152]

As we have seen in earlier Judeo-Christian history, the vision of equality was sometimes limited by the sociocultural prejudices of the day. In the face of the rhetoric about full Christian equality before the law, women, apprentices, and "such as maintain the Popes (or other foreign Supremacy)"[153] were excluded. The Levellers' movement was finally suppressed by Cromwell and disappeared as did the Diggers, a more rural, more proletarian, somewhat more radical movement sometimes grouped with the Levellers, which wanted to place all commonly held land (including the crown's) under common production by the peasants under the ancient sectarian ideal.[154]

What is important for our quest for an understanding of the grounds for and logic of a modern egalitarianism that would take seriously the moral claims generated on behalf of the weakest members of the community, such as a young, mentally retarded boy needing special intensive therapy, is not the strength and dominance of any one of these movements, but their continual, repeated appearance as reform movements constantly holding forth the ideal of equality and the commitment to those who are poor, weak, suffering, and destitute. For thousands of years of history, that ideal surfaces again and again in one form or another—in its radical communalist manifestation, its more modest ideal of almsgiving and charity, or something in between those two that we see in the Levellers and Diggers. It is not that the ideal is achieved with any regularity throughout that history; it surely is not. It is not that there are not other images of humans separated into orders, classes, castes, statuses, and power differentials; they certainly appear and sometimes dominate. But literally every few years throughout millennia of Judeo-Christian history the Biblical ideal of identification with the weak as full and equal members of the community reemerges as the foundation of the egalitarian vision.

The Methodists

In the eighteenth century it was, among others, John and Charles Wesley, tired of their high-status, elite intellectual group at Oxford, who were captured by the vision after being moved by a group of Moravian Brethren and a trip to the Moravian colony at Herrnhut. Essentially a lower-class religious and social reform movement, Methodism in its early days contained within it many of the elements of the egalitarian vision we have been tracing.[155] Though Wesley was slow to accept the contractarian basis of political, social, and economic equality, that theory, with its ultimate convenantal Biblical roots, dominated Dutch Remonstrants who were so influential in Methodist thought. Moreover, the levelling and egalitarian themes became more and more central as Methodism spread among the masses. Wesley's Arminianism led him to preach the egalitarian doctrine of universal salvation. With regard to slavery he preached equality and natural rights.[156] As with the seventeenth-century Levellers, it was not so much economic egalitarianism as a democratizing of the religious community. Historian Bernard Semmel refers to Wesley ''preaching spiritual equality and launching a campaign against clerical indifference by the undoubted levelling methods of lay preaching.''[157] By the end of the eighteenth century, Methodism had developed strongly egalitarian tendencies, especially in the more radical leadership of men like

Alexander Kilham, a principal figure in the more radical wing of Methodism. Kilham talked about a dream, a "dream of Equality," in language reminiscent of a great civil rights leader of the twentieth century who read the same prophets, trained in the same Methodist theological tradition, and absorbed the same vision.

Kilham's radical colleague, Samuel Bradburn, in a sermon on "Equality" preached in 1794, made the case for an immediate equality in the spiritual condition of man. He argued that the word "equality" is at root scriptural. All are equal in their depravity, all equally creatures, all under the same necessity of being saved by grace.[158] As we have seen so often, however, there was oscillation when it comes to the political and economic implications of this doctrine of equality. Bradburn, true to the Pauline text on which he was preaching, did not reject private property.[159] He recognized that there will be differences among members of the community. In fact, he does not go even as far as Paul, who at least held that the Corinthians, who were rich, should give to the poor "that there may be equality." By contrast, even though Bradburn was preaching on this very text, he said "this has nothing to do with levelling."[160] He did, however, to guard against the evil consequences of inequality, develop a complex theory of the "just rights of every individual" in which people in their various roles all bear responsibilities for the others within the community. He includes an unrelenting defense of equality of religious liberty and opposition to slavery. "When men of rank treat their inferiors with supercilious insolence, as if they were beings of another species," Bradburn says, the results will be "insurrections, rebellions, and revolutions."[161] The core of this Methodist egalitarianism is religiously rooted equality. As Kilham put it, "we all are redeemed by Christ, and have each a soul to save, equally precious in the sight of God."[162]

Nineteenth-Century Christian Socialism

Within a few decades this core Christian ideal—this fundamentally egalitarian, community-building, social vision—found its expression among the European intellectual elites who provided the initial impetus to what came to be called Christian Socialism.[163] In England it had its major roots, as did the earlier Methodist movement, within the Church of England—in people like J. M. F. Ludlow, F. D. Maurice, Charles Kingsley, and Thomas Hughes. To them belongs the credit for beginning to work out the meaning of egalitarian Christian heritage for the contemporary, secular Western world. They provided a contemporary manifestation of the struggle between Lucan communalism of the radical sects and more Pauline notions of charity as the expression of communal responsibility.

The movement was by no means limited to Church of England Protestantism. Christian socialism was important in France not only in Comte and Saint-Simon, but lesser known figures such as Robert Lamennais, Joseph Buchez, and August Blanqui. In Germany the leadership came from Wilhelm Weitling, Franz Baader, Victor Huber, and especially the Catholic Bishop of Mainz, Wilhelm von Ketteler.

All of these figures saw an essential link between the Judeo-Christian tradition and the egalitarian vision. Maurice, for example, in the first tract he wrote on Christian socialism, said, "I seriously believe that Christianity is the only foundation of Socialism, and that a true Socialism is the necessary result of a sound Christianity."[164] The Frenchman August Blanqui held that the problem of equitable distribution of wealth could only be solved in a religious context. Some years later Anglican Archbishop of Canterbury William Temple also made the link, saying, "Apart from the faith in God, there is really nothing to be said for the notion of human equality."[165] It is in the light of this historical link between the Judeo-Christian tradition and social egalitarianism that Marx can appropriately be viewed as a Jewish heretic. This problem of the necessity of the explicitly Christian articulation of the vision of egalitarianism will become the central theme of Chapter 4 of this study.

What is important for our investigation of the roots of contemporary egalitarianism and their meaning for concrete public policy problems of resource allocation, such as those raised by the needs of the mentally retarded, is the way the nineteenth-century religious socialists began to work out the implications of their vision for social and political practices. As might by now be predicted, the range of views on private property and the duties of charity fell within a range. Ludlow, influenced by the French, pressed for "a planned economy, abolition of the distinction between capitalists and workers, self-government, an end to class distinction and privilege, and, indeed, the abolition of private property."[166] On the other hand, Maurice favored a socialism that was much more abstract. It did not imply basic changes in the economic order, abolition of private property, or equal incomes.[167] Perhaps the most interesting view for our purposes is neither the Lucan Ludlow nor the Pauline Maurice, but the new synthesis that began to emerge with Charles Kingsley. Kingsley saw the inadequacy of purely private charity in dealing with the social problems of the day. The model of almsgiving would not do. On the other hand, his sense of communitarian responsibility was never radicalized to the extreme of collectivists who pressed for total abolition of private property. His attention was drawn primarily to social problems unamenable to private charity—to concern with what we would now identify as true public goods—public health, sanitation, and education. These were areas that of necessity required collective responsibility, yet the Kingsley mode was essentially democratic, often even voluntarist.

He once found himself a featured speaker at the first meeting of "The Ladies Sanitary Association," an organization responsible for a myriad of tracts on proper sanitary habits published in an effort to convey "the gospel of cleanliness to the dangerously insolubrious classes."[168] In his address, later published as *The Massacre of the Innocents,* Kingsley reveals how his commitment to saving the large number of babies who die each year from poor sanitation practices is grounded in an explicit sense of religiously rooted compassion for the weak. He acknowledges that saving these now doomed infants could create enormous social and economic problems for others, problems of overpopulation and finding enough food for the masses, yet it is not these larger aggregate social consequences that claim his attention. His focus is on individual children in need. In his exortation to the ladies to save the "innocents" he points out that each of them will certainly have the chance of saving three or four in the next six months. He encourages them, saying, "it is not the will of your Father that is in Heaven that one little one that plays in the kennel outside should perish, either in body or soul."[169]

It is in Kingsley's avowedly social, yet democratic and voluntarist commitment to the neediest members of the community, innocent children who can by no means stake their claim on the basis of their usefulness to the community, that we see perhaps most clearly the playing out of Judeo-Christian egalitarianism in a way that provides a framework for understanding our moral response to similarly impaired mentally retarded boy in need of the public good of education, but in need of it in a special way requiring a unique response of the community.

Contemporary Medical Ethical Egalitarianism

With the long history of Judeo-Christian egalitarianism, it is hardly surprising to find that those dealing with contemporary problems in medical ethics (such as the claims of justice for health resource allocation and the right to health care for the needy) who are working out of the Judeo-Christian tradition hardly bother to stop to justify their conviction that justice in health care means essentially distributing that care on the basis of need. The egalitarianism of their tradition leaves them with a special preordained concern for and identification with the needy. Some, as we could now predict, translate that tradition into an egalitarianism in which health care is essentially a communal responsibility. A British national health service, a one-class health care system supported out of commonly held community resources, is the model. Others, more Pauline in their commitment to the medically needy, favor less radical forms of support—universal insurance schemes, government care for the most needy, or even voluntarist charity.

One or the other of these forms of Judeo-Christian egalitarianism is the working assumption consistent in the writings on justice and health care of the contemporary religiously grounded bioethicists from the earliest strata of that literature. James Childress, of the Department of Religious Studies at the University of Virginia in 1970, in the first important argument for an equality-based theory of justice in health care in the current generation of bioethics writing, contrasts two approaches. One, which he characterizes as utilitarian, reduces the person to his social role, relations, and functions—to the contribution he can make to others. The alternative seeks to preserve ''a significant degree of personal dignity by providing equality of opportunity.''[170] The bottom line for Childress, as for anyone working within this tradition, in an assumption that equality is fundamental—an ''equal right to be saved . . . best preserved by procedures which establish equality of opportunity.''[171] It is on the basis of this assumption that he comes out in favor of a lottery as a means for allocating scarce life-saving medical resources, at least in those cases where what is being allocated is something like a kidney for transplant or a hemodialysis machine that cannot be divided more evenly among all the possible patients in need. Similar conclusions based on similar theological and ethical assumptions were reached by virtually every writer working out of this tradition since then. Paul Ramsey, in his seminal *The Patient as Person,* published in 1970, reaches a similar conclusion based on a similar set of theological presuppositions. For him equality is the decisive principle because lives are "presumed to be equally valuable."[172] Ramsey never gives a full-blown argument for that presumption nor is it clear that he could, although he has a great deal of company in the assumptions he makes.

This same set of presumptions occurs consistently in the group of bioethicists writings out of this tradition since then, in Outka,[173] Lebacqz,[174] Shelp,[175] Shelton,[176] Curran,[177] Jonsen,[178] and Walters,[179] as well as my own writing.[180] Only rarely, as in Earl Shelp's 1976 doctoral dissertation, have these authors attempted to identify the explicit foundations for the commitment to equality in health-care resource allocation. When they do they point to a series of core, theologically grounded assumptions dealing with the concept of God, the doctrine of creation, and notions of community responsibility central to the tradition.[181] It is only by setting out systematically what those assumptions are, what the foundation premises of an argument for equality would be, that we can provide a basis for understanding the conclusions of this literature and finally provide a basis for dealing with the question of Eddie Conrad's claims to extensive speech therapy. By understanding these Judeo-Christian roots of the assumptions of egalitarianism, we can begin to see whether the position has any significance for the broader secular world of health policy decision-making. We now turn to the task of setting out those core assumptions.

Notes

1. Marvin Rosen, Gerald R. Clark, and Marvin S. Kivitz, eds., *History of Mental Retardation: Collected Papers,* Vol I (Baltimore: University Park Press, 1976); and Leo Kenner, *A History of the Care and Study of the Mentally Retarded* (Springfield, Ill: Charles C. Thomas, 1964).
2. Plato, *The Republic* (495 E) (New York: Charles Scribner's Sons, 1928).
3. Rosen, Clark, and Kivitz, *History of Mental Retardation,* p. xiii.

4. William L. Langer, "Infanticide: A Historical Survey," *The Journal of Psychohistory* 1 (Winter 1974): 353–54.

5. Deuteronomy 24:17–18, see also Deuteronomy 10: 17–19; Deuteronomy 14: 28–29; Deuteronomy 27:19.

6. See, for example, Amos 4:1–3, where Amos has the Lord call those who oppress the poor and crush the needy "cows of Bashan" who will be taken away "with hooks" and "cast forth into Harmon."

7. Ezekiel 22:29.

8. Isaiah 6:1–2.

9. Ronald S. Sider, *Cry Justice: The Bible on Hunger and Poverty* (New York: Paulist Press, 1980). Many other secondary sources concur in emphasizing the overwhelming concern of the Biblical authors for the poor and oppressed. Among those used in preparing this chapter are Martin Hengel, *Property and Riches in the Early Church* (Philadelphia: Fortress Press, 1974), pp. 12–22; F. Charles Fensham, "Widow, Orphan, and the Poor in Ancient Near Eastern Legal and Wisdom Literature," *Journal of Near Eastern Studies* 21 (1962): 129–39; Richard Hiers, "Friends by Unrighteous Mammon: The Eschatological Proletariat (Luke 16:9)," *Journal of the American Academy of Religion* 30 (March 1970): 30–36; N. W. Porteous, "The Care of the Poor in the Old Testament," *Service in Christ: Essays Presented to Karl Barth on his 80th Birthday,* ed. James I. McCord and T. H. Parkes (Grand Rapids, Mich.: William B. Eerdmans Publishing Co., 1966), pp. 27–36.

10. Others not represented include Joshua, Judges, II Kings, Esther, Song of Solomon, Joel, Obadiah, and Jonah.

11. Although ancient Christians held the reference here to be messianic, recent scholars have dropped the idea and classify it as a "royal psalm with only indirect reference to the Messiah." See *Anchor Bible,* Vol. 16 *The Psalms,* ed. Mitchell Dahood (Garden City, N.Y.: Doubleday, 1966), p. 179.

12. Psalm 72:12–14; see also Ps. 82:1–5; Ps. 140:12; Ps. 146: 6–9; Ps. 10:14,17; Ps. 113:5–9; Ps. 41:1–2; Ps. 103:6–7; Ps. 15:25.

13. Exodus 23:10; Leviticus 25:1–7. For sources analyzing the Sabbatical and Jubilee Years see Robert B. Sloan, Jr. *The Favorable Year of the Lord: A Study of Jubilary Theology in the Gospel of Luke.* (Austin: Schola Press, 1977; Niels-Erik A. Andreasen, *The Old Testament Sabbath: A Tradition-Historical Investigation.* (Missoula, Mont.: The Society of Biblical Literature. Dissertation Series, Number Seven, 1972).

14. Exodus 23:10 (*Today's English Version Bible—Old Testament*).

15. Deuteronomy 15:1–4.

16. Deuteronomy 15:12–14.

17. Deuteronomy 15:14–15.

18. Deuteronomy 15:7–8.

19. Leviticus 25:8–55.

20. Aaron Rothkoff, "Sabbatical Year and Jubilee," *Encyclopaedia Judaica,* ed. Cecil Roth and Geoffrey Wigoder, Vol. XIV (Jerusalem: Keter Publishing House, The Macmillan Co., 1971), pp. 573–86.

21. *The Pentateuch and Haftorahs,* ed. J. H. Hertz (London: Soncino Press, 1960), p. 532.

22. Jeremiah 34:8–17.

23.   II Chronicles 36:17–21.

24.   Nehemiah 10:28–31.

25.   Roland de Vaux, *Ancient Israel: Its Life and Institutions,* trans. John McHugh (New York: McGraw-Hill Book Co., Inc., 1961). *Today's English Version Bible—Old Testament,* Introduction to Leviticus 25:8ff., as cited in Sider, *Cry Justice,* p. 78. Edward Neufield holds that such laws were observed occasionally, but not necessarily at regular intervals. See his "Socio-economic Background of Yobel and Semitta," *Revista degli Studi Orientali* 33 (1958): 53–124, esp. 119.

26.   Some writers contend that provisions such as Hillel's *prosbaul* prove that the remission of debts at least, was practiced during the Sabbatical years. See, for example, John Howard Yoder, *The Politics of Jesus* (Grand Rapids, Mich.: William B. Eerdmans Publishing Co., 1972), Ch. 3, esp. p. 70. Other scholars maintain that although the actual practice of the Sabbatical is questionable, the importance of the meaning of the Sabbatical is clear. See Walter Bruggemann, *The Land: Place as Gift, Promise, and Challenge in Biblical Faith* (Philadelphia: Fortress Press, 1977), p. 63.

27.   de Vaux, *Ancient Israel,* p. 175.

28.   Robert North, *Sociology of the Biblical Jubilee* (Rome: Pontificio Instituto Biblico, 1954), p. 36; "Biblical Echoes in the Holy Year," *American Ecclesiastical Review* 123 (1950): 416–36.

29.   Henry Hart Milman, *The History of the News, from the Earliest Period Down to Modern Times,* Vol. 1 (New York: A.C. Armstrong and Son, 1881, p. 206; Jans Jochen Boecker, *Law and the Administration of Justice in the Old Testament,* trans. Jeremy Maiser (Minneapolis: Augsburg Publishing House, 1980), pp. 90–91; Daniel Maguire, *A New American Justice* (Garden City, N.Y.: Doubleday, 1980), esp. pp. 123–24, and note 46 on p. 200.

30.   For a rich analysis of the centrality of the notion of the land as a gift see Walter Bruggeman, *The Land,* esp. pp. 47–54, and "Reflections on Biblical Understanding of Property," *International Review of Missions* 64 (1975): 354–61; Juan I Alfaro, "The Land-Stewardship," *Biblical Theology Bulletin* 8 (April 1978): 51–61; W. D. Davies, *The Gospel and the Land* (Berkeley: University of California Press, 1974).

31.   Deuteronomy 15:4.

32.   Exodus 19: 5; Deuteronomy 10:14; I Chronicles 29:10–14.

33.   Leviticus 25:23.

34.   Wisdom 7:3–6 (*The New English Bible* with the Apocrypha)

35.   Proverbs 22:2 (*The New English Bible* with the Apocrypha)

36.   Proverbs 29:13 (*The New English Bible* with the Apocrypha)

37.   Numbers 26: 52–56.

38.   See, for example, J. P. M. van der Ploeg, "Slavery in the Old Testament," *Ketus Testamentum* 22 (1972, supplement): 76; de Vaux, *Ancient Israel,* pp. 80–81; and S. Scott Bartchy, *First-Century Slavery and I Corinthians 7:21* (Missoula, Mont.: The Society of Biblical Literature, 1973), esp. pp. 29–35.

39.   Exodus 22:21. See also Exodus 23:9; Leviticus 19:32–34; Leviticus 24:21–22; Deuteronomy 27:19; de Vaux, *Ancient Israel,* pp. 74–76.

40.   The Hebrew term, *'ebed,* means not only slave, but also subject of the king, officer of the king, and eventually came to be used as a term of courtesy as the English term servant is used. See de Vaux, *Ancient Israel,* p. 80.

41. Deuteronomy 15:12; de Vaux, *Ancient Israel,* p. 83; M. David, "The Manumission of Slaves Under Zedakiah," *Oudtestamenliche Studien* 5 (1948), p. 73.

42. *Encyclopaedia Judaica,* p. 1655; North, *Sociology,* p. 147; de Vaux, *Ancient Israel,* pp. 80, 82.

43. *Encyclopaedia Judaica,* p. 1655; Herman Mueller, "Morality of Slavery in Holy Scripture," *American Ecclesiastical Review* 151 (1964), pp. 309–10; van der Ploeg, "Slavery," pp. 80–82, 86; North, *Sociology,* p. 135; de Vaux, *Ancient Israel,* p. 84.

44. de Vaux, *Ancient Israel,* p. 85.

45. North, *Sociology,* p. 135; cf. Bartchy, *First-Century Slavery,* p. 31.

46. North, *Sociology,* p. 150.

47. Deuteronomy 23:16–17; de Vaux, *Ancient Israel,* p. 87.

48. North, *Sociology,* pp. 135–39; Mueller, "Morality of Slavery," pp. 308–9.

49. de Vaux, "The Position of Women: Widows," *Ancient Israel,* pp. 39–40.

50. Hosea 3:1.

51. Robert J. Karris, "Poor and Rich: The Lukan *Sitz im Leben,*" *Perspectives on Luke-Acts,* ed. Charles H. Talbert (Danville, Va.: Association of Baptist Professors of Religion, 1978), p. 124.

52. For a careful discussion of the dominance of Luke as the critic of the rich see Rudolf Schnackenburg, *The Moral Teaching of the New Testament* (New York: Herder and Herder, 1965), pp. 121–32. He makes clear that while Luke is particularly conscious of the problem of wealth, "it is inadmissible to try to make the evangelist Luke alone responsible for Jesus' disowning of the rich on religious grounds."

53. Mark 4:13–20; Matthew 13:18–23; Luke 8:11–15.

54. The story is common to Luke (18:18–30), Mark (10:17–31), and Matthew (19:16–30). The labeling of the eye of the needle metaphor as hyperbole is part of a widespread, sometimes embarrassingly defensive effort on the part of modern commentators to minimize the power of the story. According to F. Albright and C. S. Mann in the Anchor Bible commentary on the version of the story in Matthew (*Matthew: Introduction, Translation, and Notes* [Garden City, N.Y.: Doubleday, 1971], pp. 232–23), it is not riches per se that are a barrier to salvation. They simply pose a "peculiar temptation to the rich man's spiritual welfare." Vincent Taylor in his important commentary on the presumably earlier version in Mark (*The Gospel According to St. Mark* [New York: St Martin's Press, 1959], p. 429) minimizes the impact by saying that Jesus was not here demanding a universal renunciation of property, but making a judgment on a case-by-case basis.

55. Luke 21:1–4; Mark 12:41–44.

56. Fensham, "Widow, Orphan," p. 1; Ernst Lohmeyer, *Das Vater-unser* (Gottingen: Vandenhoeck and Ruprecht, 1946), p. 163.

57. Andre Trocme, *Jesus and the Non-Violent Revolution,* trans. Michael H. Shank and Marlin E. Miller (Scottsdale, Fa.: Herald Press, 1973), pp. 27–40; Yoder, *Politics of Jesus,* pp. 64–77.

58. Robert B. Sloan, Jr., *The Favorable Year of the Lord: A Study of Jubilary Theology in the Gospel of Luke* (Austin, Texas: Schola Press, 1977), see especially pp. 139–46. Sloan cites, among other texts, Jesus' reading in the synagogue of the suffering servant passage from Isaiah (in which he turns the messianic prophecy into an identification of himself with the messiah). In that text, the messiah announces that he is annointed to preach good news to the poor, proclaim release to the captives and the

recovering of sight to the blind, to set at liberty those who are oppressed, and to proclaim the acceptable year of the Lord. Sloan argues that this is a conscious reference to the Jubilee with all the hard-nosed political and economic implications it contains.

59. Luke 16:13.

60. Luke 19:9–10.

61. Luke 12:13–21.

62. Luke 3: 10–11.

63. Luke 16:19–31.

64. Taylor, *Gospel According to Mark,* pp. 429–30; Albright and Mann, *Matthew: Introduction, Translation,* p. 233.

65. Matthew 6:3.

66. Matthew 6:19.

67. Romans 15:25–29.

68. I Corinthians 16:1–4; II Corinthians 8: 1–15; II Corinithians 9: 1–15.

69. II Corinthians 8:14, cf. II Corinthians 9:8.

70. I Timothy 3:2–3; I Timothy 3:8; I Timothy 6:6–10; II Timothy 3:1–5; Titus 1:7.

71. Hebrews 13:5; James 2:1–9; James 2:14–17; I John 3:16–18; Jude 1:11–12.

72. James 1:9–11.

73. Luke 1:52–53.

74. See, for example, Matthew 6:24–33; Matthew 10:42; Acts 20:32–35; II Corinthians 11:27–30.

75. Matthew 20:16.

76. Matthew 25:40.

77. Luke 14;12–23; Luke 7:18–23; Matthew 11:2–6.

78. For a thorough discussion of the collapse of the importance of the land in Paul, see Davies, *Gospel and the Land,* pp. 164–220.

79. Romans 4:10–12; see Davies, *Gospel and the Land,* p. 175.

80. Davies, *Gospel and the Land,* p. 200.

81. Galatians 3:28.

82. See Marcus Barth, "Jews and Gentiles: The Social Character of Justification in Paul," *Journal of Ecumenical Studies* 5 (1968): 241.; and Robert M. Grant, *Early Christianity and Society* (Harper & Row, 1977), p. 106.

83. Davies, *Gospel and the Land,* p. 243.

84. *Ibid.,* pp. 288–335.

85. *Ibid.,* p. 252.

86. Davies, *Gospel and the Land,* p. 255; Richard J. Cassidy, *Jesus, Politics and Society: A Study of Luke's Gospel* (Maryknoll, N.Y.: Orbis Books, 1978), p. 24.

87. Acts 2:44–45.

88. Acts 4:32–35.

89. Ernst Troeltsch, *The Social Teaching of the Christian Churches,* trans. Olive Wyon (New York: Harper Torchbooks, The Cloister Library, 1960), pp. 62–63.

90. Paul Feine, Johannes Behm, and Werner Georg Kummel, *Introduction to the New Testament,* trans. A. J. Mattill, Jr. (Nashville, Tenn.: Abingdon Press, 1966).

91. Grant, *Early Christianity,* p. 100; David L. Mealand, "Community of Goods and Utopian Allusions in Acts II–IV," *Journal of Theological Studies* 28 (1977), pp. 96–97; Hengel, *Property and Riches,* pp. 8ff.

92. Grant, *Early Christianity*, p. 99; James Downey, O.S.A., "The Early Jerusalem Christians," *The Bible Today* 91 (1977), p. 1295; Mealand, "Community of Goods," p. 99; and Hengel, *Property and Riches*, pp. 9, 32; but some, such as Hengel, argue that the communalism of Acts must be distinguished from Qumran in that Qumran's sharing is rigidly fixed by law, whereas the community in Acts shares spontaneously and voluntarily.

93. Karris, "Poor and Rich," p. 118.

94. Downey, "Early Jerusalem," p. 1296; Hengel, *Property and Riches*, pp. 29, 39–41.

95. Luke T. Johnson, *Sharing Possessions: Mandate and Symbol of Faith* (Philadelphia: Fortress Press, 1981), pp. 21–22; Downey, "Early Jerusalem," p. 1297.

96. Grant, *Early Christianity*, p. 99; Downey, "Early Jerusalem," p. 1297.

97. Johnson, *Sharing Possessions*, p. 110; Hengel, *Property and Riches*, p. 35; Grant, *Early Christianity*, p. 102.

98. Feine, Behm, and Kummel, *Introduction to New Testament*, pp. 117; cf. Troeltsch, *Social Teaching*, p. 62.

99. Luke 10:38–42; Luke 8:3.

100. Luke 7:36–50.

101. Ena P. Gould, *A Critical and Exegetical Commentary on the Gospel According to St. Mark. The International Critical Commentary*, ed. Charles A. Briggs, Samuel R. Driver, and Alfred Plummer (New York: Charles Scribner's Sons, 1907), pp. 256, 259.

102. *The Manual of Discipline* (IQS), trans. P. Wernberg-Moller, Pl. vi. 19; cf. Millar Burrows, "The Damascus Document XVIII," *The Dead Sea Scrolls* (New York: The Viking Press, 1955), p. 363; see also Grant, *Early Christianity*, pp. 100–101.

103. Grant, *Early Christianity*, p. 101.

104. Rudolf Schnackenburg, *The Moral Teaching of the New Testament* (New York: Herder and Herder, 1965), pp. 127, 131–32.

105. *The Didache as Teaching of the Twelve Apostles* 4:8, trans. Francis X. Glimm, *The Fathers of the Church* (New York: CIMA Publishing Co., Inc., 1947), p. 174.

106. See "The Passing of Peregrinus," *Lucian*, Vol. 5, trans. A. M. Harmon, The Loeb Classical Library (Cambridge, Mass.: Harvard University Press, 1936), p. 13.

107. This summary is based on Grant, *Early Christianity*, pp. 105–7.

108. Clement of Alexandria, *Quis Dives Salvetur?* trans. G. M. Butterworth, ed. T. E. Page, et al. Loeb Classical Library (Cambridge, Mass.: Harvard University Press, 1919, 1953), 27. 6–7; Grant, *Early Christianity*, pp. 108–9.

109. Clement, *Quis Dives Salvetur?* 33. 2–5.

110. Clement, *Quis Dives Salvetur?* 31. 21.

111. Gen. hom. XVI 5, *Origen: Homilies on Genesis and Exodus*, trans. Ronald E. Heine (Washington, D.C.: Catholic University of America Press, 1981), p. 222.

112. Tertullian, Apology, Ch. 39, *The Ante Nicean Fathers: Translation of the Writings of the Fathers Down to A.D. 325*, ed. Alexander Roberts and James Donaldson, Vol. 3, *Late Christianity: Its Founder, Tertullian*, (New York: Charles Scribner's Sons, 1926), p. 46.

113. *Ibid.*

114. Cyprian, Epistle IV, 1. 13–17, *The Ante Nicean Fathers*, Vol. 8, *The Writings of Cyprian*, trans. Robert E. Wallis (Edinburgh: T. and T. Clark, 1870), pp. 18–19.

115.   Cyprian, *The Writings of Cyprian*, Epistle LX 2. 9–12, p. 203.

116.   Lactantius, Vo. 2, *The Divine Institutes, The Works of Lactantius, Ante Nicean Christian Library* (1871), Book 3, Ch. 22, pp. 193–94.

117.   *Ibid.*, Book 6, Ch. 12, esp. pp. 382–83.

118.   Grant, *Early Christianity*, p. 112.

119.   Chrysostom, Homily X, 5. 6–13. In *A Select Library of the Nicene and Post-Nicene Fathers of the Christian Church*, ed. Philip Schaff, Vol. 12, *Saint Chrysostom: Homilies on the Epistles of Paul to the Corinthians*, The Oxford translation with notes by Talbot W. Chambers (New York: The Christian Literature Company, 1889), p. 56.

120.   William Walsh and John P. Langan, "Patristic Social Consciousness—The Church and the Poor," in *The Faith That Does Justice*. ed. John C. Haughey (New York: Paulist Press, 1977), p. 128.

121.   St. Augustine, *Faith, Hope and Charity*, trans. Bernard M. Peebles (New York: Fathers of the Church, Inc., 1947), pp. 357–472, esp. Ch. 18, pp. 425–26; see also *Expositions on the Book of Psalms by Saint Augustine*, edited and condensed from the Oxford translation by A. Cleveland Coke, Vol. VIII of *The Nicene and Post-Nicene Fathers of the Christian Church*, ed. Philip Schaff (New York: The Christian Literature Company, 1888), Ps. XLIX. 9, p. 171, and Ps. CXLVII, 13, p. 668. Augustine expressed the idea that the greatest almsgiving is the forgiveness of debtors in *Enchiridion*, trans. J. F. Shaw, ed. Philip Schaff, Vol. III, 1887, Ch. 73, p. 261; also in the Sermons 60, 61, and 72 "On Almsgiving," and "Commentary on the Lord's Sermon on the Mount," in *The Fathers of the Church: St. Augustine, Vol. VIII*, trans. Denis J. Kavanagh, Roy Joseph Deferrari, et al. New York: Fathers of the Church, Inc., 1951), pp. 259–99, and 113–18.

122.   David Knowles, *The Evolution of Medieval Thought* (New York: Vintage Books, 1962).

123.   Troeltsch, *Social Teaching*, p. 290.

124.   Knowles, "Religious Poverty: Traditional Approaches," *The Way Supplement.* (No. 9, Spring 1970): 18–21. : 16–27.

125.   *Ibid.*, p. 22.

126.   Barbara Tuchman, *A Distant Mirror* (N.Y.: Alfred A. Knopf, 1979), p. 35.

127.   Ibid., p. 30.

128.   Knowles, "Religious Poverty," p. 24.

129.   Troeltsch, *Social Teaching*, pp. 369–71, and note 191 on p. 442.

130.   A particularly readable account appears in Tuchman, *Distant Mirror*, p. 372–75.

131.   Cited in Tuchman, *Distant Mirror*, p. 374.

132.   *Ibid.*

133.   *Ibid.*, p. 375.

134.   Thomas More, *Utopia*, trans. Paul Turner (Harmondsworth, England: Penguin Books, Ltd., 1965 [1516]), p. 7.

135.   *Ibid.*, p. 66.

136.   *Ibid.*, p. 129.

137.   *Ibid.*

138.   *Ibid.*, p. 131; see also p. 118 where More has Raphael say that "Christ prescribed of His own disciples a communist way of life" still practiced in the

monasteries and convents, which he describes as "the most truly Christian communities."

139. John Calvin, Commentary on II Corinthians 8:13–14 in *Calvin's Commentaries* Vol 10, trans. T. A. Smith; ed. David W. Torrence and Thomas F. Torrence (Grand Rapids, Mich.: William B. Eerdmans Publishing Co., 1964), pp. 112–113.

140. For two major sources see George Houston Williams, *Radical Reformation* (Philadelphia: Westminster Press, 1962) and Hans J. Hillerbrand, *The Reformation: A Narrative History Related by Contemporary Observers and Participants* (New York: Harper & Row, 1964), pp. 214–97.

141. Martin Luther, "Against the Robbing and Murdering Hordes of Peasants" (1525), *Luther's Works* (46) (Philadelphia: Fortress Press, 1967).

142. The translation of many of the key documents appears in Hans J. Hillerbrand, *The Reformation* (New York: Harper & Row, 1964), pp. 223–28.

143. *Meister Heinrich Gresbeck's Bericht.* The text is translated in Hillerbrand, *The Reformation,* p. 257.

144. Troeltsch, *Social Teaching,* p. 703, note 488.

145. *Die Alteste Chronik der Hutterischen Bruder,* p. 87, translated in Hillerbrand, *The Reformation,* p. 271.

146. John Lilburne, "England's Birth-Right Justified," *The Levellers in the English Revolution* [Documents of Revolution], ed. G.E. Aylmer (Ithaca, N.Y.: Cornell University Press, 1975 [1645], p. 61.

147. "The 'Large' Petition," [1647], *Levellers,* p. 80.

148. William Walwyn, "A Manifestation," [1649], *Levellers,* p. 153.

149. "An Agreement of the Free People of England," *Levellers,* pp. 160–68.

150. Troeltsch, *Social Teaching,* p. 710. I have been unable to locate these words in original Leveller documents. They do, however, reflect the clear spirit of the belief upon which Leveller doctrine is based.

151. See, for example, Lilburne, "Postcript to Londons [sic] Liberty," *Levellers,* pp. 71–72.

152. Walwyn, "A Manifestation," pp. 153–54.

153. "An Agreement of the Free People of England," pp. 162, 166.

154. A brief account appears in Troeltsch, *Social Teaching,* pp. 711–12. Both of these groups must be kept separate from the movement reflected in the pamphlet, *Tyranipocrit,* which advocated strict economic equality, but not common ownership.

155. For a fascinating defense of the thesis that Methodism functioned for England as its eighteenth-century democratic revolution, thus sparing England the violent experience of the French, see Bernard Semmel, *The Methodist Revolution* (New York: Basic Books, 1973). See also Troeltsch, Social Teaching, pp. 721–24.

156. John Wesley, "Thoughts Upon Slavery [1774]," *Works of the Reverend John Wesley* XI (Bristol, England: William Pine, 1771–1774), pp. 61–79.

157. Semmel, *Methodist Revolution,* p. 112.

158. Samuel Bradburn, "Equality" [sermon preached at the Methodist Chapel, Broad Mead, Bristol, February 28, 1794], in *Sermons Preached on Particular Occasions* (London: T. Blanshard, City Road, 1817), pp. 215–67, esp. pp. 218–21.

159. *Ibid.,* p. 237.

160. *Ibid.,* p. 243.

161. *Ibid.*, p. 248.

162. Cited in Semmel, *Methodist Revolution,* p. 122.

163. For a critical account of the movement's origins, see Bernard Murchland, *The Dreams of Christian Socialism: An Essay on Its European Origins* (Washington, D.C.: American Enterprise Institute for Public Policy Research, 1982).

164. F. D. Maurice, *Christian Socialism. Dialogue between Somebody (a person of respectability) and Nobody (the writer).* Tracts on Christian Socialism, No. 1, February, 1850, London, p. 1. Cited in Torben Christensen, *Origin and History of Christian Socialism in 1848–54* (Copenhagen: Universitelsforlaget I Aarhus, 1962), p. 137.

165. William Temple, *Christianity and Social Order* (New York: Seabury Press, 1977), p. 136.

166. Murchland, *The Dream,* p. 7.

167. *Ibid.*, p. 6.

168. F. B. Smith, *The People's Health* (New York: Holmes and Meier Publishers, Inc., 1979), p. 218.

169. Charles Kingsley, *The Massacre of the Innocents,* originally given as a speech to the Ladies Sanitary Association, July 1859. Reprinted in *Charles Kingsley: His Letters and Memories of His Life,* Vol. 2, ed. Frances Kingsley (London: Henry S. King and Co., 1877), p. 86.

170. James F. Childress, "Who Shall Live When Not All Can Live?" *Soundings* 53 (Winter 1970): 339–54.

171. *Ibid.*, p. 349.

172. Paul Ramsey, *The Patient as Person* (New Haven: Yale University Press, 1970), p. 253, cf. p. 275.

173. Gene Outka, "Social Justice and Equal Access to Health Care," *Journal of Religious Ethics* 2 (Spring 1974): 11–32, esp. pp. 21–24.

174. Karen Lebacqz, *Prenatal Diagnosis: Distributive Justice and the Quality of Life.* Thesis. (Harvard University, Cambridge, Mass., August 1974), esp. pp. 266, 308, 352–53.

175. Earl E. Shelp, *An Inquiry into Christian Ethical Sanctions for the Right to Health Care.* Thesis. Southern Baptist Theological Seminary, Louisville, 1976. (Ann Arbor, Mich.: Xerox University Microfilm, 1977).

176. Robert L. Shelton, "Human Rights and Distributive Justice in Health Care Delivery," *Journal of Medical Ethics* 4 (December 1978): 165–71, esp. pp. 167–69.

177. Charles E. Curran, *Transition and Tradition in Moral Theology* (Notre Dame, Ind.: University of Notre Dame Press, 1979), pp. 139–79.

178. Albert R. Jonsen, "Justice and the Defective Newborn," in *Justice and Health Care,* ed. Earl E. Shelp (Dordrecht, Holland: D. Reidel Publishing Co., 1981), pp. 95–108, esp. pp. 98, 102.

179. LeRoy Walters, "Ethical Issues in Genetic and Reproductive Engineering." Paper presented at the American Association for the Advancement of Science annual meeting, January 4, 1982, esp. p. 9.

180. Robert M. Veatch, "What is a 'Just' Health Care Delivery?" in *Ethics and Health Policy,* eds. Robert M. Veatch and Roy Branson (Cambridge, Mass.: Ballinger Publishing Co., 1976).

181. Shelp, *An Inquiry,* especially the sections beginning on pp. 25 and 62.

3

The Religious Basis for Equality: The Theological Premises

The commitment of the Judeo-Christian tradition to the weak, the needy, the poor, and disabled is overwhelming and consistent. True, there is internal bickering between those in the Pauline tradition who accept some notion of private property and express this obligation in terms of a voluntaristic commitment to charity and the more robust Lucan egalitarian communalism where equality comes from the abandonment of private property altogether. The important point, however, is that both versions of the tradition push toward a wholehearted equality. For the followers of Paul, the rich within the community give to the poor ''that there may be equality.'' For Luke's descendents, everything is to be held in common and distributed ''as any have need.''

This consistent voice from a long and complex tradition has immediate implications for anyone who is trying from within that world view to resolve the problem of our obligation to the retarded and rest of us who are handicapped. But it raises a more complicated problem of what its significance is for the modern secular world, saturated with the history of that tradition, but seen by many as standing on its own intellectual base. Are there some basic premises that lead to the Judeo-Christian egalitarian conclusion that are shared by those working in the world of secular philosophy and public policy? Are those who are less persuaded by the faith commitments of that tradition able to build an alternative philosophical base for these social policy decisions that escapes the requirements of a radical egalitarianism?

In order to deal with these questions it will be necessary to summarize succinctly the central premises, the faith commitments, upon which the Judeo-Christian version of equality is based. Then we can, in the next chapter, see what place, if any, similar premises have in a more secular theory of justice for responding to the needs of the handicapped.

It is perhaps overly ambitious to summarize the core faith commitments of three thousand years of very complicated history in three basic premises, but, with admitted oversimplification, that is what we will attempt in this chapter. The key premises are contained in what theologians will recognize as the doctrines of God, creation, and stewardship. First, God is absolute, the ultimate center of value in comparison to which all humans are equal in their finitude. Second, the earth and all that is in it was created and given as a gift to the community such that there never was a time when there were unowned resources in the state of nature waiting to be appropriated by anyone clever enough, ambitious enough, or powerful enough to take them. Then, finally, because the resources of the world are in some critical sense a common possession of the community and because all are bound together as equals in that community, people individually and collectively bear within limits a responsibility to see that those resources are used to recreate or maintain the equality that is the appropriate relation among humans. Each of these premises requires some exposition. Expressed in this form, each of these core premises has a very traditional, religious ring to it, but intellectually identical moves are an essential part of any secular theory of justice as well.

The Equality of Humans Before an Infinite God

Radical Monotheism and Human Equality

The first and most fundamental commitment of the Judeo-Christian tradition that leads to a commitment to equality is that God is absolute, the ultimate concern, the infinite center of value in comparison to which all humans are equal in their finitude. The God of Israel is a radically transcendent, omnipotent creator God, who rescued a helpless people. In comparison to the Absolute, humans, in their finitude, are nothing, and any differences among us count as nothing. In comparison to an infinite, all finites are equal.

This was the opening line of argument used by the Methodist Samuel Bradburn at the end of the eighteenth century in his sermon on the Pauline text, "that there may be equality." Commenting on the radical gap between the transcendence of God and the finitude of man he says, "It is a humbling consideration; a little while ago I was nothing! I had no more being than the meanest reptile! The same divine power that produced me, produced also the lowest and least of insects; and considered with relation to God, I am no way superior to them, let alone to mankind; for all are equally his creatures."[1]

The idea of an absolute God as the foundation for equality is captured well in H. Richard Niebuhr's discussion of *Radical Monotheism*.[2] He makes precisely this argument. He acknowledges that commitment to human equality is a dogma, a commitment based on faith. That faith is radically monotheistic. He contrasts this with pluralistic faiths committed to "finite centers of value." With such petty commitments humans are surely unequal in their usefulness, merit, or claim. But, he says, with a radical monotheism relying on "the ultimate source of being and the ultimate power that conserves being,"[3] humans are radically relativized. Equality becomes the only plausible conclusion. A similar logic underlies Paul Tillich's commitment to human equality.

Salvation by Faith and Human Equality

A key element in the Christian commitment to human equality is its understanding that salvation is by faith rather than any merit that one earns through good works, social usefulness, or the brute strength of human accomplishment. Anglican Archbishop Temple, who was an important part of Christian socialism, put it bluntly, "Apart from faith in God, there is really nothing to be said for the notion of human equality."[4] Here he follows the logic of Bradburn some 150 years earlier. Bradburn's sermon on equality, after contrasting human finitude with God's ultimacy, makes the link to the traditional Christian doctrine of sin. Men are all equal, he argues, with respect to their total depravity. All are under the same necessity of being saved by the free grace of God.[5] The doctrine divorces any consideration of moral claim from merit, productivity, or usefulness.

The same idea was central to Karl Barth's commitment to human equality. Analyzing the text in Paul's letter to the Romans in which Paul says "there is no distinction: for all have sinned, and fall short of the glory of God," Barth argues that no positive possession of men is sufficient to provide a foundation for human solidarity. The positive factors, he says, are the making of differences. Genuine solidarity is grounded in what men lack.[6] All are radically inadequate in comparison with the infinite; in this there is no distinction. Barth, continuing this line of Pauline thought emphasizing salvation by faith, concludes that it is this that makes possible equal rights for all God's children.[7]

Equality in Creation and Common Fatherhood

Alternatively, instead of basing the commitment to the equality among humans in salvation by faith, the equality of human depravity, and need for grace, scholars working within the Judeo-Christian tradition have traced it back to an equality in creation. "Small and great alike are of his makings and all are under his providence equally," says the writer of the Wisdom of Solomon.[8] Gregory of Nazianzus, as we have seen, spoke of an "original equality" symbolized by our common and equal need for the necessities of air, water, and so forth.

Richard Overton, one of the seventeenth-century Levellers, brings this theme of equality in creation to the personal level when he bases his case for equal rights in our common origin. In "An Arrow Against All Tyrants," he argues, "For by natural birth, all men are equally and alike borne to like propriety, liberty and freedom, and as we are delivered of God by the hand of nature into this world, every one with a natural, innate freedom and propriety . . . even so are we to live, every one equally and alike to enjoy his Birthright and priviledge."[9]

Often, as in the sermon of Samuel Bradburn on equality, the recognition of an equality in creation is carried one step further by developing the parent-offspring metaphor. Bradburn, reflecting on our common creation, asks "Have we not all one father?"[10] The parent-offspring metaphor has been a dominant one since Biblical times.[11] John Lilburne, Richard Overton's fellow Leveller, writes from prison a postscript to a pamphlet in which he sets out a general statement of equal rights. He bases it on the fact that we are all "Sons of Adam."[12] The same claim is made by the nineteenth-century French Christian Socialist, Robert Lamennais.[13]

The metaphor seems to serve two functions in the logic of the argument for equality. First and most relevant to the present discussion of the equality of finite humans in comparison to the transcendence of God as the ultimate center of value, the fatherhood metaphor conveys a sense of equality like that that a parent might feel toward his or her children. It is impossible for many parents to conceive of comparing the value or worth of their children. Even though the children have differences, they are utterly trivial when it comes to comparing their moral worth in the eyes of the parent. So much more so would finite differences collapse to insignificance in the eyes of a parent who could be conceived of as an infinite.

The second function of the parent metaphor is to convey a bondedness between the offspring. Through no doing of their own they find themselves in a family-like relationship with others who are their brothers and sisters, offspring of the same parent. This basic assumption of a bond linking individual humans will be important when we discuss the third basic assumption of the Judeo-Christian tradition, the assumption of responsibility for the welfare of others in the moral community.

The parent-offspring metaphor suggests the most critical interpretive problem in the Judeo-Christian notion of equality. To what extent is the commitment to equality through the tradition limited to a kind of spiritual, ethereal quality? How radically does this equality cut through the superstructure and demand real, material equality of welfare, happiness, education, and health? Constantly within the tradition have been attempts to escape the more radical concrete social and economic implications. Bradburn, for example, having argued that humans are equal in their finitude, their creatureliness, their need for grace, and in their right to impartial justice, starts to vascillate in the second part of his sermon where he begins to acknowledge certain necessary inequalities. Mankind, he says, is surely not physically equal. Unequal talents in fact are necessary, he says, for our common comfort and safety. From this he acknowledges a doctrine of *temporary* private property and a division of labor, clearly in conversation with British political philosophers such as Locke.

But at this point Bradburn places a severe constraint on the notion of private property. In comparison with modern libertarians who have taken Locke down the path to pure private property under the unrestrained control of those who justly acquire it, Bradburn turns down the left-hand fork in the path, returning to the Biblical text on which he is preaching. He considers and rejects the communitarianism of Acts.[14] He writes this off as a peculiarity created by the persecution of the early church in Jerusalem by the Romans. Instead, he turns to the Pauline text, arguing, "The plain meaning of which is that the Christians at Corinth who were rich should out of their abundance supply the wants of the poor brethren of Judea; and if ever the Corinthians should be in want, and those of Judea should abound, they should be equally ready to relieve them, that there might be no want on one side, and no superfluity on the other. And wherever the love of God and our neighbor is experienced it will always produce such an equality as this."[15]

The Lucan communalism is not required for Bradburn, but Pauline equality in the context of private property and almsgiving is. This does not necessarily mean a levelling.[16] People will differ in their tastes and life-styles and those with particular talents will be encouraged to develop them in order that they may serve the common good. This is, however, a radical movement beyond the ethereal, spiritualizing equality of dignity or equality of worth, to a hard-nosed, practical, robust social and economic doctrine of equality in which there will be no want and no superfluity.

Creation and the Rejection of the Notion of Unowned Property

The idea that there is an ultimate value, an ultimate concern, an absolute transcendence—in short, a god—in comparison to which all humans are equal in their finitude is the most important presupposition of the Judeo-Christian view of justice as equality. By itself, however, it does not lead to the conclusion that members of the moral community bear a responsibility to use whatever resources there are to improve the lot of those who are most in need, most in distress, or most handicapped. Two other premises are needed for an argument to lead to that conclusion.

In fact, by itself, equality in creation, equality in finitude, or even equality in moral worth can be used to escape the full, radical implications of justice within the Judeo-Christian tradition. Some interpreters (such as Bradburn and, to some extent, Maurice) attempt to squirm out of the jaws of the rigorous egalitarianism called for by the tradition by arguing that this equality before the eyes of God is merely a commitment to equal respect, equal dignity, or equal humanness without any tough implications for resource redistribution.

Two other premises are needed to complete an argument that justice requires whatever resource redistribution necessary to provide at least an opportunity for equality of outcomes insofar as possible. Yet that is clearly what is talked about in both the Lucan and Pauline versions of the Judeo-Christian vision. Their notion of equality pushes beyond some vague equality of dignity; it takes into account unequal needs because of physical and mental differences to attempt to give people a chance at equality of welfare. One of these premises establishes whether there are any resources available to be redistributed. The other provides a basis for saying that humans have some responsibility to redistribute those resources according to the relationship of equality called for by a vision that sees humans as equals.

The Creation Myth

If the notion of human equality stood by itself without some functional equivalent of the doctrines of creation and stewardship, it would hit head-on against the libertarian view of property we have inherited from the modern social contract theorists. Hobbes and Locke (or at least the secular versions of them), regardless of their differences, both share an individualism in which resources in the state of nature are originally unowned and, within certain limits, up for grabs. The Judeo-Christian creation myth is a way of challenging that view of nature and nature's resources. There was, for anyone who adopts some version of the set of presuppositions implied in that story, never a time when there was any such thing as unowned resources to be claimed on a first-come-first-served basis by anyone who had need. All that is, first belonged to God—that ultimate transcendence. Certain portions are transmitted—by gift—to individuals or, more often, to communities. But they are always transmitted with strings attached.

This is the image conveyed in the Jubilee restoration. ''No land shall be sold outright, because the land is mine, and you are coming into it as aliens and settlers.''[17] The land is a gift, a public good, a community resource or, if not, then a privately held trusteeship to be used responsibly according to the needs of others.

Two Views of Property

Thus the two views about property we have identified began to emerge within the framework of the presumption that natural resources were a gift from God subject to the duties of responsible trusteeship. The first, and most straightforward, was the view that property should be held in common. This was a view common in utopian communities not only in the Judeo-Christian world, but with the Greeks as well. But it found particularly rich soil in the communities influenced by the Judeo-Christian story: the Qumran community as well as the Christian church in Acts. It is well represented in the earliest Christian writers including the Didache, the charmingly naive Epiphanes, and Origen. According to all of them, property not only starts out as a common trust, but is to be kept that way.

The alternative is the more Pauline view in which some form of temporary private control is exercised. It is seen in the limited ownership addressed by the Jubilee restoration as well as in the acts of charity of the Pauline churches. Clement's stress on almsgiving as well as the limited acceptance of private property in Cyprian, Tertullian, and Chrysostom all fit into this second view. What is important, however, is that even for those who accept some notion of private ownership, it is limited. The right of private property for Clement was limited by the needs of others.[18] The obligation was an individual one; the almsgiving was an act of charity, but it was nevertheless morally required. The view is totally at odds with the modern libertarian's view of private property in which once individuals acquire resources they are theirs to do with as they please. For the Judeo-Christian tradition property was never unowned and can never be appropriated without strings attached.

Stewardship and Human Responsibility

Thus far we have found two critical premises. The first is that people are equal in their finitude and in the claim to have a chance to have their needs met. The second is that resources are available to meet these needs. Property is a community resource. There is no such thing as unowned property to be appropriated by individuals clever enough or powerful enough to take it. What is still needed is a moral premise linking the two in such a way that persons in the moral community would have an obligation to use the community property to respond to the claims of the retarded. That comes in the form of what has traditionally been referred to as the doctrine of stewardship.

The idea has deep Biblical roots. We see it in the Old Testament idea of land as a gift to be used for the needy and in the New Testament parables that see the human as a laborer tending the vineyard or as a sower of the mustard seed. Over and over again members of the Judeo-Christian community are active agents. They take what resources they have been given, mix their labor with them, and responsibly use the gifts they have received to create something better. Acquisitiveness, in which goods are hoarded or hidden, in which the human is mere passive possessor for his or her own benefit, is roundly condemned.

Ambrose, the fourth-century Bishop of Milan, interprets the Old Testament story of Ahab, to make the point that the duty of stewardship is ever present.[19] Ahab possessed much but, in his greed, still coveted more and eventually, through a murderous plot of Jezebel, his wife, gained possession of the small plot of land belonging to Naboth. The story shows the tradition's understanding of the duty of stewardship in two different ways. First, the reason Naboth gives for refusing to sell the land to Ahab is his duty of stewardship. As the Old Testament scholar Bernard Anderson puts it:

> Properly speaking, it was not Naboth's "private property" to dispose of as he pleased. It belonged to the whole family or clan through whom it had been passed down from generation to generation as a sacred inheritance. His refusal—"Yahweh forbids that I should give you the inheritance of my fathers"—revealed an attitude toward land that was unique with Israel. According to this view, Yahweh himself was the owner of the land. Faithful to his promise, he had brought the Israelites into a cultured country and had given the land to various tribes and clans. They were to act as stewards of Yahweh's property, administering it for the welfare of the whole community. So land-grabbing and private speculation were ruled out by the very nature of the covenant community.[20]

On the other hand, the modern Jesuit scholars William Walsh and John Langan interpret Ambrose to make the stewardship point not with reference to the obligation of Naboth, but Ahab:

Ambrose uses the story of Naboth to develop the common patristic doctrine that all creation was made available for all mankind and that the rich are essentially its stewards. He deplores the ruthless greed of the avaricious, their heartless exploitation of the poor, and the ostentation of their luxury. As far as the avaricious are concerned, almsgiving is defined as restitution for stolen goods: ''You are not making a gift of your possessions to the poor person. You are handing over to him what is his.''[21]

The same theme of stewardship appears throughout the Judeo-Christian tradition. Calvin, in his *Institutes* says, ''We are the stewards of everything God has conferred on us by which we are able to help our neighbor, and are required to render account of our stewardship.'' From this, Calvin derives what he calls the ''rule for proper management of our gifts: whatever benefits we obtain from the Lord have been entrusted to us on this condition: that they be applied to the common good of the church. And therefore the lawful use of all benefits consists in a liberal and kindly sharing of them with others.''[22]

This duty of stewardship is made more comprehensible by the belief structure that sees humans as having a common origin regularly expressed by the fatherhood metaphor. If humans are brothers and sisters within the common moral community of the church and have the same parentage, bonds are established linking one to another. According to the Judeo-Christian myth system, it is not—as the modern libertarians would have us believe—that individuals originally stood isolated and alone in the state of nature only gradually building artificial and fragile links whenever it was necessary to avoid a life that was nasty, brutish, and short. A duty of stewardship in such a context would be contrived at best. But with an understanding of human relations built on the model of brotherhood and common parentage, the linkages are bound in blood, making the community the corporate protector of the welfare of those in need.

This doctrine of stewardship completes the logic of the Judeo-Christian commitment to egalitarianism. Humans are to be active co-creators constantly reordering the world. They have at their disposal resources for this project which are in one of two forms. They may be gifts held temporarily by individuals, but held with strings attached. In that case, they are private property, but private property in a very truncated sense. This private property is to be used to provide for the welfare of others. Alternatively, these resources are more literally held in common. They are dispensed from the common pot according to the needs of individuals. In either case the goal is equality of opportunity to have needs met, an equality derived from an initial acceptance of an infinite, radically monotheistic God, in comparison to which all humans are equal in their finitude and in their claims to have their needs addressed.

These three doctrines of the faith—the equality of finites in comparison with the infinite, the rejection of the idea of pure private possessions appropriated from goods not previously possessed, and the acceptance of the duty of stewardship to use these resources to maintain and restore equality—are the initial premises, the underlying presuppositions from which an egalitarian principle of justice makes sense. The needs of those in the moral community handicapped with mental or physical disability are central to the community agenda. The resources are at the community's disposal for the task and the members of the community have the duty to act.

It is now clear that theological ethical tradition could reach no other conclusion. With these basic faith commitments all else follows. What is the implication, however, for those not standing fully and consciously within this tradition?

Notes

1. Samuel Bradburn, "Equality" [sermon preached at the Methodist Chapel, Broad Mead, Bristol, February 28, 1794], in *Sermons Preached on Particular Occasions* (London: T. Blanshard, City Road, 1817), pp. 215–67, esp. pp. 218–21.

2. H. Richard Niebuhr, *Radical Monotheism and Western Culture* (New York: Harper & Rowe, 1960), pp. 73–77.

3. *Ibid.*, p. 77.

4. William Temple, *Christianity and Social Order* (New York: Seabury Press, 1977), p. 37.

5. Bradburn, "Equality," pp. 219–20.

6. Karl Barth, *The Epistle to the Romans* (London: Oxford University Press, 1933), p. 101.

7. Markus Barth, "Jews and Gentiles: The Social Character of Justification in Paul," *Journal of Ecumenical Studies* 5 (1968): 241.

8. Wisdom 6:7. For similar themes see Proverbs 22:2; Proverbs 29:13; and Wisdom 7:3–6.

9. Richard Overton, "An Arrow Against All Tyrants," *The Levellers in the English Revolution* [Documents of Revolution], ed. G.E. Aylmer (Ithaca, N.Y.: Cornell University Press, 1975 [1645]), p. 69.

10. Bradburn, "Equality," p. 218.

11.   See, for example, Romans 4:10–12.

12.   John Lilburne, "Postscript to Londons [sic] Liberty," *The Levellers,* ed. Aylmer, p. 73.

13.   Bernard Murchland, *The Dream of Christian Socialism: An Essay on Its European Origins* (Washington, D.C.: American Enterprise Institute for Public Policy Research, 1982), p. 43.

14.   Bradburn, "Equality," p. 218.

15.   *Ibid.,* p. 242.

16.   *Ibid.,* p. 243.

17.   Leviticus 25:23.

18.   Clement of Alexandria, "The Rich Man's Salvation," trans. G. W. Butterworth (Cambridge, Mass.: Harvard University Press, 1953), p. 299.

19.   Cited in William Walsh and John P. Langan, "Patristic Social Consciousness— The Church and the Poor," *The Faith That Does Justice,* ed. John C. Haughey (New York: Paulist Press, 1977), p. 128.

20.   Bernhard W. Anderson, *Understanding the Old Testament* (Englewood Cliffs, N.J.: Prentice-Hall, 1957), p. 212.

21.   Walsh and Langan, "Patristic Social Consciousness," p. 128. There is a quarrel in the literature over whether Ambrose accepted private property. Walsh and Langan cite the private ownership implied in the transaction to defend the claim that Ambrose and the other patristic fathers (except Irenaeus) accepted private property. It is, however, a concept of private ownership severely constrained by the duties of stewardship.

22.   Jean Calvin, *Institutes of the Christian Religion,* ed. John T. McNeill, trans. Ford Lewis Battles (Philadelphia: Westminister Press, 1960), Book III, Ca. vii, pt. 5, p. 695.

4

The Secular Basis for Equality

At this point we have a basis for understanding how a family with a retarded child needing special attention and special resources and a community in which that child resides might respond, working explicitly within the Judeo-Christian moral tradition. They would affirm a fundamental equality of all members of the community and strive for some kind of equality. Exactly what that equality would be is not clear yet, but if we were trying to be just, we would aim for equality. Any perceived difference in merit or usefulness among the members of the community would count for nothing in comparison to the infinite center of value affirmed by that tradition. Moreover, resources would be available with which to respond, since there is no such thing as unclaimed private property totally under the control of isolated private citizens. Finally, they would perceive a duty to become active, to rearrange the available resources to meet the needs of the retarded and others similarly deprived.

It is clear, however, that we do not live in some explicit Judeo-Christian community. We are not Essenes, Munsterites, or residents of More's Utopia. We live in a community heavily influenced by this tradition, but one that is secularized and pluralistic. The question facing the parents of a retarded child and the community of that child is what responsibility, if any, they have to meet the extraordinary needs of the most needy citizens of the community.

The Paralysis of Contemporary Analytical Philosophy

Contemporary, secular, philosophical ethics, as much as its religious counterpart, has been intrigued with the problems of justice. Often, as in the case of John Rawls, the concern is at a more abstract, theoretical level than at the level of the particular case problem of Eddie Conrad, who has been the focus of our attention. Rawls, for example, sees his task as developing a foundation for basic social practices, not resolving particular case problems of microallocation.[1] Still, his concern is with justice in allocation. If one had firmly established the principles underlying basic social practices, one would have gone a long way toward providing a basis for the answer to the question we face. One would at least know the basic commitments that would provide a guide in establishing broad social patterns of allocation.

In some ways the real puzzle is how contemporary philosophers get as far as they do, how they formulate proposals for basic principles for just social practices. A subsidiary puzzle is why these philosophers do not seem to be able to reach closure, why one group of philosophers reaches more or less egalitarian conclusions while another group views inequalities as unfortunate accidents about which individuals and society as a whole bear no active responsibility. The impasse is critical. It is true, as many claim, that we may not be able to read exactly what, if anything, ought to be done for Eddie Conrad, but the answers given to the theoretical debate over theories of justice will surely set the tone and provide the framework for answering the questions raised by his plight.

Secular persons have attempted to deal with these questions by reason alone, eschewing any explicit religious justifications of the sort we have been tracing. At their best, they exhibit a quasi-scientific mentality, insisting that well-reasoned argument, perhaps combined with solid empirical evidence, be the underpinning of moral positions taken. It is not surprising that these standards are sometimes hard, if not impossible, to meet. It is also not surprising, therefore, that the most rigorous philosophers have often turned analytic. They have become cataloguers, giving accounts of the meaning and use of moral terms and analyzing the structure of ethical arguments.

At times, in the debate over theories of justice, the contemporary analytical philosopher has been trapped at this point, suspended in analysis, unable to move on because of rigorous insistence on well-reasoned argument or definitive empirical evidence. Thus, some thinkers working in the field on theories of justice have had to be satisfied with description. Many good writers on the subject are content with describing as carefully as possible the three or four major schools of thought. These lists usually include the entitlement position of people like Robert Nozick, who hold that inequalities are merely unfortunate, but not unfair, provided the inequalities result from the natural lottery and not from unjust appropriations of other people's assets.[2] A second major position has been that of the utilitarians: that the most just allocation system is the one that produces the greatest good for the greatest number in aggregate. Holders of this position normally concede that, because of declining marginal utility, arrangements that allocate resources more equally will tend to be ethically more acceptable, but such allocation is not required in principle.[3] The third major position cited in contempory analyses is the more egalitarian one favored by Rawls in which certain goods such as liberty are to be distributed equally (on most occasions)[4] while other goods such as power, wealth, and so on are to be distributed equally unless inequalities redound to the benefit of the least well off.[5]

I have used this kind of typological classification on previous occasions, as have many others.[6] Allen Buchanan, for example (whom I take to be one of the finest minds working on these issues today), in at least one manifestation of his work, presents an analysis identifying these three positions.[7] He and some others often mistakenly collapse the Rawlsian position into a more purely egalitarian one. The real egalitarian, as we have been using the term, is committed to the position that justice requires striving for some kind of equality. Inequalities, the real egalitarian believes, cannot be considered just simply because they redound to the benefit of the least well off, as they would according to Rawlsian maximin criteria.

The exact classification of secular theories of justice is not critical at this point. What is important is the realization that if contemporary philosophers stick to the most rigorous standards for proof, many of them feel compelled to be reduced to the role of analyst. They seem to feel that no definitive argument or proof for one position or another is available. Given this widespread conclusion that no definitive argument for this (or possibly any other) moral position is going to be possible, we can understand why some feel compelled by integrity simply to analyze. The interesting question is why so many seem to be willing to move beyond analysis to reach at least a general set of principles about what is just or fair.

The Presumption of Equality in Secular Philosophers

One way or another, a remarkable number of philosophers do arrive at a set of ethical principles about justice. And what is equally remarkable is the large number who arrive at principles strikingly similar to those of the Judeo-Christian tradition. It might help us to see how they get there by looking at a number of examples, starting with Rawls.

John Rawls: Fainthearted Egalitarian

The most important contemporary philosopher in the debate over theories of justice is John Rawls. As we have seen, he is sometimes identified as an egalitarian. He at least reaches conclusions far more committed to equality of outcome than his entitlement theorist counterparts or the traditional utilitarians who would opt for practices bent on equality of outcome only to the extent that those practices would maximize utility.

It seems fair to ask how Rawls, if he is not simply going to buy into the Judeo-Christian faith, ends up where he does. His method is well known but complex, involving a hypothetical construct that he calls the "original position" and a set of hypothetical questions about what rational, self-interested people in the original position would consent to as the basic principles for social practices. His result is the set of two basic principles of justice. I will assume that the basic structure of his position is known, and press on to ask how he gets where he does.

In order for his moderately egalitarian conclusions to emerge, critical moves must take place at at least two different points. First, he must convince us that there is some reason why the truth about morality can be derived by imagining people in the original position behind the veil of ignorance and, second, he must convince us that when in that position rational, self-interested people would opt for his two principles of justice rather than some other ones. Both require some doing.

The "veil of ignorance" device is crucial in Rawls's methodology. By it, Rawls's rational contractors have knowledge of the general facts about human society: the laws of human psychology, general economic theory, and the like.[8] They are blind, however, to all particular facts that will affect their own situations: their place in society, their class, position, or social status, their fortune in the distribution of natural assets and abilities, intelligence, strength, and the like.[9] In short, they know all the general facts about human society but nothing of the particular circumstances of their own position in it.

Several critics have pointed out that once Rawls gets his contractors behind the veil of ignorance a radical change takes place.[10] While technically they remain self-interested, they do not know their own position within the society and so each person's welfare, in effect, is from that point forward counted equally. The rational contractors are, *de facto*, altruistic, out of necessity. There is no other way they can act in order to promote their self-interest except by taking the welfare of all equally into account. In this respect, there is a certain similarity to the Golden Rule or the principle of reversibility. R. M. Hare has noted the similarities in impact of the veil of ignorance and the ideal observer theory.[11] One cannot escape noticing the similarity between the Judeo-Christian commitment to the position that all are to be treated as equals in comparison to an infinite center of value who is God and Rawls's commitment to placing his contractors behind the veil of ignorance.

The key question remains: how does Rawls get to the position that moral principles can be derived by imagining people bargaining from behind his veil? Certainly, others do not insist on such a hypothetical model. Nozickeans, for example, prefer real people making real contracts, bargaining from their relative positions of strength or weakness.

Rawls never confronts this question directly. He seems to hold that the equality of claims and the altruism inherent in the veil are simply what we mean by morality or rightness.[12] If we gave special weight to our own positions or bargained out of known strengths, we might be pursuing prudent self-interest, but it would not be morality. When it comes right down to it, he simply assumes that morality involves equal consideration of the kind implied by being blind as to what position one occupies.

Although he does not, to my knowledge, admit that this is simply an assumption, he comes right out and says something very close. He says that once in the original position people are equal by supposition.[13]

Rawls *supposes* that "all have the same rights in the procedure for choosing principles; each can make proposals, submit reasons for their acceptance, and so on. Obviously," he says, "the purpose of these conditions is to represent equality between human beings as moral persons, as creatures having a conception of their good."[14]

I believe it is clear that Rawls has moved a long way toward the principle of equality by his assumptions about the original position and the veil of ignorance. It is possible, however, that rational, self-interested persons behind the veil would still opt for some substantive principles other than his two principles of justice with their heavily egalitarian flavor. Cunningham has argued, for instance, that people in that position would be gamblers; they would opt for more utilitarian principles designed to maximize net good (and therefore the average good, if the population is held constant) even at the risk of being one who, like the retarded boy, must have his interests sacrificed in order to improve average utility.[15] Cunningham believes that rational, self-interested people wanting a set of principles on which to base the practices of a society would pick the principle of maximizing total (or average) utility rather than one that distributes liberty equally and then permits certain differences in welfare if (and only if) they benefit the least well-off groups. Brian Barry and others have also suggested that such contractors might not always opt for Rawls's rather egalitarian set of principles.[16] Barry sees them sometimes opting for less egalitarian principles (such as the utilitarian ones), sometimes for even more egalitarian ones.

It is particularly important that these contractors in the original position might opt for even more egalitarian principles than those chosen by Rawls. At least insofar as justice is concerned, they might say that the fair arrangement is one that distributes resources so as to produce some sort of equality—that is, that inequalities are not justified even if they benefit the least well off. Perhaps Rawls is correct in concluding that it would be prudent under some circumstances for the least well off to surrender their claims on equality in order to improve their lot. It is not clear, however, why that would be an explication of what is fair or just. It might more appropriately be described as a situation where prudence, freedom, or utility would dictate compromising justice in order to be better off. Moreover, if, as I have argued, the Rawlsian maximin principle is a surrender of justice rather than an explication of it, the decision about whether to surrender a claim of justice might plausibly be in the hands of the least well-off group, not in the hands of, say, elites mounting the argument for inequalities (in order to improve the lot of the least well off as well, incidentally, as their own). To the extent that the least well off have a more decisive voice than the elites in deciding when the maximin inequalities are justified, Rawls's principles must be called into question. Rawls has no way of accounting for this differentiation based on who is invoking the maximin justification.

An example might help clarify the point. Suppose that Eddie Conrad and others like him could be benefitted if a talented elite of speech therapists (or speech therapy researchers) were paid unusually high wages as an incentive to expend extraordinary energies to help improve the lot of those in need of speech therapy. Assuming for the moment that the mentally and physically handicapped are the least well-off members of the moral community and therefore the focus of policy attention by both Rawlsians and full egalitarians, would it be ethical to provide the incentives necessary to produce the special efforts and, if so, why?

Rawlsians seem to say, "of course." It is fair or just that the inequalities be preserved (in fact, increased if necessary) in order to benefit the least well off. The real egalitarians would respond that the fair arrangement would be one that produces more equality in this situation. It is not the fault of the impaired that they need special speech therapy in order to have a life that is closer to that of others in the amount of welfare they possess. For the egalitarian the fairest arrangement would be for the talented elite to expend their energies out of moral commitment, thereby perhaps lowering their total welfare (at least until their joy of service is taken into account) while raising that of the least well-off group.

Now, of course, the Rawlsians might respond: what if the elite is not motivated adequately? Would not fairness require paying the elite what it took to get them to benefit the least well off? To this the egalitarian might respond that it is up to the least well-off group (or their parents, surrogates, or other voices speaking on their behalf) to decide whether to surrender the claim of justice or fairness in order to improve their lot, but it is surely not increasing justice if inequalities are increased. Should they decide to waive temporarily their claim of justice, it might be morally acceptable, though surely not just or fair. It is crucial to distinguish between what is right and what is fair, as Rawls himself says on many occasions.[17] In any case, the thought of the elite arguing for the inequality (on the ground that it improves the lot of the retarded) is certainly out of place, however. Their willingness to waive equality appears self-serving. It may, of course, be truly altruistic; the point is that it is simply a claim that carries no moral weight. That the inequalities would have to be defended as a departure from justice and that only the least well off—not the elite—are in a position to advocate the departure is what the Rawlsian maximin theorists cannot account for.

In his "Radical Egalitarian Justice: Justice as Equality," Kai Nielsen provides excellent support to the idea that it is more rational to adopt a more egalitarian principle of justice than Rawls's principles.[18] Nielsen, like Rawls, has two components to his understanding of justice. Nielsen's first principle of justice is much like Rawls's, but it is worded in a way that explicitly expresses a commitment to attain "equal moral autonomy and equal self-respect."[19] Nielsen's essential difference with Rawls may be seen in his second principle of justice in which he endorses everyone's having a right to an equal share of income and wealth. Nielsen writes:

> my claim is that, given our mutual commitment to equal self respect and equal moral autonomy, in conditions of moderate scarcity . . . equal self-respect and equal moral autonomy require something like my second principle for their attainability. There are circumstances where Rawls's second principle is satisfiable where equal liberty and equal self-respect are not attainable. In short . . . his first and second principles clash.[20] ·

While Rawls would rebut that a clash of his principles is impossible given the lexical priority of his principle of equal liberties over the "maximin" principle, according to Nielsen, Rawls's second principle permits inequalities that undermine any effective application of the first.

Nielsen anticipates Rawls's rejection of his second principle on the grounds that "an equal division of all primary goods is irrational in view of the possibility of bettering everyone's circumstances by accepting certain inequalities."[21] Nielsen answers this point contending that Rawls's understanding of bettering one's own circumstances is narrowly confined to monetary considerations—if one is better off monetarily, but notices others with more self-respect (a good to which Rawls is supposedly committed), power, authority, and autonomy, one is not likely to consider one's situation optimal. It would be more rational for one, and it seems to me more just, that greater equality obtain.

In any case, since it is now clear that there are a number of possible principles that reasonable people in the original position might choose with regard to justice, how does Rawls get to his partially egalitarian conclusions? Again, he seems to get there by assumptions about what reasonable people would do. "I assume, for one thing," he says, "that there is a broad measure of agreement that principles of justice should be chosen under certain conditions. To justify a particular description of the initial situation one shows that it incorporates these commonly shared presumptions."[22]

To be sure, he attempts to mount something he refers to as "arguments" for his two principles, especially as opposed to the principle of utility,[23] but in the end, he "assumes" agreement on his principles and only intuits that his conclusions win the day.[24] Here, as elsewhere, he acknowledges that "There is no reason to suppose that we can avoid all appeals to intuition, of whatever kind, or that we should try to."[25] His intuition here, however, is one that is rejected from the right by those more inclined to justifying inequalities—by utilitarians and entitlement theorists alike—and from the left by those even more inclined toward egalitarian intuitions such as those of the Judeo-Christian tradition we have traced.

When he comes to the question critical for our particular problem of whether the mentally incapacitated have the same claims to equality as the rest of the population, he also solves the problem by assumptions— plausibly attractive assumptions, but assumptions, nevertheless. All that is necessary for a claim of equality is for one to be a moral person, which for Rawls means having a conception of the good and being "capable of having . . . a sense of justice."[26]

This capacity is a sufficient condition for being entitled to equal justice. "Nothing beyond the essential minimum is required."[27] Moreover (again by assumption), "I assume that the capacity for a sense of justice is possessed by the overwhelming majority of mankind and therefore this question does not raise a serious practical problem."[28] He ends this discussion by confessing:

> Now of course none of this is literally argument. I have not set out the
> premises from which this conclusion follows, as I have tried to do, albeit not

very rigorously, with the choice of conceptions of justice in the original position. Nor have I tried to prove that the characterization of the parties must be used as the basis of equality. Rather this interpretation seems to be the natural completion of justice as fairness.[29]

Thus Rawls seems to leave us with some loose ends: an egalitarianism that can be overturned in the name of justice whenever the benefits redound to the least well-off group, a shaky presumption that there will be no problem in including the mentally incapacitated within the requirements of the principles of justice, and some presumptions that seem to have lost the grounding—a presumption in favor of a veil of ignorance with all its egalitarian implications and one in favor of his two principles of justice as squaring best with what rational, self-interested people would choose in the original position. What we get, however, is a set of presumptions that lead to a fainthearted egalitarianism that is compatible for the most part with the egalitarianism of the Judeo-Christian tradition. In fact, Rawls himself acknowledges that his position is one "agreeing with many theological theories on the relevance of natural attributes," but he claims that his position "needs much weaker assumptions," a claim that is surely justified.[30]

Other Egalitarians and Their Presumptions

What are we to make of all this—that Rawls has been caught making assumptions and is therefore an atypically bad philosopher? To the contrary, Rawls is quite consciously making assumptions where he makes them and knows that he must. Here he is no different, except perhaps in his level of awareness, from any other philosopher among those who reach relatively egalitarian conclusions and who would therefore provide the philosophical foundations for the educational support system the retarded need to improve their situation.

Another very important relatively egalitarian philosopher, Ronald Dworkin, recognizes the necessity of making these assumptions about equality. Commenting on Rawls, Dworkin, says:

> We may therefore say that justice as fairness rests on the assumption of a natural right of all men and women to equality of concern and respect, a right they possess not by virtue of birth or characteristic or merit or excellence but

simply as human beings with the capacity to make plans and give justice. . . .
Rawls's most basic assumption is not that men have a right to certain liberties
. . . , but that they have a right to equal respect and concern in the design of
political institutions.[31]

Dworkin himself makes similar assumptions:

> I presume that we all accept the following postulates of political
> morality. . . . Government must not only treat people with concern and
> respect, but with equal concern and respect. It must not distribute goods or
> opportunities unequally on the ground that some citizens are entitled to more
> because they are worthy of more concern.[32]

Dworkin, like all other rights theorists, takes for granted the
independence of rights from consideration of law, utility, or other
foundation.[33] For Dworkin one such right that he presumes is a right to
some version of equality.[34]

Some other distinguished philosophers with egalitarian leanings
have used slightly different language to accomplish the same thing.
They do not necessarily talk of assumptions, but they use language with
similar connotation. Thomas Nagel in his essay entitled "Equal
Treatment and Compensatory Discrimination" talks about what he
"suggests" and what he "believes." His "suggestion" is that while
certain characteristics are relevant to what one deserves, "If people are
equal in *relevant* respects, that by itself constitutes a reason to distribute
benefit to them equally."[35] What he "believes" is that people "deserve
to be treated equally."[36] Of direct relevance to our concern with the
retarded, Nagel observes in a footnote that people do not deserve
rewards on the basis of intelligence.[37] He adds to this general discussion
of what he believes about equality in distribution of benefits and
burdens that he "won't try to defend these views here."[38]

Gregory Vlastos uses language to ground his egalitarianism that is
harder to characterize. In his essay entitled "Justice and Equality" he
gives an account of our possible response to a visitor from Mars
observing our allocation of resources in order to try to equalize benefits.
In reply to the visitor's question, "But why do you want this sort of
equality?" Vlastos suggests, "My response would have to be: Because
the human worth of all persons is equal, however unequal may be their
merit."[39] Later in the essay he uses the quasi-descriptive language of
what "we acknowledge." This discussion, which has some of the

character of an argument, but is really simply the reiteration of the premise, begins, "we acknowledge personal rights which are not proportioned to merit and could not be justified by merit. Their only justification could be the value which persons have simply because they are persons."[40]

Bernard Williams' essay, "The Idea of Equality," is one of the most important, but also one of the most difficult to interpret in this genre.[41] On the one hand, he is explicating the idea of equality—that is, carrying out the analytical task. On the other, it is clear that he is very much attracted to the idea. He sees his essay as an attempt to "build up something that in practice can have something of the solidity aspired to by the strong interpretations" of the idea of equality.[42] He ends up simultaneously favoring equality in the distribution of opportunity to obtain certain goods and equality of respect for persons as persons.

He claims to be giving reasons for his notions of equality. With regard to health care, for example, he says, "Leaving aside preventive medicine, the proper ground of distribution of medical care is ill health: that is a necessary truth."[43] Envisioning a world where both wealthy and poor are receiving different treatment, though the needs are the ground of the treatment, he concludes, "This is an irrational state of affairs."[44] Again, he adds, "It is a matter of logic that particular sorts of needs constitute a reason for receiving particular sorts of good".[45]

I find Williams' conclusions plausible, in fact, compelling; but in what sense do his statements constitute reasons? Why is it a matter of *logic* that only need, rather than wealth, status, usefulness, or power be the basis of distributing health care? Why would these other states of affairs be irrational? Williams' conclusions may well be the only ones someone steeped in and committed to the Judeo-Christian tradition with its egalitarian assumptions could reach, but he has a great deal of difficulty showing that logic requires his conclusions. Perhaps that is why his essay has been difficult to interpret. When Williams says with regard to the notion of equality, "I think it is reasonable,"[46] it is hard to see him saying anything more than that it is compatible with certain core assumptions about the human and about moral obligations.

This same pattern of secular philosophers resting their case for equality on some core assumptions—assumptions that to them "seem reasonable"—occurs throughout the literature on egalitarian justice. Christopher Ake, in an insightful article on "Justice as Equality," asserts that "Justice in a society as a whole ought to be understood as a complete equality of the overall level of benefits and burdens of each member of that society."[47] Hugo Bedau, though casting his essay on "Radical Egalitarianism" as a set of qualifications on the extreme and implausible notion that all differences among people—all social inequalities—ought to be eliminated, ends up with a substantially egalitarian position.[48] He does so by introducing a set of four fundamental principles that are, in fact, the basic presumptions of the egalitarian.[49] The result is a plausible egalitarianism (Bedau calls it a "sound egalitarianism") where the burden of proof is on those attempting to justify an inequality. It is, however, an egalitarianism resting on what Bedau variously calls practical arguments, convictions, or "presumptions."

Kai Nielsen, whose arguments against Rawls's specific interpretation of justice we have traced, also reveals an egalitarian first premise that leads him to the conclusion: "We should start with this presumption, a presumption showing an equal concern for all human beings, and a belief—rooted in that equal concern—that there should be an equality of the overall level of benefits and burdens.[50] Nielsen permits departures from the equality presumption only on very specific grounds; they are to be permitted "first on the basis of different genuine needs and differing situations (where differences in rank do not count as being in a different situation) and secondly on differing preferences where the first two are satisfied or irrelevant."[51] This, he points out, is not to treat everyone the same and, therefore, avoids the persistent criticism that radical egalitarianism results in a dull, uniform world.

Secular Philosophy as Disguised Faith

What are we to make of this apparent inability of secular philosophers of egalitarian persuasion to build a definitive case for the notion of justice as equality? We find them asserting that justice is equality, presuming it, acknowledging it, intuiting it, and finding it reasonable—everything but providing a decisive proof for it. Since some answer to the question of what justice is, what fairness requires, is necessary in order to understand what our duties are as parents and as a society to the retarded and others in special need, it looks as if we find ourselves in a terrible predicament if we cannot get any further than this. These philosophers appear to be presuming equality among persons, the availability of some resources to use to increase equality, and a moral activism that sees persons as having a duty to use those resources to increase equality. Have these secular philosophers gone any further than the Judeo-Christian tradition, which accepted these same premises on faith? If so, how have they reached such similar positions?

Bootlegging Faith Statements

We may find a clue to resolving these questions in a fascinating essay by Baylor philosopher Baruch Brody. In "Health Care for the Haves and Have Nots: Toward a Just Basis of Distribution,"[52] Brody argues for taking funds from better-off taxpayers to provide health care for the indigent, and he argues that society has a claim on those resources to justify such taxation. He argues for taxing the better off on the grounds that "justice demands this equalization of capacity to obtain basic needs."[53] The scheme is "to be viewed in the context of programs of redistribution aimed at promoting greater equality."[54] As might be expected, there is no place in the article where these basic presumptions in favor of egalitarian redistribution are defended. They seem to be taken as the given starting point for the analysis suitable for justifying a particular taxation plan, but not themselves in need of justification. This basic notion that people are equal in their claim to have basic needs met is the same one that we found in the Judeo-Christian tradition as well as the secular egalitarians'.

The particularly innovative and important part of Brody's analysis is his justification of taking the resources of the well off in order to meet these basic needs. Brody offers what he calls a "quasi-libertarian" position. Tracing the libertarian doctrine of private property from Locke, he acknowledges what libertarians have held: that we have the right to the fruit of our labor. What he challenges is the libertarian's position that there are unowned resources that can be justly appropriated and to which we can add our labor. Brody argues that wealth consists both of the initial value of resources and the value added by our labor to the resources we have acquired. He never challenges the libertarian's claim to the value of labor added, but attacks the idea that one is entitled to the initial value simply because one acquires the resource. "Some wealth which exists is simply the initial value of natural resources, and neither Locke nor anyone else in the libertarian tradition has ever really explained why anyone should have an entitlement to that wealth."[55]

Brody's proposal is that reasonable people would agree to allowing the formation of private property provided that those who would lose the rights to use the natural resources be compensated in the form of socially recognized welfare rights. The natural resources, according to Brody, were never unowned—out there to be appropriated by the first Nozickean who came along. They are "leased," and those using the resources "owe a rental to everyone."[56] It is clear to Brody that such a thing as unowned resources never existed. They presumably belong to "everyone" since it is everyone who is entitled to the rent.

We are now very close to seeing Brody meet the three basic assumptions of the Judeo-Christian tradition. He never says there is an infinite center of value—a god—that makes people equal in their claim to have basic needs met, but equality is a presumption of his theory of justice. He never says a god is the original owner of the world's natural resources since he was their creator, but he does take the position that there is no such thing as never-owned resources and presumably "everyone" is their owner. All that is needed is the doctrine of stewardship, that members of the community have a responsibility to use those resources to bring about greater equality. He never argues that or even says it, but he clearly believes it.

Here is a first-rate philosopher who appears to build his theory of justice in the distribution of resources to meet the needs of members of the community on a set of assumptions that are strikingly parallel to the assumptions of the Judeo-Christian tradition that justify its egalitarianism. At no place in the essay does Brody hint at this source of his assumptions; in fact, there is no evidence either direct or indirect that he has derived them from the religious tradition. There is no evidence, but I am prepared to suggest that he is in fact bootlegging the presuppositions, the faith commitments, of that tradition. As an active practitioner standing within that tradition, where else could he get answers to these basic questions of ethics?[57]

In fact, I suggest that this provides an answer to the more general question of where those working within apparently secular philosophical camps are getting their premises to fill in the starting points of their justifications of their egalitarian ethical positions.

Brody is by no means the only one who makes basic assumptions in his theory of justice that are compatible with those of the Judeo-Christian tradition while simultaneously being an active member of that tradition. Others working within the theories of justice debate have done the same while leading religious lives committed to Judaism[58] or Christianity.[59] The only plausible explanation of the conclusions they reach is that they have drawn on the basic faith commitments of their tradition to get their philosophical analysis started in an egalitarian direction.

For this one group the link is easy to draw. It is less so for the larger group of philosophers I have identified with the egalitarian position. Nevertheless, they have all made a set of assumptions; the better, more honest among them acknowledge that to be the case. Whether they are doing so consciously or not, whether they have drawn these assumptions directly from that tradition or not, I am convinced they are transmitting basic Judeo-Christian assumptions, or at least assumptions compatible with the Judeo-Christian tradition, in their philosophical theory.

When this is not done consciously and explicitly, it would be too much to expect the match to be perfect. Some (Rawls, for example) do not hold out for the notion that justice is equality in those cases where inequality would improve the welfare of the least well-off groups. When the assumptions have lost their roots, they may drift with the winds of culture and be modified in their character. The chain of connection seems unavoidable, however. We move from mere finite human beings equal in comparison with an infinite god to Tillich's equality in the face of an infinite, if impersonal, god-like center of value, to an equality of respect and equality of opportunity to have needs met. Holders of this last position, which is the position of many of the philosophers we have reviewed, may have no imaginable way of explaining why people ought to be viewed as equals, but they start with that presumption.

We also see a progression with regard to our second assumption. We start with God as a creator of property that is given as a gift with strings attached making it available to meet the demands of equality to some version of a doctrine of communal ownership. For Brody "everyone" owns the resources and therefore those who are in possession must pay "rent." For Vlastos, the resources of the natural universe are the "means of well-being" from which all of humanity may derive benefit.[60]

In dealing with our third assumption, we move from a theologically grounded doctrine of stewardship—in which members of the moral community owe it to each other to use the commonly held resources to produce greater equality—to an almost unanalyzable position of most secular philosophers that people ought to take active steps to right the wrongs of distribution, that they ought to act, for example, so as to promote equality. For example, Charles Fried, while not by any means ending up with a fully egalitarian position, does make the assumption that humans share positive duties to act toward the assistance of other humans. He writes: "I assume that one has at least an obligation to meet some of the needs and perhaps some of the wants of those who coexist with him in cooperative units—economies, states, societies."[61] In supporting this claim, Fried stresses the idea that we are bound together by common humanity and by certain things that we have because of others: fruits of common labor, cultures, language, civil society. But Fried more or less acknowledges that his assumption about positive duties is just that—an assumption: "the theory must carry conviction by virtue of its riches and overall plausibility,"[62] not by some sort of proof. Thus, philosophers like Fried are making statements of faith just as surely as the more explicitly religious egalitarians.

The Necessity of Faith Statements

The reader might at this point easily be misled into thinking that I am offering this as an attack on the egalitarian philosophers. Nothing could be further from the truth. The point is a logical one. When philosophy pushes back far enough, it eventually reaches the point where reasons can no longer be given. Brody favors taxing the well off to meet basic needs of others. He can give reasons for that position. He could first state as a reason that the tax money would help meet needs. If asked why, he could give various empirical arguments. Eventually, however, he will be asked why society should meet basic needs. He can give a reason here as well: justice demands this equalization of capacity to meet basic needs. If again asked why, he might still state further reasons such as that reasonable people contracting to articulate the basic moral principles (perhaps behind the veil of ignorance) would opt for this interpretation of justice. If asked why again—and again—he will eventually run out of reasons; he will have to acknowledge that, by assumption, by intuition, or by faith, he has certain starting points, which, by definition, cannot be defended with further reasons. The premises of a syllogism are established by citing reasons that themselves are foundational, by intuition, by empirical observation, by assumption, by faith—or by induction, which is a first cousin of these. Logically, there is no other escape from this infinite regress. Faith statements are of necessity the starting point.

It is, of course, embarrassing for purportedly secular philosophers to admit this, so often they find it necessary to bootleg these faith moves by using phrases like "it is reasonable to assume that," "reasonable people will agree that," "we acknowledge that," "let us assume that," or "all will agree that." I did no less in *A Theory of Medical Ethics* when I claimed that reasonable contractors taking the moral point of view about justice would conclude that justice requires that people be given an opportunity for equality of net welfare.[63]

Increasingly, philosophers of knowledge are recognizing the necessity of faith moves or their equivalent. The Kuhnian revolution in thinking about scientific revolutions is built on that recognition. Scientific systems are built upon paradigms—on gestalts, metaphysical speculations, or world views—that are prelogical, pre-empirical, and must be accepted on faith.[64] According to Kuhn, choices among metaphysical systems closely resemble choices between scientific theories.[65] Neither involves testing. Decisions about whether there is an infinite value in comparison to which all finites are equal are of this kind. So are decisions about the existence of unowned natural resources available for appropriation. The latter is a position that purportedly secular environmentalists reject just as surely as do Christian theologians or Baruch Brody.

The theologian Paul Tillich recognizes the necessity of what I am calling faith moves to provide a foundation for reasoned thinking. In his effort to use vocabulary that will not offend, he speaks of a "depth of reason" that "precedes reason and is manifest through it," a kind of intuitive beginning that provides the basic premises for reason.[66] He could just as easily have spoken of foundational faith moves. "Even in the means-ends structure of 'reasoning,'" he says, "assertions about the nature of things are presupposed which themselves are not based on technical reason."[67]

As the Catholic theologians are wont to argue, the tension is not between the faith of theology and the reason of philosophy; both are required in both fields. The faith moves of some philosophers—the egalitarians—are compatible with, if not based upon, those of the

Judeo-Christian tradition. For Tillich, "Every creative philosopher is a hidden theologian."[68] Or as H. Richard Niebuhr puts it in a way more directly relevant to our concern for equality and the retarded, the argument over equality is not between faith and reason, it is between two faiths.[69] The world cannot be divided into theologians who accept on faith that justice is equality and tough-minded philosophers who reject all such faith moves. Instead, it is divided between one group made up of theologians and philosophers who accept by assumption—by faith—the premises leading to equality and another group who accept on faith premises leading away from it.[70]

Anti-Egalitarian Faith Moves

If this is correct, then the theologically inclined and their egalitarian philosophical counterparts are by no means alone in making faith moves when pressed to the foundations of their thought. We see this most conspicuously in the thought of Plato and Aristotle, the pair whose thought has been so influential, yet so alien to the Judeo-Christian tradition whose basic assumptions we have been tracing into modern thought on justice.

For Plato, in Book VIII of the *Republic,* nothing is more foolish than the permissive democracy that treats unequals alike.[71] Similarly, Aristotle, in the *Nichomachean Ethics,* articulates his conception of the principle of justice as being, "If the persons are not equal, their (just) shares will not be equal."[72] Injustice results when unequals get equal shares, just as when equals get unequal shares. To Aristotle justice means to each according to his desert, but he immediately concedes there is dispute over what constitutes a reasonable basis for the proportion. He considers three possibilities: free birth (the basis of the democrats), wealth or noble birth (the basis of the oligarchs), and excellence (the basis of the aristocrats). On any basis, however, justice is proportional. Thus justice is often referred to as "geometrical," that is, based on proportion. The idea of justice being based on simply being human is so alien that it does not even make his list of possibilities. For neither Plato nor Aristotle is there ever any argument beyond this point. The idea of each having an equal claim, of justice requiring opportunity for equal welfare outcomes, is so outside the framework of the Greek culture of the day that it does not merit refutation. The Hebrew equality of all as children of a common creator is so out of the Greek world view that no refutation is thought of, much less needed. The Greeks—and their modern spokespersons—make basic assumptions about the inequality of persons that contrast sharply with the assumptions of the Judeo-Christian tradition.

Alien to them is the basic intuition of the Judeo-Christian tradition that leaves humans with a sense of gratitude for a gift bestowed equally upon all and that binds them together in a community of common responsibility to use the commonly shared resources to meet needs where they arise. In place of this sense of gratitude is an equally fundamental and equally pre-rational intuition giving the Greeks— ancient and modern—a sense of human difference, difference based on birth or wealth or excellence. Differing excellences, differing virtues, differing merit, differing fortunes dictate differing treatment. For Aristotle it was simply obvious that people were unequal in morally relevant ways although there was some room for dispute over exactly what the relevant ways were.

In order to understand the basic assumptions—the faith moves—of those who reject egalitarianism, it may be helpful to see how various anti-egalitarians handle the problems dealt with in the three basic assumptions of the Judeo-Christian tradition. We shall see that it is plausible to end up an anti-egalitarian if different moves are made in handling any one of the three assumptions. When all three are handled differently the result is likely to be anti-egalitarianism with a vengeance.

Assuming Inequality of Finite Humans

The first point of potential difference over these assumptions is that some anti-egalitarians assume inequality at the point that the Judeo-Christians and their secular egalitarian counterparts assume equality. We have seen that the Judeo-Christians have a God, an infinite center of value, in which they easily ground their conviction of an equality of humans as mere finite creatures as well as children of a common creator. The secular egalitarians have more trouble justifying this assumption, but they manage to get there by talking about equality of respect and equality of opportunity.

Those who finally reject egalitarianism may place their emphasis on the assumption of a fundamental moral inequality among persons as Plato and Aristotle do. J. R. Lucas is an important critic of egalitarianism who illustrates this kind of anti-egalitarian faith move.[73] He begins his discussion of the relation of justice and equality by stating, "At first sight, it is obvious that justice is not the same as equality."[74] Since it is "obvious," that pretty well settles the matter. He backs this up with some of the obvious ways in which humans are unequal, picking up from Bedau,[75] Benn,[76] and others by observing that the guilty are not the same as the innocent, men not the same as women, and so on. After a page he concludes with what was obvious in the first place: "So justice is not equality."

After this preliminary argument against what Bedau has called "radical" egalitarianism, an egalitarianism in which all differences in the way people are treated would be eliminated (which is an absurdity that no one takes seriously), he gets down to business with several arguments against more serious kinds of equality such as equality based on need and equality of opportunity. He first, beginning with Bedau's "presumption of equality," argues that without considerable qualification the presumption "is bound to prove internally inconsistent."[77] It is hard to understand exactly what he means by this. It is hard to see how there could be any internal inconsistency from at least starting with a presumption of equality. There may be unsatisfying contradictions with other ethical principles or counterintuitive implications if pressed to extremes, but hardly internal inconsistency, say, of the sort Kant thought he found in some applications of the categorical imperative. He goes on quickly to argue that "egalitarian sentiment leads easily to totalitarianism."[78] That seems patently false as well as irrelevant. One of the most obvious implications of egalitarianism, as we have seen throughout the history of commitment to equality, is equality of political and legal rights. One can imagine that some version of egalitarianism might lead to totalitarianism as, for example, in Munsterite or Leninist corruptions of egalitarianism, but it surely will not get there easily. Hubmaier, Bradburn, and the democratic Christian egalitarians show us that. Moreover, even if it did lead to totalitarianism, at best this would be a kind of utilitarian case against egalitarianism. It would be an argument that people cannot be equal because, if they were, an awful form of government would result. If, however, what we are debating is the nature of people's relative moral status, it is hard to see how a bad political consequence could be used to refute a "fact" of equality such as that envisioned by the Judeo-Christian vision of equality of finites before an infinite god. It would be akin to arguing that people cannot come with different skin colors because awful racial prejudices would be inevitable.

When it comes down to it, Lucas really wants to argue that egalitarianism is wrong because he is convinced in his heart that people are really in morally relevant respects not equal. He starts with the premise that people are unequal in morally relevant respects. He argues, "If we give everyone the same, then someone who deserves more, or who merits more, or who is entitled to more, will have cause for complaint."[79] That, of course, would be true, provided people really do differ in desert, merit, or entitlement, and provided inequalities on these bases justify unequal distributions. Lucas never argues for this. He states it: "The general argument from justice to equality is mistaken. . . . A decision not to give [someone] what he deserves, or merits, or is entitled to, is an adverse decision."[80] It may well be, but if it is, it is because of Lucas' assumption that people are unequal in morally relevant ways. Lucas can reach his conclusion only by making an assumption—a faith move—that people are fundamentally unequal, different in morally relevant ways, and separate from one another.[81] This is a faith move directly contrary to the one made by the Judeo-Christian tradition and by the secular philosophers who, whether they know it or not, are transmitting a basic world view based upon or compatible with that tradition.

An important and complex group of thinkers who make faith moves that are in some sense contrary to egalitarianism are the utilitarians. They do not jump immediately to the assumption that people are fundamentally different and unequal, but, in some sense, that is where they end up. The utilitarians all begin with the assumption that the morally correct action is the one that in one way or another maximizes utility. As Mill puts it, being exempt from pain and as rich as possible in enjoyments "being, according to utilitarian *opinion,* the end of human action, is necessarily also the standard of morality."[82] There are, of course, many internecine disputes over how utility is calculated: whether different goods are counted differently or all are counted on some hedonistic scale, whether the utility of individual acts is calculated or the utility of alternative sets of rules, whether the utility of the set of rules conformed with fully or only generally accepted, and even whether some objective measure of good is used or people's preferences. For our purposes all holders of these positions share a commitment to the norm of utility and they share it by assumption. As Mill put it, it is their opinion. When pressed, Mill is smart enough to realize that no ultimate justification can be given for this opinion. He slips into one of the code phrases whereby philosophers bootleg their faith moves. He says, "It seems natural to suppose that all actions take their whole character from the end to which they are subservient."[83] Over and over again in the development of his argument he acknowledges that he is dealing with questions "not amenable to direct proof"[84] and for which "no reason can be given."[85]

This norm of utility is not totally lacking in a commitment to equality. The utilitarians, in calculating the net benefits of alternative sources of action, aggregate the net benefits over all the people affected.[86] In doing so they hold that the benefits and harms that accrue to each person much be counted equally. Bentham has argued that "everyone is to count for one, and no one for more than one."[87] This means that the joy of the peasant counts as happiness, just as the joy of the elite. Or, to apply this to our example, the happiness of the retarded counts as much as that of the intellectual. This is an insight that is by no means obvious, but is taken as a given by all utilitarians. In this sense they are egalitarian in their assumptions.[88] Mill sounds downright egalitarian when he says, "Society between equals can only exist on the understanding that the interests of all are to be regarded equally."[89]

Regarding the interests of all equally in the sense of making sure that the benefits and harms of each person are included in the aggregate when we make the utilitarian calculus is radically different from holding the interests of all equally in the sense of striving for equality of outcome. In this latter sense the utilitarians are consistently non-egalitarian in principle, although as a practical matter the effect may often work toward greater equality of outcome. Because of decreasing marginal utility, it may often turn out that greater equality in distribution of resources or of welfare will produce the greatest aggregate good. But, as Mill recognizes, there will be cases where inequalities turn out to be efficient or expedient. At this point Mill and the other utilitarians acknowledge that reward for effort, for desert, for talent, or for any other attribute that might increase total utility would not only be justified, it would be just.[90] There would apparently be no residual pull in the direction of equality. Mill retreats to the old Greek ideal of justice as proportionality,[91] in thus case proportional to aggregate net goods, resolving any possible conflict among different considerations by appeal to social utility.[92]

The implications for the retarded and others with handicap are significant. It is in precisely these groups that substantial transfers from the relatively well off to the relatively needy may actually decrease the total welfare in the society. In Eddie Conrad's case, for example, we see a situation where a youngster particularly disadvantaged in the natural lottery will benefit marginally from substantial expenditures, but the commitment to his speech therapy may, at least in the short run, cost many other children art, music, and physical education. Of course, it is easy to argue that the school system ought to have both—that some other expenditure in the community ought to be eliminated. But insofar as the choice before the parents and the school board is a forced one, it really is not obvious that more total good is done by helping the one particularly disadvantaged boy rather than the large group of more nearly normal children. In fact, if we are only concerned about total good, the case of the retarded is a very shaky one. It is fairly obvious, however, that the one boy has an unusual need to make him more like the other children, and that depriving the others of their music and art will not leave them worse off than Eddie Conrad is even with his speech therapy.

Many utilitarians—not just Bentham and Mill, but contemporary scholars such as Joseph Fletcher—believe that their intuition is compatible with the Judeo-Christian tradition.[93] They miss, however, the radical difference between treating people as equals in the sense of counting their benefits and harms and treating them as equals in the sense of striving to meet their needs even if it means decreasing the total amount of good in a society.[94] It is simply a different vision, a different starting point, a different initial premise about the way people are equals. It is a vision in which the welfare of one may be traded for the welfare of another if the trade increases the aggregate welfare. This vision misses the fundamental equality among finite persons based on a comparison to an infinite that leads to equality of outcome even if it means less total good in the society. If we assume that people are unequal in the sense that their welfare may be traded for another's when it increases total welfare, the utilitarian's view of distribution makes sense; without that assumption, it is incomprehensible.

Assuming the Existence of Unowned Property

One way to get to the anti-egalitarian conclusion is to assume the inequality of human beings and the interchangeability of individual welfare. That is not the only way, however. Another group of anti-egalitarians reached their conclusion by assuming there is such a thing as unowned property. The egalitarians believe that the natural resources of the world are already owned. They are God's because he created them and gave them as a gift with certain strings attached, or they are "everyone's" so that they can be leased to certain users provided the users pay rent in the form of honoring the welfare claims of the needy. Some of the critics of egalitarianism make a radically different set of assumptions about the ownership of the natural resources. Even if one were willing to grant the equality for finite human beings and somehow include in that equality a claim of equality of outcome, this egalitarian move with regard to the first assumption would have no significance unless there were some resources to which one justly had access for the purpose of distributing them in a way that would increase equality.

Robert Nozick, the Harvard philosopher whose volume *Anarchy, State, and Utopia* is perhaps the most significant contemporary, anti-egalitarian manifesto, appears to assume the inequality among people. He never argues for that position, but he recognizes and attacks the presumptive quality of the egalitarian starting point. "The entitlement conception of justice in holdings," he says, "makes no presumption in favor of equality, or any other overall end state or patterning. It cannot merely be *assumed* that equality must be built into any theory of justice.[95] Here he has caught the egalitarians in the same bootlegging operation we found them in earlier in this chapter. At the same time, Nozick seems not to recognize that he is engaged in a competitive bootlegging business—bootlegging a presumption against equality.

We see the depth of Nozick's presumption against equality in a footnote where he argues by example in a way that is particularly relevant to our problem of what would count as a fair allocation to a retarded child when others of more normal mental ability could profit by withholding marginal benefits from the retarded one. Nozick attempts to refute Rawls with a rhetorical question: "Should a family devote its resources to maximizing the position of its least well off and least educated child, holding back the other children or using resources for their education and development only if they will follow a policy through their lifetimes of maximizing the position of their least well off sibling? Surely not."[96] While Nozick's intuition about his case is apparently clear, I believe others would be less convinced that it would be right to avoid bringing the less talented one to greater equality in order to permit the already talented siblings to flourish. Perhaps it is because Nozick is making assumptions against equality that he is able to answer so clearly and without elaboration on his intuition.

Another interesting possibility is that Nozick is (silently) appealing to a respect for potential, the idea that in this case the children should have equal opportunities to meet their potentials. But people with vastly different starting points in life who are given equal chances to meet their potentials are really quite unequal in their lives. In the next chapter I argue that mental and physical resources distributed in the natural lottery are, in fact, part of the resources individuals possess. If the goal is to strive for opportunities for equality of overall well-being, it is wrong to devote even more resources (for the purpose of helping realize potential) to those who already are richly endowed.

Nozick faces a logical problem here. On the one hand, he argues against any patterned distribution. Presumably that would include a rejection of patterning in which people were given an equal opportunity to fulfill their potentials. On the other hand, he may be appealing intuitively to distribution according to a pattern based on equality of opportunity. If he does, he appeals to a pattern, not the equality of outcome pattern of the egalitarians, but a pattern focusing on equality nonetheless. In that case he needs to defend or at least articulate his assumptions that lead to the "equal-chance-to-realize-potential" position. In any case, if he is incorporating an intuition that within families there should be equal chance to realize potential, that intuition does not follow from, indeed, appears incompatible with, his entitlement theory.

That is not the most significant assumption he is marketing, however. He is also in the business of pushing an unproven theory of private property. He begins his volume with the premise that "individuals have rights, and there are things no person or group may do to them (without violating their rights)."[97] Nowhere in the entire volume does Nozick argue for that sweeping moral assumption. Without it the rest of his position collapses; with a theory of rights, especially the kinds of rights he assumes, his position seems rock solid. The most significant of these rights, according to Nozick, is the right of ownership of private property acquired through just appropriation of unowned resources or through just transfer.[98] Since just transfer in the end traces back to someone else having acquired private property through appropriation of unowned resources, the interesting notion is Nozick's unowned, or what he sometimes calls unheld, property.

The key is what Nozick calls the principle of justice in acquisition, for which he is heavily indebted to John Locke. Property rights in an unowned object, Nozick summarizes without defense, originate through someone's mixing his labor with it.[99] Here Nozick has already set up his bootlegging business. Nowhere is it defended that the mere fact of mixing one's labor with an unowned object gives one a property right to the object as well as the value his labor adds. More basically, nowhere is it defended that there exists such a thing as unowned property.

There are several levels of assumption in Nozick's thinking. He realizes that one might ask why adding labor to an unowned object should give one ownership of the whole object rather than merely the added value. This is the kind of challenge Brody and others offer. Nozick's weak reply is that "no workable or coherent value-added property scheme has yet been devised." But that could just as easily be an argument against *any* notion of private property, thus requiring that unowned objects be left unowned.

More fundamentally, it begs the question of whether any unowned objects ever existed in the first place. Nozick and, in a more modest way, Locke before him, clearly believe that they did. Nozick seems to presume an object is unowned until proven owned. And here he is back to his basic assumptions, to his faith moves that are so different from the faith moves of both the Judeo-Christian tradition and its secular egalitarian counterparts. The notion of a collective ownership—by a god, a transcendent ground of being, or even by "everyone"—simply escapes him, while a belief in the existence of unowned property and a (limited) right to appropriate it for one's own purposes by adding labor to it seems to be acceptable.[100]

Nozick has a problem at still another level. Even if his initial assumptions are granted, he accepts Locke's proviso that, in order for the right of private property to be created, there must be "enough and as good left in common for others.'' But as he realizes, even if that were imaginable in some primitive day of wilderness appropriation, it leaves little room for private property in a time of acute scarcity. Moreover, he recognizes that if there eventually comes a time when one final appropriation would not leave ''enough and as good for others,'' then the penultimate appropriation would not leave enough and as good for others (since no further appropriation would be permitted). He tries to maneuver out of this bind by distinguishing between a stronger and weaker sense of the Lockean proviso. The strong sense would prohibit appropriations depriving others of the opportunity to improve their situation by a particular appropriation and also those that leave others no longer able to use freely (without appropriation) what they previously could. The weaker sense—the one Nozick apparently favors—would prohibit only the second. Nozick seems to believe that softening the Lockean proviso in this way makes it feasible. It is hard to see why; complex interdependency and severe scarcity are as likely to make private property violate the weaker formulation as the stronger. More critically, it is no more obvious why Nozick should be able to waive the stronger version of the Lockean proviso than why Locke should consider the right to private property annulled when it would leave others without ''enough and as good'' in the first place. All of this has the tone of inventing a set of principles that square with one's preconception of the way the moral world ought to be. In Nozick's case that means one where the notion of unowned property makes sense and where appropriating it by adding one's labor to it is justified.

These Lockean/Nozickean assumptions about ownership and the original existence of unowned resources show up explicitly in anti-egalitarian discussions of the ethics of health care and the care of the retarded. Baylor professor H. Tristram Engelhardt, for example, incorporates Nozick's discussion of private property and ownership into his analysis of health resource allocation. Since people own what they possess (provided they have acquired it justly), society simply has no right to appropriate it for charitable purposes such as providing speech therapy to a retarded adolescent, no matter how noble and worthwhile such an act.[101] The resources are simply not at the disposal of society.

Assuming Lack of Human Responsibility

Nozick, Engelhardt, and the other anti-egalitarians tend to combine an assumption about the inequality of finite persons with their assumption about the existence of unowned property in order to support their anti-egalitarian conclusions. They have available to them one other assumption by means of which they can distinguish themselves from religious and secular egalitarians. They could assume humans have no responsibility to be active in using resources to increase equality.

The anti-egalitarians do not make much of this third assumption; they really do not need to. They have already rejected by assumption the first two pillars of the egalitarian faith. If pressed, however, they seem to take a position consistently opposed to that of their rivals. Nozick, and Engelhardt following him, take the position that a sharp distinction must be made between the unfortunate and the unfair.[102] Many natural events, such as being retarded by losing in the natural lottery are, according to Nozick or Engelhardt, unfortunate, but not unfair, they are pitiable, but do not have any moral claim for redress. This conclusion is, in part, based on the assumption that people are just naturally unequal. But it seems also to reflect a belief that the mere existence of suffering, deprivation, or lack of well-being in the world implies no moral responsibility for remedial action on the part of society. According to Engelhardt, a society that does not respond may be despicable, indecent, or unfeeling, but not unjust or unfair because it has no human duty to respond. In fact, feeling such a duty seems to be for Engelhardt (whether by rationalization or not) an act of hubris. It is "seeing ourselves in the image and likeness of God."[103] One might see no need to respond to an inequality, even if he or she believed that inequality violated the fundamental equality that existed among humans, and even if one knew that resources were available to respond. If so, he or she would still be anti-egalitarian. If one assumes inequality, the existence of unowned resources that can be appropriated as one's private property, *and* a lack of human duty to act, there is little chance for the egalitarian conclusion.

In the end, the anti-egalitarians are in no better position than the egalitarians; their starting point is no more logical or assumption-free than that of the egalitarians, whether explicitly religious or secular. The anti-egalitarians are simply in a different position. They assume inequality among finite humans; they assume the existence (at least at one time) of unowned resources to be appropriated without strings attached according to the principles of just acquisition; and they assume no necessary human responsibility to act in situations even where one has the capacity to meet the needs of another. Theirs is a different position indeed, one that cannot be refuted by any definitive proof any more than assumptions of the egalitarians.

Public Policy as Forced-Choice Faith: Why Justice Is the One Issue Where Theology May Make a Difference

That school board that must decide whether to fund speech therapy by eliminating the physical education, music, and art programs for more nearly normal children is strangely uncomfortable. Their choice seems to depend on some apparently arbitrary assumptions about equality, private property, and human responsibility to compensate for what the libertarians call misfortune in the natural lottery. Is there a way out?

Pluralism and Conflicting Underlying Assumptions

Realistically, if there existed definitive, irrefutable proof for one position or the other, the collective wisdom of the best minds in human history would have found it by now. Plato and Rawls, Luke and Nozick would not be giving that school board contradictory advice. But in reality there is no definitive solution to this most basic human moral problem. When we reduce the problem of morality to its most fundamental starting point—the basic assumptions with which we get an argument going—we are forced to posit a set of faith moves by which existence in a coherent, morally comprehensible world is possible. For many issues of abstract morality and belief this has led modern humans to a liberal pluralistic stance. Since we must start with some basic faith and we cannot all agree on precisely the same faith, we agree to differ, to live and let live. That works fairly well for many problems of philosophy and even religion. We divide ourselves into smaller and smaller communities of belief, giving up consensus for freedom of belief and the excitement of sectarianism that rigorously affirms belief.

The Necessity of Choice in Public Policy

Public policy, however, is the one area where we are not really afforded that option. Some decision to act must be made and that action is collective. A school board cannot simultaneously opt for an egalitarian policy that distributes resources on the basis of need, a more utilitarian one that distributes on the basis of aggregate utility, and an entitlement view, which allocates on the basis of ability to pay. Some implicit or explicit decisions must be made on the basic questions that provide the assumptions to fuel the logic of decision-making.

Some discussions of church-state relations offer the stock answer that the burden of proof for supporting assumptions rests on those grounding their actions on a belief system. If I am correct, however, the debate is not between a religiously grounded set of assumptions leading to egalitarianism and a tough-minded, rational, secular skepticism that is anti-egalitarian because it rejects the faith moves of the religious community. It is rather between two radically different sets of faith moves that initiate thought processes—sometimes religious, sometimes secular. The basically egalitarian faith moves, whether those of theologians or those that purport to be secular, are moves that have their roots in or at least are compatible with the Judeo-Christian tradition. The opposite set has its origins elsewhere, perhaps influenced by Greek or Indian thought, or modern individualism. One style or the other, however, is a necessity if a community is to make critical choices in matters of public policy. Some consensus faith assumptions become essential.

Is There a Logical Priority for One Set of Assumptions?

If both egalitarians and anti-egalitarians are grounding their systems of thought in what amounts to faith moves, thus making it impossible for the more purely secular pattern to claim priority on that basis, is there some other logical ground for selecting one pattern? After all, a great deal is at stake. Under one set of assumptions people are equals, resources are available, and humans carry the responsibility for using those resources to meet needs; under the other set, people are unequal and lack any activist duty in the first place. Even if they had such a duty, once unowned resources were appropriated there would be none left for the community to meet needs and restore equality. With a few assumptions along the way, one set of moves leads to a policy of giving Eddie Conrad his speech therapy while the other set does not.

The defender of the apparently more secular, anti-egalitarian set of assumptions might argue that the egalitarian is making positive assumptions while he or she is only making negative ones and that positive assumptions carry the burden of proof. If a religious cult claimed that the world was going to end within a year so that all public policy should be based on that assumption, surely the opponents of that policy recommendation would be correct in saying that the defenders of the assumption bear the burden of proof. By the same token, do those who assume the equality of finite humans (perhaps in comparison with an infinite god or center of value), who assume that a god or that everyone retains some ownership rights in the natural resources, and who assume human moral responsibility, carry the burden of proof? Since we have seen that proving these basic assumptions is probably not possible, whoever is determined to carry the burden of proof is likely to lose the public policy debate. The argument that positive assumptions carry that burden, therefore, is a very important one, if successful.

There are two problems with the claim that positive assumptions carry such a burden, however. First, each set of assumptions can be stated in a positive form. While egalitarians can be burdened with the defense of the assumption that God or everyone owns the natural resources, the anti-egalitarian position can be stated as one of assuming that unowned resources exist (or once did). While the egalitarians can be burdened with the assumption that an infinite center of value exists in comparison to which humans are equal in their worth, the anti-egalitarian position can be seen as starting with the assumption that people differ in their merit or worthiness. The distinction between the two is a semantic one.

Moreover, even if positive assumptions do carry the burden of proof, some positive assumptions are simply so overwhelming that they may be able to meet it at least in a practical sense. For example, it is overwhelmingly plausible that the laws of physics that hold today will hold tomorrow. Yet this is no more than an assumption. One is tempted to say that the certainty of the consistency of the laws of physics is based on experience and is, therefore, not merely an assumption. But for experience to carry any evidential weight, the law of induction—that if things behave similarly over and over again in the same situation, they will (or are likely to) behave that way in the future when in identical circumstances—must be presumed. But induction does not seem to be derivable from logic; nor can it be confirmed by experience, for the evidential weight of experience itself depends on induction, so that relying on experience would be circular. So the belief that the laws of physics will be the same tomorrow is simply an assumption, albeit an overwhelmingly plausible one [or is, at least based on the (mere) assumption of induction].

It is also virtually impossible not to assume the existence of other minds. This is indeed an assumption because, in order to *prove* the existence of other minds, one would have to experience the experience of others—not the behavior that is supposedly a concomitant of those experiences, but the experiences or thoughts, pains, pleasures, and so on, themselves. For those of us who do not have the sort of extrasensory perception that allows one to dive into others' streams of consciousness, such proof is impossible to give. Yet it is extremely difficult to imagine one not carrying this assumption.

As a final example, the positive assumption of freedom of the will is overwhelmingly believable. To recognize this, one need only observe the consequences of holding the denial of this assumption. If the actions of man are determined entirely by the laws of nature, precluding his being able to select among alternative possible actions, the notions of responsibility, guilt or blame, virtue, and the entire field of ethics as well as the system of law become farcical illusions. Admittedly, a minority of philosophers probably think that this is the case. They are likely to argue, of course, that though these ideas and institutions are absurd, they are necessary absurdities, since humans had no *choice* in inventing them. Yet presenting this (or any other) argument seems to presuppose that one is giving reasons for a point, *good* reasons, reasons that one might not have chosen if one were not being intelligent enough. Thus for an argument to seem to have any strength at all, one must assume that the reasoning was *not forced upon one by physical necessity,* but was arrived at by free thinking. To be sure, free will is an enormously plausible assumption, but an assumption nevertheless.

Thus some sets of assumptions, even if stated positively, are simply overwhelmingly plausible. They are more believable than their contraries. Deciding which assumption is stated positively surely cannot settle the question of which carries the burden of proof.

So even if there is not a logical priority for one set of assumptions, there might be some sort of priority. Historically, in the West, especially in the post-Constantinian West penetrated by the Judeo-Christian tradition, the more egalitarian assumptions have prevailed. That, of course, is not to say that Western society has always been egalitarian; far from it. But it is to say that the core assumptions about the relations of humans to an infinite, about the creation of natural resources, and about the duty of stewardship have consistently been affirmed. Moreover, the explicitly religious manifestations of the assumptions converge with some of the secular, philosophical manifestations, something that cannot be said with any consistency for the anti-egalitarian pattern.

None of this, of course, is anything like a definitive justification. We have already conceded that that is impossible. We are left in a devilish position, however. We must make a forced-choice faith move, at least on matters of public policy. Two radically different patterns of assumptions present themselves, neither of which is capable of carrying the logical burden of proof. The world is divided, not between the religious and the secular, the people of faith and those of reason, but between two diametrically opposed faiths, between the grateful and the demanding. Were the pluralistic answer available to us, many would be attracted to it, but it is not. If one position carried the burden of proof, we would surely reject it, but it does not. In the end, this most critical question of public policy, this issue upon which the welfare of Eddie Conrad and the rest of us who are less than perfect depends, comes down to a matter of faith. From where the Judeo-Christian tradition, the egalitarian secular philosophers, and I stand, the faith of the anti-egalitarians is simply not plausible. Surely this faith is not as difficult to hold as the negations of any of the assumptions I have argued to be overwhelmingly believable. Although a few philosophers do hold the anti-egalitarian assumptions, I submit that the egalitarian assumptions are much more plausible than the anti-egalitarian ones and that holding some position here is necessary just as it must be done when assuming the consistency of physical laws, the existence of other minds, and the freedom of the will. I invite any thinker to open-mindedly consider these two sets of assumptions. If I am correct, the most natural response to such a consideration is an endorsement of the egalitarian assumptions. This vision seems overwhelmingly attractive from the moral point of view. There is nothing explicitly religious about the alternative faith moves required of those who accept the more egalitarian starting point.

Traditional theological premises are not necessary to hold that there is an infinite center of value in comparison to which all are equal in their worthiness or that some form of collective rights of ownership remains with property even if it is, for the time being, in the possession of private individuals. Certainly we do not require theological premises to believe that humans are agents bearing moral responsibility. A religious tradition may make these assumptions easier to transmit, understand, and apply. It may help avoid the confusions in application that come to an isolated, secular individual who tries to go it alone in deciding what these premises mean for a school board or a health care system. The real gap, however, is not between the philosophers and the theologians; it is between those whose faith moves are egalitarian and those whose moves point them in the opposite direction.

Why Theology May Make a Difference

Despite the claim that the definitive gap is not between those who are explicitly religious in their starting point and those who believe they are more secular, the question of justice may be one area of ethics where theology does make a difference. For the other basic ethical principles in most ethical systems—for the principles of beneficence, autonomy, truth telling, promise keeping, and perhaps avoiding killing as well—there is, in one way or another, substantial agreement among the philosophers and the theologians. Some argue that these principles are derived from an overarching teleological principle such as utility maximizing and that the principles are merely rules that maximize the end being valued. But both philosophers and theologians make such moves. Others argue that these principles are inherent right-making characteristics of actions. But both philosophers and theologians adopt these positions as well. More significantly, one way or another there is substantial convergence around these basic principles. When there is dispute—over paternalism, for example—the philosophers and theologians seem to sort themselves out quite randomly among the positions. There is no reason to expect anything else since no essentially theological premises are inherent in the dispute.

In the dispute over the principle of justice, however, we have found something of a pattern. The pattern is not a simple one with theologians opting for egalitarianism and secular philosophers opting for anti-egalitarianism. Rather, it is one in which those working out of religious ethics have, for the most part, made egalitarian assumptions while those working in secular philosophy are split. At first the split seems random, but, if we are correct, it really is not. The key working assumptions of the egalitarian secular philosophers are based upon or compatible with the theological assumptions of those in religious ethics: an infinite making finites equal, some prior claim on apparently unowned resources, and a notion of human responsibility. It looks strangely like Judeo-Christian theology once removed, bootlegged at the point some assumptions are needed. It looks like the doctrines of God, creation, and stewardship. If those are really Judeo-Christian theological assumptions, while the anti-egalitarians are making contrary faith moves derived from some other sources, then here is one point where at least indirectly theology makes a difference.

The members of Eddie Conrad's school board may not be able to escape an essentially theological task—the choice of some assumptions upon which they must start their moral reasoning process. They will have to take a stand on some tough issues. They could opt to reject equality in comparison to an infinite; they could take the view that some unowned resources exist (or once existed) that gave rise to private property that cannot be appropriated even for Eddie Conrad's good cause. They could simply accept the idea that humans have no moral agency, no responsibility to act. They could make any of these assumptions, but they seem strange and are inconsistent with another set of assumptions that seem much more plausible, much more attractive, much more believable, at least for those who stand on the Judeo-Christian tradition and for a large part of the secular community. If they make the egalitarian faith assumptions rather than the anti-egalitarian ones, they will not have any proof of their position, but they will have a view of the world that is more plausible and more attractive from the moral point of view. They will also have the task of deciding just what it would mean to treat Eddie Conrad as an equal. It is to that question that we now turn.

Notes

1. John Rawls, *A Theory of Justice* (Cambridge, Mass.: Harvard University Press, 1971), p. 64.

2. Robert Nozick, *Anarchy, State, and Utopia* (New York: Basic Books, 1974), esp. pp. 150–60.

3. John Stuart Mill, *Utilitarianism,* ed. Oskar Priest (New York: Bobbs-Merrill, 1957 [1863]), Ch. 5.

4. Rawls, *Theory,* pp. 62–64, 202.

5. *Ibid.,* p. 302.

6. Robert M. Veatch, ''What is a 'Just' Health Care Delivery?'' *Ethics and Health Policy,* ed. Robert M. Veatch and Roy Branson (Cambridge, Mass.: Ballinger Publishing Co., 1976), pp. 127–53.

7. Allen Buchanan, ''Justice: A Philosophical Review,'' *Justice and Health Care,* ed. Earl E. Shelp, (Dordrecht, Holland: D. Reidel Publishing Co., 1981), pp. 3–21.

8. Rawls, *Theory,* pp. 136–37.

9. *Ibid.,* pp. 137–38.

10. See, for example, R. M. Hare, ''Rawls' *Theory of Justice*—I,'' *Philosophical Quarterly* (July, September 1973): 151.

11. *Ibid.*

12. *A Theory of Justice,* p. 111, provides an example of a place where Rawls connects ''the concept of something being right'' with the principles that would be acknowledged in the original position. He never argues for the link. Rather, he describes it as an ''intuitive idea.''

13. ''It seems reasonable to suppose that the parties in the original position are equal.'' Rawls, *Theory,* p. 19.

14. *Ibid.*

15. Robert L. Cunningham, ''Justice: Efficiency or Fairness?'' *Personalist* 52 (1971): 423–81.

16. Brian Barry, *The Liberal Theory of Justice* (Oxford: Clarendon Press, 973), esp. pp. 94–95, 99, 103.

17. Rawls, *Theory* pp. 3, 9, 17, 110. It is unclear exactly how other principles relate to Rawls's concept of justice. Rawls distinguishes between principles for institutions and principles for individuals (p. 108). Even for institutions, there are principles other than justice (p. 3, 9). At times, however, it appears that Rawls considers justice to be synonymous with right distribution in institutions (pp. 9,10). To the extent he is equating justice with right distribution, he implies that the other principles for institutions (such as efficiency and liberality [p. 3]), must have no bearing on ethically correct distributions or are incorporated into the principles of justice. If that is Rawls's position, we are in disagreement over what is the best usage. I would prefer to use the term justice to refer to the equal opportunity for equal well-being, which is one among many principles for institutions, all of which may have a bearing on distributive matters.

The conflict between justice and the other principles would, as Rawls often notes, have to be resolved using a set of priority rules (see the chart on p. 109)

18. ''Radical Egalitarian Justice: Justice as Equality,'' *Social Theory and Practice,* Vol. 5, No. 2.

19. *Ibid.,* p. 211.

20. *Ibid.,* p. 213.

21. Rawls, *Theory,* p. 546.

22. Rawls, *Theory,* p. 18.

23. *Ibid.,* pp. 175–82.

24. See R. M. Hare, ''Rawls' *Theory,*'' in which he stresses the same point, pp. 145, 155.

25. Rawls, *Theory,* p. 44.
26. Rawls, *Theory,* p. 505.
27. *Ibid.*
28. Rawls, *Theory,* p. 506. While this assumption works nicely for the overwhelming majority of humans, it has the potential of raising serious problems for the discussion of justice and the retarded. The problem is this: Can the retarded be included among those who have claims for equality even though they may lack a capacity for a sense of justice and, if so, do the criteria for inclusion also mean that other animal species are also included?

First, how are the retarded included? Many of the retarded do, in fact, satisfy Rawls's minimal condition; they do have a sense of justice. But what of those who do not? Are they excluded from the moral community and therefore from any claims to equality?

It should be noted that Rawls explicitly refers to possession of this sense of justice as a sufficient rather than a necessary condition, leaving open the possibility that other characteristics are also sufficient. Rawls includes infants and children by referring to the potentiality for moral personality, potentiality "that is ordinarily realized in due course" (p. 505). That might not, however, include all of the retarded (or the senile). I have argued (largely in conjunction with the problems of the definition of death) that what is critical is not rational capacity or moral personality, but rather the capacity to experience and interact socially. [See *Death, Dying, and the Biological Revolution* (New Haven: Yale University Press, 1976), pp. 38–42; "The Whole-Brain-Oriented Concept of Death: An Outmoded Philosophical Formulation." *Journal of Thanatology* 3 (1975): 13–30; and "Definitions of Life and Death: Should There Be Consistency," *Defining Human Life,* ed. Margery W. Shaw and A. Edward Doudera (Ann Arbor, Mich.: AUPHA Press, 1983), pp. 99–113.] Thus I differ from Rawls not only in identifying experience and social interaction as critical, but also in emphasizing actual capacity rather than a potential. If experience and social interaction capacity are critical, then most (but not all) of the retarded are included. Those who absolutely lack any such capacity (the anencephalic is the obvious example) would be excluded from any claims to equality. In fact, I have argued they would be excluded from any claim to be considered living in the sense of being part of the moral community.

In order for those who have the capacity to experience and interact socially to be part of the moral community and have claims to opportunities for equality of welfare, some modifications of the hypothetical contract model are necessary. If the hypothetical contract is a model of rational self-interested people inventing a set of basic principles for governing their society, then it is understandable why only those with capacity for rationality might be thought to be the only bearers of moral claims. If, however, as I would maintain, the hypothetical contract is merely a metaphor for how we can "discover" rather than "invent" basic principles, there is nothing inconsistent about having principles serve as the source of duties toward some who are not envisioned as original contractors.

This solves the problem of how the retarded (as well as infants and animals) can be included among those to whom we have moral obligations, but it may create a new problem: the problem of opening the door too wide. If those who experience have moral claims and that includes the claim to equality of welfare, does every rodent have a claim to welfare equal to that of humans retarded and otherwise? That, I take it, is absurd. How can I avoid this implication short of being guilty of speciesism?

First, it should be clear that resting moral claims on the capacity to experience and interact socially at least excludes non-sensate animals. That is the conclusion that even Peter Singer and others interested in morality involving animals reach. Moreover, it should also be clear that we can grant certain morally relevant interests to sensate animals of other species (the interest in avoiding pain, for example) without being reduced to an absurdity. For example, we tend to believe it is wrong to torture animals. But if we grant claims to opportunities for equality of welfare to the retarded, do we also have to grant the same claim to all sensate animals? It seems intuitively obvious that we do not. But articulation of the reasons why the line can be drawn is extremely difficult. Arguing that the retarded have claims because they are ''conferred'' on them in ways that they are not conferred on other species seems to me implausible. It is implausible, first, because some groups at least may be quite willing to confer similar status to other species and moral status should not depend on whether someone is around who chooses to confer it. Second, it is implausible because infants, the retarded, and other humans seem to bear the moral status they have not simply because it is conferred, but rather because it actually exists independent of any conferring.

This is emerging as a major problem in ethics. I am not prepared to develop fully at this time the justification on limits to animal claims. My theory of justice is, thus, incomplete when it comes to the problem of the claims of other species. I am prepared, however, to argue that the capacity for experience and social interaction is sufficient and necessary for humans to have moral claims including the claims of justice. It may be that including the capacity for social interaction as well as experience is the key to differentiating the claims of humans from other species. While members of many other species surely have the capacity to experience and interact in certain ways, perhaps the social-psychological interaction among members of the other species (at least those known to exist) is qualitatively different from that among humans. Were I to develop the theory of justice further with regard to other species I would have to explore these empirical as well as conceptual issues further. I am at this point inclined toward the conclusion that if other species show similar capacities for social interaction as well as experience, then they would have to be included among those who bear claims to equality, but that the likelihood of finding such species on this earth is remote.

29. Rawls, *Theory,* 509.

30. Rawls, *Theory,* 508.

31. Ronald Dworkin, *Taking Rights Seriously* (Cambridge, Mass.: Harvard University Press, 1977), p. 182.

32. *Ibid.,* p. 272.

33. David Lyons, ''Introduction,'' *Rights,* David Lyons, ed. (Belmont, Calif.: Wadsworth Publishing Co., Inc., 1979), p. 2.

34. Ronald Dworkin, ''What is Equality? Part II: Equality of Resources,'' *Philosophy and Public Affairs* 10 (Summer 1981): esp. pp. 341, 345.

35. Thomas Nagel, ''Equal Treatment and Compensatory Discrimination,'' *Philosophy and Public Affairs* 2 (Summer 1973): 354.

36. *Ibid.*

37. *Ibid.,* note 5.

38. *Ibid.,* pp. 354–55.

39. Gregory Vlastos, ''Justice and Equality,'' *Social Justice,* ed. Richard B. Brandt (Englewood Cliffs, N.J.: Prentice-Hall, 1962), p. 43.

40. *Ibid.,* p. 48.

41. Bernard A. O. Williams, "The Idea of Equality," *Justice and Equality*, ed. Hugo A. Bedau, (Englewood Cliffs, N.J.: Prentice-Hall, 1971), pp. 116–37.

42. *Ibid.*, p. 118.

43. *Ibid.*, p. 127.

44. *Ibid.*, p. 128.

45. *Ibid.*, p. 129.

46. *Ibid.*, p. 127.

47. Christopher Ake, "Justice as Equality," *Philosophy and Public Affairs* 5 (Fall 1975): 71.

48. Hugo A. Bedau, "Radical Egalitarianism," *Justice and Equality*, ed. Hugo A. Bedau (Englewood Cliffs, N.J.: Prentice-Hall, 1971), pp. 171–74.

49. Bedau, see pages 173–74 where language of presumption is used.

50. Nielsen, "Radical Egalitarianism," p. 225.

51. *Ibid.*

52. Baruch Brody, "Health Care for the Haves and Have-nots: Toward a Just Basis of Distribution," *Justice and Health Care*, ed. Earl E. Shelp (Dordrecht, Holland: D. Reidel Publishing Co., 1981), pp. 151–59.

53. *Ibid.*, pp. 151–52.

54. *Ibid.*, p. 151.

55. *Ibid.*, p. 156.

56. *Ibid.*, p. 157.

57. Baruch Brody, "The Use of Halakhic Material in Discussion of Medical Ethics," *The Journal of Medicine and Philosophy* 8 (August 1983): 317–28; "Marriage, Morality and Sex Change Surgery: A Jewish Perspective," *Hastings Center Report* 11 (August 1981): 8–9.

58. Martin P. Golding, "Justice and Rights," *Justice and Health Care*, ed. Earl E. Shelp (Dordrecht, Holland: D. Reidel Publishing Co., 1981), p. 33; "Preventive vs. Curative Medicine: Perspectives of the Jewish Legal Tradition," *The Journal of Medicine and Philosophy* 8 (August 1983): 269–86.

59. James F. Childress, "Who Shall Live When Not All Can Live?" *Soundings* 53 (Winter 1970), esp. pp. 348–49; Paul Ramsey, *The Patient as Person* (Princeton, N.J.: Princeton University Press, 1970), pp. 239–75, cf. p. xi; Robert M. Veatch, *A Theory of Medical Ethics* (New York: Basic Books, 1981), pp. 250–87.

60. Gregory Vlastos, "Justice and Equality," p. 59.

61. Charles Fried, *Right and Wrong*, p. 118.

62. *Ibid.*

63. Robert M. Veatch, *Medical Ethics*, pp. 265–66, as modified to adjust for different uses of opportunities, p. 278.

64. Thomas Kuhn, *The Structure of Scientific Revolutions* (Chicago: The University of Chicago Press, 1962), p. 157.

65. Thomas Kuhn, "Logic of Discovery or Psychology of Research?" *Criticism and the Growth of Knowledge*, ed. Imre Lakatos and Alan Musgrave (Cambridge, England: Cambridge University Press, 1970), p. 7.

66. Paul Tillich, *Systematic Theology* Vol. 1 (Chicago: University of Chicago Press, 1953), p. 88.

67. *Ibid.*, p. 73.

68. *Ibid.*, p. 25.

69. H. Richard Niebuhr, *Radical Monotheism and Western Culture* (New York: Harper and Brothers, Publishers, 1960), p. 77.

70. An astute critic of an earlier draft of this chapter has pointed out that I repeatedly liken the assumptions in the philosophical case to the premises in the theological argument, not the other way around. Thus I refer to initial philosophical assumptions as "faith moves." The critic suggests that maybe the theological premises get moral punch through the use of some intermediate, essentially nonreligious moral principles (such as the premise that anything that is as different from an infinite and perfect being as a normal human being is has no morally superior standing to that of the not discernably *more* different, handicapped human being). The point is well taken. I, like the Catholic theologians I have cited, am attempting to emphasize the convergence of the two kinds of reasoning. Both require some initial starting assumptions (the term more amenable to philosophy) or faith moves (the term more compatible with theology). I never mean to imply that one discipline is dependent upon the other.

71. Plato, *The Republic* VIII, 558c. (New York: Charles Scribner's Sons, 1928), p. 336.

72. Aristotle, *Nichomachean Ethics,* Book V, 3, trans. Martin Ostwald (Indianapolis: Bobbs-Merrill Co., Inc., 1962), p. 118.

73. This account is based on John Randolph Lucas, *On Justice* (Oxford: Clarendon Press, 1980); "Again Equality," *Justice and Equality,* ed. Hugo A. Bedau (Englewood Cliffs, N.J.: Prentice-Hall, 1971), pp.138–51; "Justice," *Philosophy* 47 (1972): 229–48.

74. Lucas, *Justice,* p. 171.

75. Hugo A. Bedau, "Radical Egalitarianism," *Justice and Equality,* pp. 168–80.

76. Stanley I. Benn, "Egalitarianism and the Equal Consideration of Interests," *Justice and Equality,* pp. 152–67.

77. Lucas, *On Justice,* p. 173.

78. *Ibid.*, p. 174.

79. *Ibid.*, p. 184.

80. *Ibid.*

81. Lucas, himself, recognizes this. See *On Justice,* p. 174.

82. Mill, *Utilitarianism,* p. 16, emphasis added.

83. *Ibid.*, p. 4.

84. *Ibid.*, p. 7.

85. *Ibid.*, p. 44.

86. See, for example, Jeremy Bentham, *An Introduction to the Principles of Morals and Legislation,* Ch. IV (Oxford: Clarendon Press, 1879), pp. 30–31.

87. Jeremy Bentham. "L'Esssai sur la Representation" translated in M. P. Mack, *Jeremy Bentham: An Odyssey of Ideas* (New York: Columbia University Press, 1963), p. 449.

88. See Richard B. Brandt, *Ethical Theory* (Englewood Cliffs, N.J.: Prentice-Hall, Inc., 1959), pp. 414–15.

89. John Stuart Mill, *Utilitarianism,* p. 40.

90. See, for example, Amartya K. Sen, *On Economic Inequality* (New York: W. W. Norton, 1973), p. 16.

91. John Stuart Mill, *Utilitarianism,* p. 75.

92. *Ibid*, p. 71.

93. Joseph Fletcher notes, "The *procedural* principle of utilitarianism ('the greatest number') and the *normative* principle of the commandment ('love your neighbor') result in the greatest amount of *agape* for the greatest number of neighbors possible. That is justice." *Humanhood: Essay in Biomedical Ethics* (Buffalo, N.Y.: Prometheus Books, 1979), p. 56. See also his *Moral Responsibility: Situation Ethics at Work* (Philadelphia: The Westminister Press, 1977), especially Chapter 3, and his *Situation Ethics: The New Morality* (Philadelphia: Westminster Press, 1976), especially Chapter V and the foreword. Mill likewise addresses this theme. He maintains that, "In the golden rule of Jesus of Nazareth, we read the complete spirit of the ethics of utility." *Utilitarianism*, p. 22.

94. Charles Fried is quite sensitive to this sort of distinction. In arguing against a purely market-oriented approach to ethics, Fried uses the dramatic example of rape to establish that our justifications for doing or not doing certain things are not always matters of utility or efficiency. Rape does not seem to be wrong because of the expense and extreme inefficiency of the financial transactions between a man and a woman that would be necessary to prevent the former from raping the latter whenever he was so inclined. As Fried writes:

> Our moral intuition is that rape is wrong in itself—that it is a grievous violation of the rape victim's rights. Now the economic model has no place for a right to personal security as such. . . . Efficiency demands that the balance between assailants and victims be struck in such a way that the total level of gratification of interests be maximized. "Rights and Health Care—Beyond Equity and Efficiency," *New England Journal of Medicine* 293 (July 31, 1975): 242.

95. Fried further develops the concept of physical integrity, as well as that of intellectual integrity, as the basis of negative rights in Chapter 6 of *Right and Wrong*.

96. Robert Nozick, *Anarchy*, p. 233.

97. *Ibid.*, p. 167, footnote.

98. *Ibid.*, p. ix.

99. *Ibid.*, pp. 153; 172–73.

100. *Ibid.*, p. 174–82, for basis of this discussion.

101. *Ibid.*, p. 32–33, cf. p. 178.

102. H. Tristram Engelhardt, Jr., "A Response to the Unjust and the Unfortunate," *Justice and Health Care* ed. Earl E. Shelp (Dordrecht, Holland: D. Reidel Publishing Co., 1982), p. 123.

103. Robert Nozick, *Anarchy*, pp. 236–38; cf. Engelhardt, pp. 125–27.

104. Engelhardt, "Response," p. 126.

5

What Does Equality Mean?

If equality of persons is the only reasonable option, what, exactly, does that mean? If we are going to use it as a basis for some hard-nosed policy decisions regarding the handicapped, we will need much greater specification of the policy impact of the equality of persons. Do we mean merely equality of worth or respect? If so, we might be able to deliver that very cheaply (although respect comes hard when persons appear so unequal in their economic, physical, or mental assets). Do we mean equality of opportunity in the sense of everyone having the opportunity to show his or her ability on job application tests or that everyone should have access to a certain fraction of a teacher's attention? If so, we probably can deliver on that as well (although resistance even to equal chance to be tested for a job seems incredibly strong in some circumstances). If, however, equality of persons means something more—say, a chance for equality of outcome or some more sophisticated modification of that idea—then our school board and all other public policy-making bodies face an enormous challenge. We will have to be very specific about what equality means.

Even if we come to agree that equality of persons has to be taken in its most rigorous form as meaning equality of outcome, we still will need more clarity. Is equal subjective outcome sufficient, as in equal happiness or want satisfaction? If so, the retarded may once again let us off the hook rather easily because as a general rule they seem remarkably easily satisfied (a point that has caused no small problem for those who want to argue that retardation might justify a parental decision to abort or even end the life of an infant on the grounds that it is a life not worth living). Or, on the other hand, must we strive for some more objective measure of outcome, for equal wealth, equal intelligence, equal physical ability, or objective net good, whatever that might be? Do we have to consider outcome at all? Perhaps it is sufficient to strive for equal resource commitments for each person in order to satisfy the requirements of the principle of equality. That is what at least one distinguished philosopher has argued.[1] And if we strive for equality of resource expenditures, do we take into account only the economic resources expended or do we consider the resources each of us has received as natural endowments, as mental and physical abilities as well? Equal dollar expenditures for someone with a severe physical or mental handicap will not take us very far. On the other hand, if we take into account natural assets, our task of moral calculation is much more complex and the demands generated may be virtually infinite.

When we begin looking at physical and mental ability as part of our natural assets, we face another problem in understanding the meaning of the principle of equality of persons. Do we calculate the equality of persons at one point in time or do we consider the degree of the person's well-being over a lifetime? Who has a greater claim based on equality: an infant who is comfortable and happy, but will die soon if not treated, or an elderly millionaire who has had a joyous and rewarding life, but who is now in intractable pain from a cancer? Taking such factors into account will make the calculus very complex.

The puzzle gets even more complicated when we consider that some persons may have opportunities for equality and not take advantage of them. They may in effect bring on their own inequality on themselves by their poor health habits or their refusal of sound medical advice while others (such as the retarded) are in no way responsible for their positions of relative inequality.

Finally, we have to clarify the relation among equality, justice, and the morally right course. It may be, for example, that the just thing to do is to strive for equality of resources per person over a lifetime, but that other moral considerations—considerations related to autonomy or promise keeping or maximizing the amount of good done—press us to override justice.

Equality of Worth, Opportunity, and Outcome

When Americans learn as a basic part of their heritage that all men are created equal, that equality is not defined. If anything is obvious, it is that people are not equal in talent, social usefulness, or willingness to serve the welfare of the community. Yet that kind of equality is obviously not what the founding fathers or the writers in our great religious traditions standing behind our founding fathers had in mind when they talked about equality in creation. Whatever it is they had in mind, it must be something other than an equality of social usefulness and commitment.

Sometimes, to be sure, their vision has been short-sighted. When they said men were created equal, they really meant men and not women; they meant white men, not black, yellow, or brown; they meant property holders, not landless peasants. Here, and throughout the history of the tradition we are tracing, humans have often had difficulty grasping the full impact of the radical equality among all persons, but that has always been the direction in which the vision of equality has been pushing: the landless, indebted Israelite, as well as the well-to-do; the widow as well as the widower; and in at least proleptic ways the foreigner as well as the member of the community. The real problem is not how inclusive the equality must be, but how real. Are we to take the social, political, and financial implications of equality as seriously as the ethereal, spiritual, and moral implications?

Equality of Moral Worth

It is sometimes said that persons are equal in their moral worth, whatever that might mean. The concept of equality of moral worth is a difficult one to grasp, but I take it to be an essential starting point for understanding the meaning of equality. Surely it is not the claim that people are equal in the quality of their moral praiseworthiness or in their moral conduct. On both counts people differ widely. The core notion is something like the following: underlying obvious and radical differences in natural capacities is an equality of moral status, an equal claim of all persons to have moral rights. Suppose, for example, that all agree that freedom is a basic right. The notion of equality of moral standing conveys the idea that insofar as there is such a right, everyone bears it equally. It is unacceptable for one person's claim to freedom to be more weighty than that of someone else on the grounds that the first person is more worthy of having his or her moral claims considered. To take another example, insofar as morality is a matter of responding to the welfare of various parties, each person's welfare counts equally in the moral calculus.

What is striking about this notion of equality of moral worth is that it is shared by the holders of virtually all major ethical theories. Nozickean libertarians, for example, would agree that all are the holders of liberty and each person's liberty counts equally (although because of different natural endowments weaker individuals may freely surrender some of their possessions in what appear to be deals in which the power is very one-sided). Utilitarians would agree that in calculating the net utilities of various courses of action each person's goods counts for one and no one's good for more than one. Thus it would be unacceptable, in principle, for a utilitarian to treat the happiness of certain individuals as more weighty than the happiness of other individuals (although if making certain talented individuals unusually happy has indirect effects that also increase the happiness of other parties, then all of this indirect happiness is to be taken into the calculus of happiness). Equality of worth is the notion that stands behind each person having one vote or each having equal protection of the law. In this sense all the major ethical theories have some notion of equality of moral worth. Where does it come from if not from the basic assumptions made by egalitarians in their theory of justice?

For the theologically explicit theorists there is an equality of finites before an infinite god. That all are equally children of God is the more metaphorical, anthropomorphic way of putting it. This, of course, does not necessarily mean that all are equally elevated or exalted in their high moral status. Traditionally, at least in the Judeo-Christian tradition, it is more that all are equally low in their moral status, equally weak, equally sinners in need of grace. Still in this radical finitude there is equality.

Bernard Williams recognizes that Kant and others have provided a thinly veiled secular analogue for this transcendent basis for equality of moral worth:

> Accordingly, the respect owed equally to each man as a member of the
> Kingdom of Ends is not owed to him in respect of any empirical characteristics

that he may possess, but solely in respect of the transcendental characteristic of being a free and rational will. The ground of the respect owed to each man thus emerges in the Kantian theory as a kind of secular analogue of the Christian conception of the respect owed to all men as equally children of God. Though secular, it is equally metaphysical: in neither case is it anything empirical *about* men that constitutes the ground of equal respect.[2]

This equality of moral status is the beginning of an exegesis of the notion of equality, but it does not get us very far. In fact, equality of respect is sometimes taken as an interpretation that waters down the full impact of the concept. As we saw, the Methodist preacher Samuel Bradburn could retreat to this notion of equality of moral rights to defend himself against the charge that his preaching of equality would lead to the excesses of levelling. If both libertarians and utilitarians can share this element of equality of moral worth with the egalitarians, just where does the concept of equality have its bite? Equality of moral worth may give us such principles as one person/one vote or such obligations as that of counting everyone's good equally in a utility calculus, but is that all that is meant by equality? This notion of equality of moral worth does not answer the question of what equality really means in dollars and cents and in claims upon scarce common resources for the lame, the halt, the blind, and the mentally retarded in need of marginally beneficial, expensive speech therapy.

Equality of moral worth or equality of respect for persons as persons appear to be an important element of the concept of equality. It is essential in one way or another in every important normative ethical theory. It provides a basic starting point for morality, but does not by itself tell us how we should respond to the most critical questions of resource allocation faced by our society. It does not tell us whether it is legitimate for those bargaining from strong positions to take advantage of those in weaker positions. It does not tell us whether in calculating benefits and harms it is acceptable for aggregate benefits for a majority to override the welfare of weak minorities who happen to be poorly off. To determine that we must turn to additional elements implied in the concept of equality and our basic assumptions that underlie it.

Equality of Opportunity

If we are to move beyond equality of worth or equality of respect for persons as persons, an obvious second element in our concept of equality is equality of opportunity. Equality of opportunity has become a fashionable, liberal slogan of justice in the era of civil rights and the movement for racial and gender equality. At the same time it is a much more complex notion than it at first appears. Offering Eddie Conrad the same opportunity as others to compete in a fair entrance examination for college or for a job to earn his own livelihood is hardly what could be called justice.

A first stab at figuring out the principle of equality of opportunity might lead to a formula like the following: if people are competing for a scarce resource not available to all, their chance of success should not be influenced by extraneous social, psychological, or biological factors. Two terms in this initial statement of the principle of equality of opportunity need special attention: "scarcity" and "extraneous factors." First, equality of opportunity arises only when there is a scarcity such that not all can have a piece of the scarce resource and thus satisfy the requirements of equality in that way. If the scarce resource were like pie that could be cut into any given number of equal shares, we would not have the equality of opportunity problem that arises when the scarce resource cannot be divided. It is scarce either by its very nature (such as prestige or a leadership position) or is contingently scarce because there is simply not enough to go around.[3]

The second and more problematic term in this initial statement of the principle of equality of opportunity is "extraneous factors."[4] Without some clear idea of what makes a factor extraneous, we will not get very far in understanding equality of opportunity. Some factors are clearly extraneous: race of applicants for positions as trainees in the police academy, marital status or gender in applicants for almost all employment positions. Some factors are not so obviously extraneous, however. Have we failed to provide equal opportunity if we exclude a male from competing for an executive position in the National Organization of Women? Or if we exclude atheists from teaching in church-sponsored schools, or prevent unmarried persons from becoming marriage counselors in a therapeutic setting that stresses the experience of the counselor?

The notion of equality of opportunity, it seems, may not get us as far as it first appears. It tells us that social, psychological, and biological classifications unrelated to performance are morally excluded in distributing scarce resources. If Eddie Conrad, a white child of middle-class parents, and a black girl of working-class parents were similarly in need of speech therapy, the notion of equal opportunity would tell us that they each should get the same amount or at least have an equal shot at getting the therapy if it cannot be divided between them.

A case of current interest reveals how difficult it is to determine whether equality of opportunity has been provided. Jamie Fisk, an eleven-month-old child suffering from biliary atresia and in need of a liver transplant, received a cadaver organ after her father, an articulate medical administrator, appealed to his Senators, Congressmen, the White House, the American Medical Association, and the American Academy of Pediatrics, all of whom then helped publicize his daughter's need for a liver donation for transplant.[5] No one can question the integrity and dedication of a father who would go to such efforts for his daughter. In fact, one might argue that as a father he has a special "role specific" duty to seek such an advantage for her (a concept we discuss in the next chapter). The question faced in this case, however, is whether the father's unique social position and skill in reaching the media gave his daughter an unequal opportunity for access to a life-saving liver transplant in comparison with other similarly situated infants whose parents were not in a position to generate this publicity. If our society is to commit itself to equal opportunity, it must create institutions that will give all such children equal opportunity of access to organs for transplant regardless of parental skills and dedication. This parental skill, then, seems to be an extraneous factor in the distribution of cadaver livers.

The positive formulation of equal opportunity might, therefore, be stated in a more limited way as follows: people of equal need and ability desirous of a scarce resource not available to everyone should have an equal opportunity to obtain it.

The most critical problem arises when we ask whether need and ability are relevant factors in distributing scarce resources or whether they are also extraneous. Should two individuals with differing needs have equal opportunity for access to medical resources? What, for example, if both Eddie Conrad and a classmate with a slight speech impediment and the desire to become an actor wanted intensive private speech therapy? Here it seems that equality of opportunity is more complex. Two radically different and competing conceptions of equality of opportunity present themselves. The libertarian conception would focus on procedurally equal opportunity. Each should have an equal chance at getting the therapy. Need would not, per se, be a reason to favor one student over the other. Various allocative devices such as the free market, the bargaining power of parents, the vote of the school board based on personal whim, or even a lottery might be used. This libertarian conception would still exclude extraneous social categories such as race and sex, but would also consider need an extraneous factor.

Equality of Outcome

By contrast, a holder of an egalitarian conception of equality would strive not for an equal chance to get the therapy, but what we may tentatively call equality of outcome. In this case he or she might strive for an equal opportunity to speak (or more generally an equal level of well-being). If we take this more egalitarian conception of equality, we would want to discriminate on the basis of need, at least in this case. That is the only conclusion consistent with our basic assumptions about the equality of finite persons and the availability of some common resources that people have a responsibility to use to increase equality. When people have differing needs, inequalities of opportunity for access are necessary in order to have movement toward equal opportunity for outcomes.

It is striking that John Rawls, who offers a powerful egalitarian interpretation of the notion of equality of opportunity, always qualifies his discussion with the word "fair." He speaks of "fair equality of opportunity."[6] or simply of "fair opportunity"[7] making clear that in cases of differing need, opportunity of access will not be equal. His goal is a "just outcome."[8] The result is what Rawls calls "the principle of redress," which applies explicitly to the problems of educating people of differing intellectual needs. "The idea is to redress the bias of contingencies," he says, "in the direction of equality. In pursuit of this principle greater resources might be spent on the education of the less intelligent than the more intelligent."[9] The result is equality of opportunity to be educated, but this means unequal opportunity to get the use of the school's resources.

One set of cases where many are inclined not to distribute on the basis of need is in the distribution of rewards for some talent or ability. When we compete, we expect the rewards of the contest—praise, prizes, grades, or job offers—to be based on ability. Here the common wisdom has it that there should be equality of opportunity to compete and that rewards should be distributed on the basis of ability: grades for intelligence, the most valuable player award for athletic skill, a beauty queen's title for beauty, or a job to the one who best meets the placement requirements. Normally, we would feel it absurd to distribute any of these on the basis of need, or even to distribute them equally.

But this creates an odd situation. The mathematical skill of the genius, the physical ability of the athlete, the beauty of the beauty queen, and the various skills of the successful job applicant are, at least in large part, natural endowments over which the competitor has little control.

At most, natural abilities were nurtured and developed. It is hard to see why those with generous natural endowments *deserve* these rewards. The reward, it appears, should at most be for the marginal increment for which the individual was responsible. Equality of opportunity in the libertarian sense of fair procedure in which each competitor starts at the same point and must complete the same test to be rewarded is, in fact, a device for producing inequalities of outcome, inequalities that are based at least in large part on "God-given" natural endowments over which the rewarded one has little control. Equality of opportunity in this context is really a rationalization for inequality of outcome. Natural endowments do not deserve reward; such rewards do not contribute to greater equality. If our goal is equality, in competitions where there is differing ability we should handicap if necessary to assure the one less endowed of a fair shot. If we do this in golf, should we not in the rest of life where the stakes are much higher? Once again the principle is not equality of opportunity to compete, but equality of outcome.

Here Rawls follows the core assumptions of the Judeo-Christian tradition and the sense of community the tradition conveys. He views the natural endowments of more talented individuals as a common asset, a rigorous application of the faith commitment to common ownership of natural resources.[10] Moreover, we have a responsibility to use these assets in such a way that there is a "tendency toward equality" since no one deserves his or her advantage. There is a common fraternity among persons such that those with natural endowments use them to the advantage of the least well off.

There are two exceptions to this dissociation of equality of outcome and equality of opportunity (which rewards ability). First, some level of performance in such competitions does, in fact, result from human effort, training, persistence, and fortitude. If two people start with equal natural talents and one develops her talents more fully, to that extent it seems reasonable that she should be rewarded. Here equality of opportunity—

to train, to develop talent, and to compete—does seem to lead to a reasonable inequality of outcome. More about this in a moment.

Second, sometimes people with an unusual degree of natural skill are rewarded not simply because they have won a competition, but because others in the society find it useful to reward them. We reasonably distribute sensitive jobs in our national defense on the basis of ability (or at least we think we should do so). This is not simply because we feel it is just to reward talent. Rather, it is because we realize that it is in everyone's interest to get the job done well even if it is unfair to reward the one whose unusual ability is the result of unusual natural endowments. It seems plausible that one of the few circumstances in which it is legitimate to reward natural ability in such competitions is when it is in the interests of others, particularly others who are least well off, to do so. Here we are rewarding ability not because it deserves reward, but because it serves some moral purpose to do so.

It is in accounting for this legitimate rewarding of ability that Rawls and the Judeo-Christian tradition part company even though they may reach very similar conclusions. For Rawls such rewards are not only legitimate, they are just and they are actually an expression of fraternity, of common bonds, between the elite and the less well off. When (even if only when) the least well off gain by inequalities, those inequalities are just and are a manifestation of community. The real egalitarian is much more uncomfortable about such rewards for talent than is Rawls. There may, in fact, be circumstances where rewarding ability and thereby increasing inequalities nevertheless produce some advantage to the least well off. For the egalitarian to justify this, the least well off would, at a minimum, have to approve of the inequality. But this is a condition that Rawls never requires. Moreover, the real egalitarian would view even this inequality as unfortunate even if necessary. Far from being an expression of fraternity, of community cohesiveness, it is a breakdown of community. Far better that the talented use their talent for the benefit of the least advantaged without the inducement of rewards that actually increase inequality. Finally, from the point of view of the real egalitarian—the one who shares the common assumptions that lead one toward placing high value on equality—it does not follow that it is fair or just to reward ability in this way, even though it may be the right thing to do in the sense that it is the action that best resolves the conflicts between justice and other *prima facie* principles.

Where does that leave us with regard to equality of opportunity as a supplement to equality of moral worth? First, people of equal need and ability desirous of a scarce resource that not all can have should have an equal opportunity to obtain it without regard to extraneous social, psychological, or biological considerations. Second, people of different need desirous of such resources should have a fair opportunity—that is, opportunity in proportion to need. Finally, people of different ability desirous of such resources should have an equal opportunity to obtain them even if that requires handicapping so as to compensate for some individual's lack of ability. The only exceptions to this general rule are when the differences in ability are attributable to individual effort when all had an opportunity to expend such effort and when rewarding those with greater ability will benefit the least well off and those least well off approve.

Ultimately, what we are really after is something like equality of outcome (with some very limited qualifications). Exactly what this means will require more analysis. It is neither equality of moral worth nor equality of opportunity. Equality of moral worth will be a necessary precondition, but it will not be sufficient. Equality of opportunity will often further that goal as in cases where extraneous social, psychological, or biological factors are excluded from consideration. In some cases, however, when people have differing needs or differing abilities, this kind of procedural equality of opportunity will actually hinder equality of outcome. In those cases we abandon equality of opportunity as defined by everyone having an equal chance to compete for some resource. When needs are different, we distribute on the basis of need replacing equality of opportunity with equality of outcome. When abilities differ we, with some exceptions, give special consideration to those with lesser ability—we give them a handicap—so that they have an equal shot at a desired outcome. That may be considered equality of opportunity, (i.e., opportunity for a given level of well-being), but it is a far cry from the liberal, procedural notion of equality of opportunity.

Momentary Equality and Equality Over a Lifetime

Even if we agree that equality of outcome is a significant part of the content of our concept of equality to supplement equality of worth and equality of opportunity, some complex problems remain. One of these is whether we are striving for equality at a given moment in time or over a lifetime. Consider the choice a city government might face in deciding about Eddie Conrad's speech therapy. Let us assume that Eddie is not acutely uncomfortable, that he has his essential life requirements fulfilled; he has adequate food, clothing, shelter, and the like. He may have love, family support, and a competent school staff striving to educate him, but he still might be said to be in considerable need. His life would be better if he could speak more clearly, thus communicating his desires and interacting more effectively with others.

Suppose that the city must choose between spending its resources to meet Eddie's needs and to meet the needs of terminally ill, suffering cancer patients most of whom are elderly people who have lived long and happy lives in the community. They also have needs. If our goal is equality of outcome, we must determine which of the two types of need is the greatest. Let us assume that foolish expenditures have already been cut or are politically impossible to cut, thus forcing the city into the choice between these two groups.

It might be reasonable to say that looking at the choice from the perspective of the present moment—as a slice of time—the terminally ill cancer patients may have greater need than Eddie and other mentally retarded persons needing similar speech therapy. Summing the calculations over time, however, may give a radically different perspective. The elderly cancer patients who have had good lives over many years might be said to have had more well-being even taking into account their present misery. Moreover, if one considers future time as well as past time, the speech therapy will amount to more well-being than the intervention for the terminally ill cancer patients.

We face the question of whether, when we consider equality of outcome, we mean at any given instant or over a lifetime. It is not obvious which perspective is the correct one. Looking at the aggregate amount of well-being over a lifetime would mean that the acute needs of the elderly at the moment would be subordinated to the claims of justice of those who are so sickly that they will never have a chance to get to the frailties of old age. Equality of outcome over a lifetime would mean that the needs of the sick, the retarded, and the otherwise poorly off young would take precedence over those of older people who are suffering acutely and could be treated easily, but have at least lived through the good times as well.[11] If one has the intuition that a previously well-off elderly person should not be left to writhe in agony in order to expend scarce resources on an extra speech lesson for a retarded boy rather than on a morphine injection, this suggests that the slice-of-time perspective is relevant for assessing acute needs that can be met inexpensively. On the other hand, if only the slice-of-time perspective is used, persons inevitably dying in old age who have had long and happy lives will get very high priority in resource allocation. The plausible compromise is to assess well-being primarily in a longitudinal fashion accumulating well-being over a lifetime, but adjusting for intense immediate needs that can be met easily and cheaply. The logic of this compromise is not obvious. It, however, has the quality of rational calculation of equality over a lifetime tempered with compassion for a special group of immediate needs.

If that is our perspective, then the goal with several qualifications is equality of outcome determined as the net welfare considered over a lifetime. The quality of life at the particular moment when the determination is being made is not decisive. This formula requires several qualifications, however. In addition to taking into account easily met overwhelming immediate needs, adjustments must be made for the differences in outcome that result from different efforts that people make. Moreover, we will have to determine how to go about measuring equality of outcome.

Overall Equality and Variations in Life-Style

We are making some progress toward understanding the meaning of equality and how it might apply to such concrete problems as allocating a school budget between the almost infinite needs of a retarded youngster and the lesser needs of a large number of more nearly normal children who could benefit from physical education, music, or arts programs. Equality includes equality of moral worth and equality of opportunity, but these must be supplemented with and subordinated to something approximating equality of outcome measured over a lifetime.

To clarify further this notion of equality of outcome, we must return to the problem of rewarding those who take their quite ordinary abilities and, through great effort, develop them to extraordinary levels. We need to decide whether the Pete Roses of the world deserve the rewards that come from their own efforts to develop their talent. We also need to refute the anti-egalitarian argument that equality of outcome makes for a world of sameness, a world where everyone would be exactly alike.

Both of these are elements of the problem of variation in life-style. A liberal, pluralistic society values variety. We are generally repulsed by regimentation and by any social policy that would require everyone to lead identical lives. This, of course, rests on an aesthetic judgment and depends on the assumption that we have an obligation to make the world more pleasing aesthetically—a very questionable assumption. Nevertheless, if that were the implication of egalitarianism, many would reject it.

Fortunately, that is not the implication at all. Egalitarianism strives for an opportunity for an equal level of well-being for all—not for sameness. At first it may appear that we could achieve an equal level of well-being by giving everyone identical resources: a fixed ration of foods, a standard allotment of clothing, and a standardized shelter. In fact, there is no need for such regimentation, and it probably would lead to very unequal well-being. With regard to these basic goods (excluding health care and education for the moment), we can assume that people have approximately the same needs. There is surely nothing wrong with a scheme that would distribute some fixed amount of these goods and let people trade so that they could improve their well-being. As long as the needs and desires are approximately equal, and the marginal increases in well-being resulting from the trades are about the same, each person in the trade would have his or her well-being improved without significant abandonment of equality. Alternatively, we could distribute some general medium, like money, and let people buy whatever mix of food, clothing, shelter, and other goods they desire. There is no reason why equality of well-being would require sameness. Any society that values freedom would permit such variations as long as they do not lead to serious deviations from equality of overall well-being as an outcome.[12]

Before trying to determine how different needs for education and health care fit into this scheme of overall equality of outcome, let us consider the problem of different effort. If two people with about the same ability and the same resources start out with equal well-being, but one of them uses all her spare hours struggling to improve her abilities or enhance her resources, do we still insist that there be equality of outcome?

There may be a technical solution to the problem. If we really keep track of well-being over a lifetime, it may turn out that the one who expends great effort to improve abilities or enhance resources is no better off than a more slothful counterpart. Consider the one who spends every spare hour cultivating a rose garden and therefore a year later has the joy a beautiful roses. His counterpart with roughly similar needs and abilities may have spent his spare time watching television or eating steaks or going on long walks in the woods. At first it would appear that after a year the one who planted the rose garden is better off. He has a beautiful garden while his counterpart does not. Calculated from that moment of time he may have greater well-being, but if the burden of the past year is included and the memories of television, steak, or walks in the woods are counted as part of his counterpart's well-being, the two may actually still be in about the same relative position if we try to measure overall well-being over a lifetime.

More basically, however, it may not make a difference morally whether the two are actually equal in their well-being when one has a rose garden and the other does not. What the egalitarian is striving for is really opportunity for equality of outcome measured over a lifetime, not the actual well-being. In this example, where our two actors had roughly similar needs and abilities, we can say that they had an equal *opportunity* for the garden (or the walk in the woods). Had the second person been unable to cultivate his garden because of some severe physical handicap or because of lack of time to devote to anything but providing the basic necessities, the case would have been different, but in this simpler situation, they both could have had the garden. If we value freedom, we will not insist on actual equal outcome (even if we are only talking about equal well-being rather than actual sameness). We insist only on equal *opportunity* for a level of well-being comparable to that of other people.

From this point of view, there is nothing wrong with rewarding real effort (even if a different level of well-being results after taking into account the stress and strain of making the effort). The only problem is a technical one: knowing how to separate real effort from differences in ability that make it easier for one person to develop a garden or a skill beyond that person's natural endowment. The distinction is almost impossible to make in practice. A rough rule of thumb might be of help here. It seems very unlikely that differences in outcome purely as a result of effort could result in much more than the range of one-half to double the average well-being. Thought of in terms of working hours, if we consider that the typical person puts in, say, sixty hours of occupational and/or domestic work per week, it is unlikely that anyone could exert an effort that results in more than double that output. The overachiever might work twice as hard for the sixty hours or work at the standard pace for one hundred twenty, but not much more than that. If this overachiever's output is much more than double the average, the chances are good that it is in part accounted for by unusual natural endowments: unusual physical or mental skills, an unusually aggressive personality, or some other essentially nonvoluntary element. If we are to reward this overachiever for true effort, any reward that exceeds double the average should be suspect. It is likely to include reward for nonvoluntary natural endowments, which need a different justification than rewards for real voluntary effort.

The underachiever's situation is somewhat more complex. It is possible to imagine someone so lazy that he achieves less than half the average well-being and yet is not deficient in natural endowment. It is more likely, however, that such underproductiveness is attributed to some biological, psychological, or social aberration rather than slothfulness.

If this is a rough approximation of the range of variation that we can attribute to real human effort, the range of one-half to double the average would give us the outer limits of the amount of variation in well-being that we can tolerate in the name of justice. This toleration of variation up to a factor of four (ranging from half to double the average) would still be unfair to some with less natural ability, but it at least sets limits on the injustice and accepts the variation in life-style that we all value. We value it not in the name of justice, but in the name of freedom. Thus, if in the name of freedom we want to avoid the regimentation of regulated work patterns and work levels, all we can insist on in the name of justice is an opportunity for equal level of well-being, not its actual achievement. In any case, differences in well-being over a lifetime that result from real voluntary choices of individuals to express themselves in unique ways and to develop their talents extraordinarily are no problem for an egalitarian. All that they are striving for is equality of opportunity for an equal level of well-being over a lifetime.

Equality of Well-Being vs. Equality of Resource Commitment

These adjustments for equality over a lifetime and for differences in effort are only the initial problems we encounter in determining exactly what we mean by the notion of equality as equality of outcome. A more serious problem arises when we realize that outcomes, thought of in terms of well-being, may be highly subjective.

Subjective vs. Objective Well-Being

We are drawn back once again to the purported fact that Eddie Conrad and others who are mentally retarded apparently can lead quite happy lives. Supposing this to be so, should we be permitted to argue that in comparison with his classmates who are endowed with extremely high intellectual capacities, Eddie can look forward to a happy life and that therefore he has achieved a level of well-being equal to others? He will escape the agony of rejection by the best colleges, the search for a prestigious profession, and the burdens that go with keeping up with the Joneses.

Some people are easily satisfied with just the basics for food, clothing, shelter, and a loving, caring family, while others have extravagant tastes that are extremely expensive to satisfy. If our goal is an opportunity for an equal level of well-being over a lifetime, must we take into account this subjective variation in our understanding of an egalitarian theory of justice as equality? The answer is not at all obvious. Should one be condemned to unhappiness because the natural lottery has bestowed on one a taste for exotic travel, elegant food, or owning fine art? Perhaps not, but the problems associated with this subjective notion of well-being are enormous. We would have to distinguish between the one who would be miserably unhappy without a distinguished art collection and the one whose happiness would simply be greater for having it. About all we would have to go on is self-reporting, which could be extremely unreliable. Moreover, it is not clear that the one who is really miserable when expensive tastes are not satisfied is really endowed with those tastes as part of his or her nature. Often these tastes appear to be cultivated, sometimes at the discretion of the individual himself. In that case, they are more akin to voluntary variations that should perhaps be tolerated in the name of freedom, but as needs they are hardly comparable to the need of the child with biliary atresia for a functioning liver or to Eddie Conrad's for speech therapy.[13]

Amy Gutman considers the hypothetical case of a social commitment to dental care.[14] She notes that replacing carious teeth with dentures could preserve dental functioning without exorbitant cost. But the sort of full mouth reconstruction for which many rich persons opt today, involving periodontal and endodontal treatment and capping, might be only slightly more effective, but much more satisfying. Of course, such treatment is quite costly. While the social commitment to dental care might seem to confer an equal right to the preferred treatment, "it is unclear whether the satisfaction of subjective desire is equivalent to fulfillment of objective need."

Given the difficulty of measuring subjective well-being and the doubt that these variations are a natural occurrence in the first place, a plausible alternative is to pursue some more objective notion of well-being. This would-be well-being not based on happiness, but on the meeting of basic human needs thought to exist independent of tastes, preferences, whims, or other individual variations. This would prevent society from being made the captive of the deviant individual with extraordinarily exotic tastes. There have been several attempts in the philosophical literature, primarily in the literature of philosophy of medicine, to develop a notion of objective needs.[15] Norman Daniels, for example, develops the notion of "species typical functioning," implying that an objective set of needs can be derived from this notion. Someone incapacitated by pain needs relief in order to function typically; someone without food needs a certain level of sustenance; someone who is cold needs shelter; someone like Eddie Conrad needs speech therapy in order to function more nearly like a normal member of the human community. If our concept of equality is to include a notion of equality of outcome, it surely must be based on objective needs of this kind rather than desires to achieve a predetermined level of happiness no matter what bizarre exotic resources are needed to achieve it.

Daniels and others who have sought some objective notion of needs have run into difficulties however. At the very least we must recognize that Daniels' notion of species typical functioning, just as the more subjective formulations, requires value judgments. Some quite typical functioning of the species may, in fact, be awful. Dental caries and their associated pain are quite typical for the human species, but the need for a dentist is no less because of that statistical fact. On the other hand, some quite atypical functioning—outstanding athletic endurance, brilliant intellectual performance, or saintly character—may be highly valued and we would hardly recommend altering them to restore the holders of these characteristics to more species typical functioning.

The notion that we are striving for is neither the statistical feature of "species typicalness" nor the absence of value judgment. It is rather a value judgment so consistent and so predictable that we can treat it as fixed, as if it were an objective part of nature. It may in fact *be* an objective part of nature—depending on the truth of metaphysics (if there is any)—although we could never prove this. The dislike of pain, the desire to think, feel, reason, walk, and enjoy are all value judgments of this sort. The dislike of pain is so universal that, were we to encounter someone who said he enjoyed the pain of a toothache and wanted it to continue, we would tend to doubt the veracity or the mental stability of the speaker rather than decide that liking or disliking of pain is simply subjective, a matter of taste, like ice cream flavors.[16]

This may mean that we face what appears to be a very complicated task: trying to reach a consensus on the value judgments made by people who claim they need particular resources to function in such a way as to have an opportunity to be as well off as others. We have to be able to treat these judgments as objective, as if they were part of nature.

That task may not be as complicated as it sounds. Many needs claims obviously satisfy this criterion. Some minimum of food, clothing, and shelter, and many medical and educational basics all seem obviously essential to some minimal well-being. Other items that some people might claim as needs to be equal to others seem obviously to fail this criterion: a claim of an objective need for fine art, caviar, or cosmetic surgery for a slightly enlarged nose just will not stand the test of this kind of objective equality of well-being.

The project is made more difficult once we accept the modification based on freedom that permits persons to reject opportunities that are made available to them. Suppose we allocate to each person enough funds for basics of food, clothing, shelter, and medical care and education. Consider two men who have no special needs, one of whom uses his freedom to buy routine dental check-ups and restorative services. The other may forego the dental service in order to buy more opera tickets. He would have had an equal opportunity for dental services, but would have chosen to spend his resources elsewhere. If both now develop a toothache, they might stand in very different relationship with regard to the "objective" need for emergency dental treatment. The first surely has such a need, but the second may have a toothache that could have been prevented through his own voluntary choice. It is really quite hard to determine whether the two men have identical "objective needs" in order to have an opportunity for equal well-being. This makes clear that two people suffering exactly the same pain may nonetheless be in quite different relation to the claims of justice. One has done what he could voluntarily to avoid his need. For the second, we do not know if the voluntary behavior could have avoided his present crisis. The idea of striving for equal objective well-being over a lifetime may be so complicated that it can serve as nothing more than a conceptual model of what the egalitarian is striving for.

The concept of ethical and other values being objective may sound controversial. For some it is hard to imagine how values can be objective the way scientific claims purporting to describe objective reality are. It may not be as difficult as it appears, however. In the first place we must remain modest in the claims of objectivity we make in science. It is now well recognized by philosophy of science that even apparently non-controversial descriptive statements contain buried within them conceptual and metaphysical presumptions. For most everyday work we get by quite nicely treating these culturally tainted statements "as if they were objective." A similar treatment is in order regarding certain evaluative claims. For example, we need not settle the ultimate metaphysical status of the dislike of intense pain in order to treat the dislike of such pain "as if it were an objective fact" that pain was undesirable. Likewise we can safely treat the undesirability of severe retardation as if it were objective. Those working from a religious tradition and certain secular philosophical traditions will have no trouble with this. For others it will require a more conscious commitment to treat certain evaluative judgments "as if objective."

Objective Well-Being and Equality of Resource Commitment

In order to avoid some of these problems of basing policy on efforts to provide opportunities for objective well-being, philosopher Ronald Dworkin has suggested that instead we strive for equality of resource commitment.[17] Dworkin seems to believe that even the egalitarian is not striving for equality of outcome (or even opportunity for outcome), but rather is going to be satisfied with equality of resource commitment.[18] I cannot follow him in his apparently principled rejection of equality of outcome as a goal (once we have made the suitable adjustments for effort, variation in life-style, and lifetime rather than momentary equality). He gives no argument for this shift. Rather, he seems to think that equality of resource commitment is all that justice requires in the first place. On that, if I understand him correctly, I cannot agree. If we get to equality by making some primary assumptions about the relationships among people—that they are equal in their finitude, that some resources are held in common, and that people are bound together in a common community that leads them to use available resources to attempt to restore equality—then surely it is opportunities for equality of outcome, not mere resource commitment, that count.

Still, Dworkin may be on the right track. If equality of outcome is so difficult to measure, especially in a world that values variation in life-style, and people really have about the same needs, then we might short-circuit much of the confusion by simply using equality of resource commitment as an approximation for equality for outcome, assuming that within some limits, people who are given equal resources—equal food, clothing, and shelter—will end up with about equal well-being even after one takes into account the trades they make, the differences in marginal utility of those trades, and the wisdom they show in pursuing their welfare.

For food, clothing, and shelter—those things we all need in about the same amount—equal distribution of resources is probably not a bad approximation of equality of outcome. It is surely far closer than the radically unequal resource distribution that exists in the present world. It might even be more equal than trying to produce equality of outcome by direct welfare interventions, especially when we take into account the problem of just differences in result that can be attributed to differences in real effort and differences in the timing of resource use.

It appears to be not a bad approximation at all. Dworkin is perhaps too timid actually to affirm the assumptions that would be necessary to reach this conclusion and he, for some reason, loses sight of the fact that equality of resources is only a pragmatic substitute for our real goal of equality of opportunity for objective net outcome, but he is surely on the right track.

He is, that is, until we reintroduce the problem of education and medical resources. For food, clothing, and shelter where needs are about the same, equal economic resources would do the job quite adequately, but what about education and health care? Here surely the objective needs are radically different. As Daniels argues, while many of our basic needs are roughly equal, "In contrast, many other needs are not roughly equal at all. Indeed, it is often these unequal needs it is most expensive to service."[19] Giving everyone equal resources to cover these items of unequal need would surely not lead to equality of outcome. Eddie Conrad and the mentally retarded would be fighting a losing battle in the purchase of education. The physically impaired would be equally disadvantaged in the purchase of health care.

Dworkin considers and finally rejects what I think may be the real solution to this problem,[20] though his reasons for rejecting it are not at all clear. He considers the possibility that when calculating the resources distributed to each person we include not only the economic resources or their equivalent (the food, land, livestock, etc.), but the mental and physical assets as well. Dworkin finally rejects this, but then is forced to a formula in which we strive for equality of resources "corrected to provide for [mental and physical] handicaps."[21] Instead of coming up with this rather complex formula, which then requires a justification for the correction—a justification he does not really provide—it seems far simpler to take as our operational goal (our approximation of equality of outcome) equality of resource allocation *including mental and physical assets.*

The effect would be to require a preliminary drawing on the commonly held assets to compensate as best we can those who have lost in the natural lottery and then to distribute what is left equally to everyone (perhaps accepting a variation of a factor of four to accommodate different efforts). This would still be only an approximation, but a very good one. It would unfortunately reintroduce one of the problems we are trying to avoid. It would require some effort to quantify or rank the extent of people's handicaps in order to know how much compensation to render. Dworkin, in fact, recognizes that this must happen whether one includes mental and physical ability as part of the natural assets or whether one corrects the equal (economic) asset distribution for these differences in natural endowment. He proposes a sophisticated scheme that he refers to as a kind of auction to determine what a fair amount of compensation might be. An alternative, which seems more plausible and more directly relevant to our real goal of equality of outcome, would be to use the common resources first to provide actual services that could restore as much as possible the abilities of which the losers in the natural lottery have been deprived. This seems to be the ethical conclusion to which the egalitarian assumptions drive us. The mentally and physically handicapped—the mentally retarded, the physically deformed, and the chronically ill—have a first claim of justice on society for the use of common resources to compensate for their handicaps.

In-kind and Financial Compensation

This strategy of using assets first to restore those with handicaps to a somewhat more equal starting point faces several challenges. One comes from those favoring the free market solution who would simply give the handicapped a just amount of money and let them buy either the needed educational and medical services or else. They argue that buying other goods might make them even better off. Charles Fried has made a strong case for distributing money rather than in-kind services such as health care.[22]

In an ideal world where the handicapped were rational, autonomous agents capable of making free choices of this sort, we must concede that the free market alternative is attractive. It would permit trades of resources allotted to education and health care just as we have already permitted trades of other essentials like food, clothing, and shelter.

The arguments against this approach are in part pragmatic. In the first place, many of the needy handicapped, such as Eddie Conrad, are in no position to act as free, rational, autonomous agents to trade away their education and therapy for some other desirable goods. The entire scheme requires some judgment of objective needs in the first place. It would take additional justification to permit some third party presumably acting on behalf of the incompetent needy one to trade away the resources supplied to meet an ''objective need'' in order to provide what the third party takes to be a more valuable good.

Another reason to supply actual education and medical resources rather than some generalized compensation like money is that the services needed to respond to these purportedly objective needs are complex and social. They require complex educational and health care research, development, and service networks. It is not clear that the services would be available to buy if some of those who were entitled to compensation used their resources to buy other goods instead. If the compensation for physical and mental disability has a first claim because it is designed to meet what has been determined to set a so-called objective need, then society, if it has an obligation to strive for equality of outcome, also has an obligation to provide the social institutions necessary to provide the services needed to move as close as possible toward equality of outcome. That may well mean providing the educational and health care institutions that can only be provided if this initial compensation is in kind rather than in money.

There is a final reason for this in-kind initial compensation in order to make the total resource allocation as equal as possible. Consider the people with the dental problems once again. Let us suppose that two women have severe dental pain attributed to a congenital malformation of the jaw resulting in abnormal growth of the teeth. Let us agree that this pain constitutes a physical abnormality, a shortcoming in natural endowment deserving of compensation in order to get their allotment of natural resources up to an even starting point. If we gave each some money (presumably equal to the cost of getting oral surgery to correct the condition) and permit each to spend it as she saw fit, one might buy the surgery and the other some other good. That would be permitted on the principle of variation in life-style we have defended. But then a year later we would have two women who, although in fact approximately equal in outcome in our sense, would look very different. They would be approximately equal because one would have the freedom from the dental pain and the other would have the joy of the television or whatever she bought that she considered more valuable. The trouble is not a moral one but a pragmatic one. Should the television-preferring woman present herself at the dental clinic a year later and ask for compensation for her awful dental pain, society would not know how to respond unless it had a full set of records to distinguish this woman with ''voluntary'' dental pain from another like our first woman whose pain is a result of the loss in the natural lottery for which she has not been previously compensated.

If we opt for the compensation in money and permitted freedom of choice, we buy a small increase in marginal utility for the woman preferring the television, the price of which will be an enormous bureaucracy keeping tallies on how all those compensated for losses in the natural lottery spend their money. The fact that many in a position to be compensated are not competent, rational decision-makers, that the response called for is a complex social institutional one, and that complex bureaucracies would be needed to monitor compensations and distinguish the voluntarily deficient in ''objective needs'' from those who had lost in the natural lottery and never before been compensated, all lead to a case for providing educational and health care resources to the losers in the natural lottery in kind as compensation to get their resource allotment back up to an equal starting point. Then and only then will equality of resources allocation approximate equality of outcome, which is what we are really striving for while still offering a socially manageable set of welfare institutions.[23]

This leads us to the conclusion that justice in dealing with the handicapped requires that resources be channeled into in-kind medical and educational services so that all have, insofar as possible, opportunities for equality of objective net outcome and that this, at least as an approximation, amounts to equality in resource allocation taking into account the fact that physical and intellectual resources have been distributed very unevenly in the natural lottery. Outcome will not be exactly the same for several reasons: people will use their discretionary resources differently and make trades that are mutually advantageous; some people will increase their share somewhat through extra effort; and some people will never be able to be compensated adequately—a problem to which we turn in the next chapter. It is the limiting of health care and education to in-kind aid together with a confidence that trades of other goods will leave people approximately equal that provides a basis for concluding that persons would not end up with radically unequal outcomes if there were an initial equal distribution of resources. With these qualifications, however, justice requires striving for equality of objective net outcomes.

Conflict between Justice and Other Ethical Principles

There remains one more conceptual point in clarifying the meaning of the term justice and its relationship to equality before turning to policy questions such as the infinite resources that this kind of compensation of the severely handicapped would seem to demand. We need to be clear on the relation between justice and other ethical principles. Many ethical systems recognize that there are potentially conflicting ethical principles, rules, or rights claims. Each of these principles, rules, or rights claims may have merit. Considered by themselves they tell us one element of moral duty, what is often referred to as a prima facie duty.[24] When we take into account the other competing principles, rules, or rights claims we must decide priority according to some normative ethical theory. We may opt for a strategy of balancing competing claims or one of giving certain claims priority. The result will be an eventual decision about what is one's actual duty or "duty proper," possibly leading to an abandonment of our initial commitment to full compensation of the handicapped.

Whether such an abandonment—an overriding of the claims of justice of the handicapped—is ever justified will depend upon one's normative theory and how the competing ethical principles are to be related to one another. In *A Theory of Medical Ethics* I argued that the only plausible formula for dealing with competing claims involves two steps.[25] First, we must distinguish those ethical principles that are simply devoted to production of consequences—the principles of beneficence and nonmaleficence—from those that characterize certain inherent right-making characteristics of actions—what philosophers sometimes call the deontological principles. In that volume I discussed five such principles: autonomy, promise keeping, truth telling, avoiding killing, and justice.

Second, we have to decide the priorities both within and between these two groups of principles. I developed an argument (that cannot be repeated here) that the deontological principles are each equally morally weighty and that, if more than one of them arises in a particular moral conflict, the only solution is to balance the prima facie claims of the competing principles. That is a position taken by many, including W. D. Ross. Likewise, I have argued that the two principles oriented to production of consequences—beneficence and nonmaleficence—are equally morally weighty so that they should be balanced.

The novel part of my argument was that, taken together, the moral requirement determined by considering the deontological principles takes precedence over the principles that deal only with consequences. While some, such as W. L. Sumner, have criticized this position, saying that non-consequentialist duties cannot always take such precedence and that no modern philosopher would take such a position,[26] in fact, many of the greatest ones have, including Kant, Nozick, Rawls, and most rights theorists. My formula is not novel because it gives priority to the deontological principles over the consequentialist ones. There is no other way to account for many of our most deeply held moral convictions including the priority of rights claims over aggregate good consequences. The novel feature is combining of this priority for the deontological principles with a balancing strategy to relate those deontological principles as co-equal in the moral deliberation. We will see in the next chapter that this solution to the normative problem of the relation among ethical principles may provide a solution to certain public policy problems, such as the infinite demand problem, without running the risk of sacrificing the justice claims of the handicapped whenever they would promote the aggregate social good.

Notes

1. Ronald Dworkin, "What is Equality? Part 2: Equality of Resources," *Philosophy and Public Affairs* 10 (Fall 1981): 283–345.

2. Bernard A. O Williams, "The Idea of Equality," *Justice and Equality*, ed. Hugo A. Bedau, (Englewood Cliffs, N.J.: Prentice-Hall, 1971), p. 122.

3. See Williams, pp. 130–31, where he distinguishes further between contingently and fortuitously limited resources. Contingently limited resources are those requiring certain conditions of access (such as ability to do college level work for admission to college) to be met while fortuitously limited resources are those where, although all are qualified, there is simply not enough to go around. Williams is perhaps too constrained by his environment when he treats college education (and even grammar school, that is British academic secondary school) as requiring certain preconditions of ability for admission.

4. See Amy Gutmann, "For and Against Equal Access to Health Care," *In Search of Equity: Health Needs and the Health Care System,* ed. Ronald Bayer, Arthur L. Caplan, and Norman Daniels (New York: Plenum Press, 1983), pp. 43–67.

5. Victor Cohn, "Baby Girl Gets Chance to Live," *The Washington Post,* November 6, 1982, pp. A1, A7; "Baby Reported as Improving After Transplant," *The Washington Post,* November 8, 1982, p. A5.

6. John Rawls, *A Theory of Justice* (Cambridge, Mass.: Harvard University Press, 1971), p. 83ff.

7. *Ibid.*, p. 87.

8. *Ibid.*, p. 85.

9. *Ibid,*, p. 100–01.

10. *Ibid.*, p. 101.

11. Kai Nielsen, "Radical Egalitarian Justice: Justice as Equality," *Social Theory and Practice* 5 (2):209–26. Pp. 220–21, somewhat similarly, judges that a young woman with three children who needs only a blood transfusion to return to good health should receive it if only one transfusion can be given to either her or a senile ninety-year-old. Nielsen's approach in arriving at this answer, though, is largely intuitive. A similar policy conclusion might have been reached on the grounds of utility, as well as egalitarianism with the "over-a-lifetime" interpretation. Greater good (for the patient and for her children) is likely to come from giving the treatment to the younger woman.

In the argument that the elderly get low priority based on consideration of the fact that they have had more well-being over a lifetime might force one into assessing the relative quality of life of different persons at the same age. The one with overall poor life quality might, it could be argued, get priority over someone of a similar age who has had good life quality. While that might follow from an "over-a-lifetime" interpretation, the more appropriate way to cope with these differences in quality over a lifetime is to apply the egalitarian principle of justice directly at the earlier times when objective well-being was not at a high level, thus providing compensation for whatever shortcomings there are in objective well-being. Attempting to assess different overall levels of lifetime well-being for a population at a particular age would be procedurally and administratively a nightmare.

12.   For another account of why radical egalitarianism does not entail sameness, see Kai Nielsen. "Radical Egalitarian Justice: Justice as Equality."

13.   See Norman Daniels, "Health Care Needs and Distributive Justice," *Philosophy and Public Affairs* 10 (No. 2, Spring 1981): 161–62, for an argument against using satisfaction as a basis for calculating well-being.

14.   Amy Gutmann, "For and Against Equal Access to Health Care," pp. 43–67.

15.   See, for example, Norman Daniels, "Health Care Needs and Distributive Justice," p. 146; Chirstopher Boorse, "On the Distinction Between Disease and Illness," *Philosophy and Public Affairs* 5 (Fall 1975): 49.

16.   This excludes some rare cases of people with brain pathology who are said to be able to feel pain in the sense of knowing that a sensation is present, but do not experience the "hurt." Some patients with split brain syndrome apparently experience this phenomenon. It also excludes situations where pain is "enjoyed" as a sign, as in the case of someone who had suffered a spinal injury, leaving him with no sensation in the legs, who suddenly feeling pain return might say he "enjoyed" the pain.

17.   In fact he has avoided the core philosophical problem of defending this kind of commitment by first of all assuming equality is the first goal and then by pointing out the difficulties of the notion of equality of outcome. He then proceeds to "define a suitable conception of equality of resources." He thus neatly avoids having to defend the moral legitimacy of either the commitment to the resource interpretation of equality or the equality priority itself. It seems clear, however, that he would like us to accept not only the conceptual suitability of this formulation, but the moral suitability as well. He has bootlegged his faith commitments, which in the end is not much different from simply affirming them. See Ronald Dworkin, "What is Equality? Part 2: Equality of Resources," especially pp. 283 and 295.

18.   *Ibid.*, pp. 283–84.

19.   Norman, Daniels. "Health Care Needs and Distributive Justice," p. 181.

20.   *Ibid.*, pp. 300–04.

21.   *Ibid.*, p. 304.

22.   Charles Fried, "Equality and Rights in Medical Care," *Hastings Center Report* 6 (February 1976): 33. Paul T. Menzel, *Medical Costs, Moral Choices: A Philosophy of Health Care Economics in America* (New Haven: Yale University Press, 1983), pp. 73–103, offers the most careful and detailed review of the arguments.

23.   Norman Daniels also finds himself uncomfortable with plans that allow market forces and individual decisions to be controlling after fair shares are distributed. First, Daniels argues that from the original position, an aid-in-kind scheme would seem

necessary to insure against unpredictable needs [Norman Daniels, "Rights to Health Care and Distributive Justice: Programmatic Worries." *Journal of Medicine and Philosophy* 4 (June 1979): 190]. Second, Daniels argues that the critical assumption from those who defend distribution of money is that a prudent citizen will be able to buy a reasonable package of goods. But, if some fair shares do not allow one to buy certain basic needs, there is something wrong with the system. See Norman Daniels, "Health Care Needs and Distributive Justice," p. 149.

Amy Gutmann, "For and Against Equal Access to Health Care," pp. 43–67, is another unprepared to accept free-market solutions. She rejects the claim that an aid-in-kind scheme is necessarily paternalistic, as some critics such as Fried would argue. She says, "Unlike a law banning the sale of cigarettes or forcing people to wear seat belts, the institution of a national health care system forces no one to use it. If a majority of citizens decide that they want to be taxed in order to ensure themselves health care, the resulting legislation could not be considered paternalistic. . . . It is significant . . . that for the last twenty years the Michigan survey of registered voters has found a consistent majority supporting government measures designed to ensure universal access to medical care" (p.55).

Gutmann also provides good reasoning for rejecting bureaucratic mechanisms for distinguishing those voluntarily lacking in objective needs and those involuntarily deficient.

24. W. D. Ross, *The Right and the Good* (Oxford: The Clarendon Press, 1939), p. 19.

25. Robert M. Veatch, *A Theory of Medical Ethics* (New York: Basic Books, 1981), pp. 291–305.

26. W. L. Sumner, "Does Medical Ethics Have Its Own Theory?" *Hastings Center Report* 12 (November–December 1982): 39.

6

Public Policy and Our Commitment to Equality

If the retarded and all the rest of us who are deficient in some talent have a claim of justice to an opportunity for equality of well-being over a lifetime, we have some enormous public policy problems. In particular, why in the world are we justified in rewarding the particularly talented or particularly gifted when they already have more than their share of opportunities? Why should the gifted athlete be rewarded with a multi-million dollar contract when he already has more than a reasonable share of rewards? Physical talent is something most people enjoy and physical ability makes many tasks of living easier. Why add extraordinary income as well? Why should those whose natural intellectual ability simplifies so much in life also receive the rewards of good grades, school room praise, and eventually high paying jobs while Eddie Conrad not only loses out on those rewards, but has to fight (or have others fight for him) just to receive some compensatory education?

A commitment to equality as the meaning of justice and to a sense of responsibility to use social resources—including people's intellectual and physical resources—to move society toward greater equality has radical implications for a wide range of public policies: competitive sports, competition in the marketplace and the classroom, and in just about all other phases of life.

The theme of equality, grounded as it is in the Judeo-Christian tradition, raises questions that may undercut our entire orientation toward individual competitive achievement. It forces us to reconsider the individualistic drive to achieve and excel—to beat out others to demonstrate superiority. It may be that we cannot answer the specific policy question about spending money for speech therapy for a mentally retarded boy without simultaneously reexamining the entire structure of our individualistic, competitive society.

Why do we reward talents of any kind? The answer, for one committed to equality as a foundation of a just society, may not come easily. Three justifications are given for rewarding talent rather than the opposite—distributing resources in inverse proportion to talent so that those who have less may be moved toward equality.

First, in a meritocratic society reward for talent is simply taken for granted. Aristotle posits it as obvious in the *Nichomachean Ethics* that unequals deserve unequal shares. The only room for controversy in his peculiarly inegalitarian (and therefore non-Judeo-Christian) view of the world is whether desert should be based on free birth, wealth, noble birth, or excellence.[1] Small wonder that the debilitated, the deformed, and the deficient fared so poorly in the Greek world. But if natural abilities—intellectual and physical—are, by definition *natural,* that is, a gift beyond the control of the individual who possesses them, why should they be the basis of reward?

The second argument for rewarding talent is more social—that regardless of whether talent is the result of natural endowment or human voluntary effort, rewarding it provides an incentive to use it in socially constructive ways. It is socially useful, so the argument goes, to reward talent. That is the insight behind much current social theory, especially that influenced by Rawls. The inequalities that result from rewarding talent are justified if, and only if, the rewards are necessary to induce socially constructive behavior that will benefit the least well off. Paying the speech therapist (or more plausibly innovative teachers of speech therapists) extraordinarily high wages is justified, according to this view, if it is necessary to coax better performance out of the teacher and thus benefit the Eddie Conrads of the world.

There are two problems with this defense of reward for talent. First, it is not obvious that rewarding talent produces the necessary incentive. Some would use their skills and use them about as well even without generous inducement. Second, rewards for skills do not necessarily work to the benefit of least well-off groups. The life choices of highly paid plastic surgeons and psychoanalysts attest to that. Many choose career paths that are not the most useful to the least well off.

Can we really argue, for example, that million-dollar-a-year contracts to star baseball players are justified because they bring the joy of excellent baseball to the retarded or to other least well-off groups and thus constitute better use of the funds? It seems obvious that the benefits to these groups are miniscule in comparison to other more direct help that could be given them with the funds. We should at least acknowledge the problem of surplus incentive. Realistically, a great athlete gets paid many times what it would take to make him choose an athletic career when its attractiveness is compared with other things he could do with his life. This excess incentive should at least be taxed so the surplus incentive could be used more directly for more egalitarian projects. If we want to distribute burdens equally and have high salaries go to those whose life work is made easy through natural talent, this argues for even more steeply progressive tax rates than presently exist.

We should concede, however, that sometimes rewards do induce performance and orient it toward least well-off groups. They might encourage great research or excellent teaching. That does not necessarily justify the reward, however, or at least it does not make the reward just. At least, if the purpose of the reward is to help less fortunate ones, the consent of the less fortunate to the inequality would seem to be necessary. That, at least, is what we have argued in an earlier chapter. More critically, if someone gifted with some natural talent that could be useful to others less fortunate must be bribed to use that talent constructively, such an inducement may be justified in the name of freedom of efficiency, but it can hardly be justified in the name of justice. The ethical thing to do would be to use the community resource that the individual, by luck, possesses for the benefit of the less fortunate without the inducement. If the inducement is necessary, it may be ethically justified—because we hold an ethical commitment to freedom and to doing good for others but hardly because it is what justice requires. The argument for rewarding talent based on utility is at best a shaky one, and, if it works at all, it is in spite of, not because of, what justice requires, since justice requires greater equality.

We are forced, then, to a third, rather feeble defense of rewarding talent. Some small part of talent could be the result of extraordinary voluntary effort made on the part of the talented one. Goods stewards cultivate their gifts. Some intellectual or athletic talent is the result of effort rather than natural ability or luck. We have already conceded that justice permits, indeed requires, that individuals be rewarded for true voluntary effort. But the realistic limit on such effort is performance that cannot be more than about twice the normal capacity. The result is at most a weak justification for modest reward of talent.

The egalitarian alternative is to compensate people for deficits in natural ability. The social policy implication is that we distribute resources by providing a "handicap" in direct proportion to an individual's physical or mental disability, giving everyone a chance at equality of outcome. We do make use of the handicap model in certain sports—golf and bowling, for example—but for some reason usually not in track or any significant team sports. The closest thing to it is the school yard device of letting team captains pick their teams by alternating choices or the professional analogue of letting the teams with the worst records draft available amateur athletes first. The result is indignity to those who lack talent, but approximately equal teams. The logic of the egalitarian interpretation of justice, however, urges us in the direction of doing our best to provide a compensatory "head start" for those with mental or physical handicaps. Given the incalculable, irreplaceable losses the handicapped may have suffered, the extra resource commitment should, as much as is possible, exactly compensate for the handicap so that all have a chance for equality.

Equality: Its Implications for the Retarded

The retarded stand to be affected dramatically by the concept of compensatory resource expenditure. The egalitarian concept of justice requires a whole new orientation to them. It begins with an affirmation that the retarded are fully members of the moral community, equal in moral worth to the rest of the community. They should, therefore, have equal opportunity for well-being in their lives. The bonds of community lead to the now familiar implications. We, as a community of finite human beings including the retarded, are equals in comparison to an infinite—infinite intelligence, infinite wisdom, infinite value—whether that be thought of as the God of the Judeo-Christian tradition or the secular surrogates for that god. The resources that the community holds in common, including those temporarily being used by "the gifted," are large, and they are to be used, according to the basic assumptions we have made about human responsibility, to try to do what we can as a community to make things more equal.

Several countries have made serious efforts to use resources to benefit the retarded, although, it is safe to say, none has really pushed the welfare equality commitment to its logical conclusion. In the United States both charity and governmental support from commonly held assets have been tapped.

Estimating the expenditures for care for the retarded is notoriously difficult. It is hard to define whose care should be included in such data. It is sometimes difficult to determine what counts as care. It is particularly difficult to get data on the costs of the noninstitutionalized population. Yet we have some general statistics available. K. Charlie Lakin and colleagues,[2] for example, report total expenditures of $2,626,600,000 in the year 1978–79 for residential care for the retarded in public institutions and another $484,046,000 in private facilities, a total of about 3.1 billion dollars. On this 93.9 percent came from government sources. Only 4.3 percent came from the residents or their families and only 1.7 percent came from donations. A recent summary of public expenditures for mental retardation and developmental disabilities in the United States for fiscal years 1977–1984 indicated an increase in institutional expenditures from approximately 2.4 billion to 4.25 billion unadjusted dollars. Costs estimated in 1977 dollars indicate that insitutional expenditures have plateaued at about 2.5 billion dollars, although the average daily number of residents in institutions has decreased approximately 27 percent.[3]

In 1977 institutional per diems ranged from $22 to $117 per person with a median of $40. In 1984, estimates of costs per retarded person per day range from $62 to $250 with a median of $105, depending, of course, on degree of handicap, methods of calculating, quality of care, and regional cost variations. Some states, for example, budget fringe benefits outside of the mental retardation agency resulting in underestimates of per diem costs by as much as 20 percent.[4] (One source indicates cost per resident in public institutions in 1981 to be $28,446.35.[5])

The past eight years have shown a shift in the distribution of government financing of institutions, with the federal government assuming an increasing burden of institutional costs following the advent of numerous programs in the early 1970s, most notably the financing of intermediate care facilities (ICF-MR) and P.L. 89–313 for educational aid. While close to 60 percent of the aggregate $27.6 billion spent on public institutions in the 1977–1984 period came from state revenues, 40 percent has come from the federal level, 95 percent of which falls under the ICF–MR programs. This increase in federal expenditures from $570 million in 1977 to $1.910 billion in 1984 shows an adjusted growth rate of 90 percent, or 10 percent per year. In 1983–84, however, ICF–MR reimbursements declined 6 percent as a result of the descreasing resident population and cost reduction sanctions.[6]

The shift from state to federal financing to institutional care allowed the states to increasing funding to the noninstitutional sector. The 1977–1984 period showed a rapid and continuous growth in public expenditures for community based service with the increase in state spending accounting for 70 percent of the overall rise. Total state expenditures rose 316 percent in unadjusted dollars from $745 million to $3.1 billion—a 22.8 percent adjusted increase. Compared to the average institutional per diem in 1984 of $105, community based care ranged from $7 to $40 per day with $8 to $15 given as the most realistic estimate.[7]

Overall expenditures for 1977–1984 were approximately 27.62 billion dollars for the operation of over 240 United States institutions for the mentally retarded and another $14.25 billion for community based services.[8] (By contrast, the cost of raising a more normal child at a moderate cost level in 1980 was estimated to be between $3331 and $5782 depending on age.[9]) These costs have increased sharply over the past two decades partly due to inflation, but partly also because of improved services, stimulated in part, by judicial and legislative action. Whether these changes result in improved quality of care is open to debate, but the patterns of change are so dramatic that it seems reasonable that many of them have resulted in improved quality. For example, the ratio of residents to direct-care employees changed from 4.4 in 1965 to .78 in 1981.[10]

A breakdown of 1985 federal expenditures on "training" for the mentally retarded and developmentally disabled showed $2.64 million (8.3%) for rehabilitation, $9.01 million (28.3%) for special education, and $20.17 million (63.4%) for health and biomedical costs. Since 1980 funding for special education and rehabilitation has been cut approximately 20 percent and 47 percent, respectively.[11]

Figures projected nationally indicated special education expenditures of $5.43 billion in 1984. Other data estimated that it is 1.4 times as expensive to educate a mentally retarded individual as a handicapped child without mental retardation; however, 16.73 percent of all children served under the "Education for All Handicapped Children Act" were mentally retarded.[12]

Cases like Eddie Conrad's call for a very different kind of cost analysis. His parents feel he could benefit from additional speech therapy from a fully trained specialist. This would require escalating the costs from the nominal amount under a plan to provide one twenty-minute session a week from the speech therapist to a level that is at least comparable to the three sessions a week the child received in the private facility. Salaries for speech therapists vary depending on experience and geographical location, but a salary of $24,000 (approximately the median income for speech therapists) would be a reasonable estimate. If the extra speech therapy for Eddie Conrad and others with similar needs in that school system required one additional full-time employee, that is the amount by which the budget would have to be increased.

The present levels of expenditure at the national level and in Eddie Conrad's school system are substantial, but the real question is: are they enough?

Are These Expenditures Enough?

Is it a fair level of compensatory advantage to bring the handicapped back to as close to a normal starting point as possible? From one common point of view, no amount of resources would be enough. The test question, especially for those who work in a contractarian framework, is whether a reasonable person would accept this amount in compensation for being retarded. That, of course, may be an unanswerable question; if we were able to answer, many would probably say, at least at first, that no amount of money would ever compensate.

But the question can be put in a more answerable form. Some, Ronald Dworkin, for example, would ask the question in a hypothetical form.[13] He proposes an "equal auction" where people allocate resources and determine comparative values. He discusses the specific problem of how to determine the monetary value of compensation for those born with handicaps:

> Suppose we can make sense of and even give a rough answer to the following question. If (contrary to fact) everyone had at the appropriate age

the same risk of developing physical or mental handicaps in the future (which assumes that no one has developed these yet) but that the total number of handicaps remained what it is, how much insurance coverage against these handicaps would the average member of the community purchase? We might then say that but for (uninsurable) brute luck that has altered these equal odds, the average person would have purchased insurance at that level, and compensate those who do develop handicaps accordingly, out of some fund collected by taxation or other compulsory process but designed to match the fund that would have been provided through premiums if the odds had been equal. Those who develop handicaps will then have more resources at their command than others, but the extent of their extra resources will be fixed by the market decisions that people would supposedly have made if circum- stances had been more equal than they are.[14]

Egalitarians can use such estimates to determine how much we as a society should pay to eliminate retardation if it is preventable and to compensate (in cash or services) for unpreventable retardation.

Dworkin's hypothetical calculus asking people what they would be willing to pay resembles the "willingness to pay" approaches proposed by Schelling,[15] Acton,[16] and others who are contributing to the cost-benefit analysis literature. They, however, ask real people what they would really be willing to pay to avoid or reduce risks of particular illnesses. When the question is asked in that form, individuals' biases, their knowledge of their real risks, and their capacities to pay will all influence their reports of what they would be willing to pay. A disease affecting minorities who typically have few resources would fare poorly in such a survey regardless of how serious the condition is. Sickle-cell disease, for example, would get a low score not only because the members of the white majority know that they (or their children) are at very low risk, but also because the average black person, whose children are at higher risk, has uniquely poor ability to pay.

In order to overcome these biases, if the insurance auction strategy is to be used to determine a fair level of compensation, we must ask people not what they would really be willing to pay, but rather what they think they would be willing to pay if hypothetically they did not know what position they really occupied in society. We ask people to try to imagine that they know the general probabilities of an infant being born retarded, but not whether they themselves (or their children) would be that infant. This, of course, at best, gives an approximation of what people who really did not know their own position would bid, but it at least gives us a model for establishing an approximate figure.

A critic of the hypothetical model of an "equal auction" might ask how this hypothetical average response in any way obligates *actual* handicapped persons to accept the amount generated by the auction device as a fair compensation. "I am handicapped," one of them might say, "so why should I agree to abide by the limited claims of compensation made by some unreal person who was never *me?*"

It has to be acknowledged that the problem of determining the proper amount of compensation is a complex one. The hypothetical contract solution may raise problems, but they are not the problems raised by this handicapped person's question. The question implies that the reason real persons should be bound by the amount of compensation generated by the auction is that they were parties to the contract and thus bound by the results.

The hypothetical contract, as I am using it, serves a totally different function. It is not introduced to provide an answer to the question of why people are morally bound to a particular course of action. Rather, it is a fictional metaphor for deriving answers reasonable people would give if they were totally impartial regarding their own positions. If such people determined that a fair compensation for a condition is *X*, then *X* is the amount to which such persons are entitled regardless of whether they or anyone else in their real-life situations concur with the judgment. The real problem for the hypothetical contract is not explaining why real persons ought to accept the results of the auction, but rather trying to operationalize an approximation of a hypothetical situation in which people act in total impartially.

What does this imply for the problem of whether the expenditures for the retarded in general and Eddie Conrad in particular are enough? First, this makes clear that the expenditures for the retarded would not be infinite. (More about that in a minute.) But, second, it also makes clear that the expenditures for the retarded are inadequate. It seems obvious that if we were buying an insurance policy to protect us against the possibility of being born retarded we would on the average be willing to pay more than what we currently spend to avoid the risk and would therefore be prepared under the principle of equality of resources (as an approximation of what it would take to produce an opportunity for equality of outcome) be willing to pay more to those who could not avoid the risk of retardation. Finally, since the cost of Eddie Conrad's treatments, including speech therapy, is in all likelihood less than the figure we would arrive at calculating on the basis of Dworkin's equal auction, we should be willing to pay for the therapy. Since we have not actually gone through the exercise as a society of estimating what we would be willing to pay for reducing or eliminating the risk of retardation, it is hard to determine exactly what the upper limit of compensation for the retarded should actually be. It seems clear, however, that it is much higher than what we are actually paying. Insofar as justice is concerned, chance for equality of outcome is our goal. Equality of resource expenditure is an approximation of a chance for equality of outcome. The hypothetical equal auction in which people do not know their chances of suffering from retardation is our device for approximating what would have to be given to the retarded to get them back to as close to an equal starting point with others as possible. Our task is to estimate immediately what that compensatory expenditure would be and provide it.

Equality: Its Implications for the Rest of Us

The idea that the retarded and others who have lost in the natural lottery should be given a compensatory handicap to get them back to the point where they have an opportunity for equality of outcome has broad implications for the rest of us. First, if some handicaps are so severe that no imaginable compensation would be adequate, does not the principle produce an infinite demand reducing everyone else to a position where they literally cannot survive? Second, will not the compensation, especially if it is provided in medical and educational services, increase the survival of the handicapped to the point that they will be able to reproduce, thus increasing the genetic load of defective genes in the gene pool? And, third, does not the idea of using resources to compensate for deficiencies rather than to reward the naturally talented have terrible implications for competitive sports, academic rewards, and other areas where talent is normally rewarded? The answer probably is that such an egalitarian basis for distributing resources does have serious implications for all of these areas and more, but the results may not be as radical as at first envisioned.

The Infinite Demand Problem

THE NATURE OF THE PROBLEM

The first difficult question is whether commitment to compensating the handicapped will produce an infinite demand. Especially in cases of severe mental retardation, we delude ourselves if we think that piling some resources into special education and speech therapy—even a lot of resources—will adequately compensate Eddie Conrad and get him back to an even starting point so that he has a real chance for equality of well-being over a lifetime. If we are honest with ourselves about certain mental or physical handicaps, we might say that no amount of resource commitment would adequately compensate for the loss in the natural lottery. If the condition is incurable, as Eddie Conrad's is at least to a large extent, then if our compensation strategy is to provide in-kind services to get the handicapped individual back to a normal starting point, the initial compensation, which we have argued is a priority in an egalitarian world, would produce infinite demands. Nothing would be left for anyone else; not even food and so forth. What do we do with this *reductio ad absurdum* of the egalitarian position?

POTENTIAL SOLUTIONS

The answer to the problem that compensation for the retarded and other seriously handicapped persons would bankrupt the system by producing infinite demand has already been hinted at. There are really several lines of defense against the infinite demand criticism. The insurance scheme for determining a fair level of compensation gives us some finite limit on the level of compensation. It will probably be quite large, but not infinite. The amount arrived at for compensation is the amount set by the demands of justice itself.

Looking at the infinite demand problem from the standpoint of ethical principles, there are two kinds of potential limits placed on the amount of resources a seriously handicapped person might command as compensation: limits placed by the principle of justice itself and limits placed by other ethical principles.

Limits Placed by the Principle of Justice. First, justice itself requires compensation to the handicapped only to the point where others would be reduced to a level of well-being equal to the one being compensated.

At that point those participating in Dworkin's hypothetical equal auction to purchase insurance against, say, retardation would choose to spend their resources in other ways. They would not buy the insurance at a price that would deprive them of something they value even more.

Let us confront this anti-egalitarian challenge on its own terms. Suppose that in order to compensate Eddie Conrad and provide the basics of special diet, housing, and education, his community was forced to use not only the entire school system budget, but to take all money that would be used for food for other children of the community. Could that be done in the name of egalitarian justice? If so, the implication seems absurd.

If, however, Eddie Conrad's claim of equality led to a world in which other children got no food at all, the tables would surely have been turned. Eddie Conrad would no longer really be the one needing a chance for equality of outcome; the other children would have such a claim. They would be literally starving to death. In that alternative world a claim of egalitarian justice might actually be mounted to transfer some resources back to the other children so that they might have a chance for equality of outcome.

The principle of egalitarian justice that provides an opportunity for equality of well-being would actually, therefore, set limits on how much compensation should be rendered for a handicap. At some point the compensation process might actually leave others less well off than the initially handicapped one, thus violating the principle of equality in the very name of that principle. This limit will obviously be reached only in the extreme case, but it does set a limit in the name of egalitarian justice.

In fact, more subtle versions of this limit setting might appear as well. Suppose the only way to compensate the handicapped child were to cut a polio immunization campaign. Would it be just under egalitarian justice to eliminate the immunizations in order to provide for equality for the handicapped one? Here we face a difficult problem of quantification. If we conclude, however, that the child who misses the immunization and thereby gets polio would be worse off than the originally handicapped one, then even in the name of egalitarian justice it would be unacceptable to eliminate the immunization campaign.

Note here that we are not considering the aggregate harm of eliminating the campaign. It would not do to point out that the aggregate harm would exceed the deprivation of the originally handicapped one. That would be the justification of the utilitarian, but not of the egalitarian. Defense of the retention of the immunization campaign in the name of egalitarian justice would require deprivation of at least one child to a level worse than that of the originally handicapped one. Envisioning such a severely deprived child would, if we were operating solely on the basis of egalitarian justice, trigger a demand for compensation for that now worst-off child. It would, for example, require taking from the now compensated and better-off handicapped one (or others even better off) in order to compensate the new polio victim for the deprivation. Egalitarian justice itself, therefore, does place some limit on the use of resources to compensate for even incurable handicaps such as retardation and physical disability. The limit, however, is one that is not easily reached. At least it cannot be reached merely by pointing out the aggregate advantage of noncompensation.

Limits Placed by Other Ethical Principles.   There is a second kind of limit on the egalitarian principle of justice as well. Justice was presented as a prima facie ethical principle, one potentially in competition with other principles. What do we make of the prima facie qualification?

AUTONOMY AND CONSENT OF THE LEAST WELL-OFF. The principle of autonomy gives us one straightforward basis for limiting egalitarian justice. If we accept the principle of autonomy, then surely those who bear claims of justice should have the right to waive such claims when they think it is in their interest to do so. This provides the basis for reintroducing Rawls's difference principle with the important qualifier that those who bear the claim of equality—in our case the handicapped or their agents speaking on their behalf—must consent to the inequality that results. Rawls's difference principle states that inequalities are acceptable provided they benefit the least well off. This has been used to justify, for example, large salaries for those particularly skilled in providing research or therapy that could benefit the handicapped. What is striking is that Rawls considers it justice if such inequalities are part of a social arrangement. A far more plausible account would be that this is a situation where justice may be overridden because it is in the interests of the one having the claim of justice to do so. In the name of freedom we permit the handicapped or anyone else having a claim of justice to waive that claim should they so desire. The situation where they could improve their lot by such a waiver is one plausible place for them to waive their claims of justice. Doing so, however, is not promoting justice. It is sacrificing justice in order to let the handicapped freely pursue their interest. The most obvious situation where it would be in the interests of the handicapped to waive their right to equality of outcome is in the case where exercising that right would generate such an infinite demand that no one else would be capable of meeting the interests of the handicapped. The rational thing for the handicapped (or their agents) to do in such a case would be to waive their claims of justice in order to survive and maximize their interests.

THE AUTONOMY OF OTHERS. The principle of autonomy provides another limit to the demands of egalitarian justice. That principle gives individuals the right to choose freely how they will conduct their lives. This applies not only to the holding of values and beliefs, but to certain economic decisions as well. If we can establish that there is a certain portion of what is normally thought to be private property that really is legitimately held by individuals as their own, then the principle of autonomy would give them the right to dispose of it as they see fit. Property probably is much less private than it is often regarded. Some resources (perhaps all of them) are given as gifts with strings attached or are a common community asset that is at most on loan to individuals who have a responsibility to be good stewards for the community. Still, autonomy may give individuals some limited freedom to dispose of some assets as they see fit. They are morally bound by the ethical requirements of justice so that they ought to use those resources to give everyone an opportunity for equal well-being. They may take the Lukan option of pooling resources so they are literally held in common or the more Pauline option of charity. But they may choose not to act according to the morality of justice at all. In such a situation, a society would face a conflict between the demands of justice and the demands of respecting autonomy. Any plausible balancing will be a compromise with some resources being taxed to serve morally justified common purposes such as paying for speech therapy for the retarded and some resources being left with individuals to use autonomously. At some point the principle of autonomy may limit the resources that are available to meet the demands of egalitarian justice. The trade-off will have to be made in individual cases. The important thing is that the limits are not placed in the name of justice. They come from outside. Justice is sacrificed in such cases, and we should never forget it. Commitment to autonomy might, for example, justify permitting talented experts in retardation to spend their lives (or portions of them) in ways other than serving the retarded and others in great need. To the extent that individuals have resources that are really their own and they choose to act by ignoring the demands of justice, other ethical principles may require us to tolerate the resulting injustice. In addition to autonomy, other deontological principles may compete with justice.

OTHER DEONTOLOGICAL PRINCIPLES. Under the principle of avoiding killing it is always prima facie morally wrong to kill actively another human person. That at least tells us that if compensation of the handicapped to give them an initial equality of resources would involve killing another, then the two deontological principles are in conflict and could be balanced. Since killing another would probably be thought of as leaving him worse off than the handicapped person anyway, the result of introducing this principle might lead to the same conclusion as the justice principle.

Promise keeping is another possible source of conflict. What should Eddie Conrad's city council do if it has already made a promise to use available social resources for some other purpose, one that meets a less weighty need? If there is an inherent prima facie duty to keep promises, then the council is in a head-on moral conflict between justice and promise keeping. It is inevitably thrown into a situation where it must balance competing claims. Since promise keeping is also only a prima facie duty, it is quite possible that the promise is what would give way rather than the demands of justice, but it is possible that it would come out the other way as well. Of course, in such a conflict between a promise and the demands of justice, there is often an obvious resolution: use more of the commonly held resources (including those that could be mustered into service by increasing taxes) in order to meet both ethical demands at once. If there is no such thing as unowned resources that can be appropriated as private property without strings attached, and those who hold resources must "pay rent" for their use as Baruch Brody suggests, then within some limits we may be able to tap more of these common resources to solve the problem. In short, other non-consequentialist ethical principles may justify some inequalities that would place limits on the compensation given to the retarded and others with serious handicaps, but this would be done in spite of what justice requires.

POSSIBLE LIMITS BASED ON SOCIAL COSTS. There is a final, more problematic potential limit on the demands that an egalitarian principle of opportunity for equal outcome might place on a community's resources. Some would argue that the total consequences of a policy of compensation for handicap must be taken into account in the ethical calculus. They would introduce at this point the principle of beneficence with its consideration of aggregate net welfare. They might do this not as the utilitarians would as the sole basis for deciding what is the ethically correct distribution, but as a counter-consideration to the demands of justice, claiming that the ethically correct distribution is the one that balances these two counterveiling claims.

For example, Norman Daniels, who works from a principle of equality of opportunity, writes, "clearly, health care institutions capable of protecting opportunity can be maintained only in societies whose productive capabilities they do not undermine."[17]

This is both dangerous and unnecessary. It is dangerous because once aggregate consequences are put on a balance with other ethical principles, they can eventually overpower any residual notion of individual rights or claims of justice if only the benefits are weighty enough. It is unnecessary because the other counter-considerations provide substantial leverage for limiting the potentially infinite demands of the handicapped. Any further limitation introduced out of consideration of simple aggregate net benefits would sacrifice the important claims of the handicapped to a principle that more appropriately remains subordinate.

These responses provide some rational limits on the demands of egalitarian justice. Still, the demands it does produce are very large, surely much larger than what is now spent to attempt to compensate those with severe handicaps. We should not shrink from these implications. The inequalities left to us by the natural lottery are very large, so it is reasonable that the costs of compensation will be large too. That is as it should be. Fortunately, the resources available for the community to respond to these needs are large as well.

In the case of the school board having to choose between speech therapy for the retarded and music or physical education or art for the entire student body it is hard to see how justice itself requires choosing the programs for the more nearly normal children. No other directly conflicting prima facie duty that we know of binds the school board to providing these courses. And it is hard to see how it would be in the interests of Eddie Conrad for him (or his agents) to waive his claim to equality. The case for his speech therapy is a powerful one. The school board ought to provide it.

Implications for the Gene Pool

A second potential objection to massive compensatory resource commitments to the handicapped is that it will improve their survival and capacity to reproduce such that there will be long-term effects on the gene pool. Medical and social interventions might make it possible for some young severely handicapped children to survive to reproductive age and thus risk perpetuating their affected genes. Others who presently survive might nevertheless presently be supported in ways that do not permit reproduction. Warehousing in isolated, sexually segregated institutions would have this effect. Humane social interventions for the less severely handicapped, such as providing small group homes more nearly like normal living conditions, might easily include co-educational living arrangements or even informal contacts with the opposite sex in new work and recreational environments. As part of the normalization movement some, especially the more mildly retarded, are being encouraged to marry. Surely the effect will be that these people will bear more children.

It is important to separate the effects of prejudice from the real possible outcomes here. Even assuming that some severely handicapped people will reproduce who would not have under less humane conditions, it is not clear what the effects on the gene pool will be. For starters, concern about the gene pool is not warranted for any conditions that are not genetic. This concern about the gene pool has no bearing at all on physical handicaps that are the result of accidents or retardation that is the result of birth trauma lacking any genetic component. At most, the offspring might get less than adequate care by a handicapped parent and there is no evidence that this risk should be of concern.

There are, however, handicaps that do have a genetic component. It cannot be denied that any intervention that has the effect of increasing reproduction of such individuals will have some statistical effect on the gene pool. For autosomal dominant conditions, of which there are relatively few, there will be a fifty percent chance that offspring will suffer from the parents' condition. Retinoblastoma is a serious, potentially fatal condition. Some concern has been expressed that medical intervention could save the afflicted ones long enough for them to reproduce and transmit the gene.[18]

These conditions are extremely rare, however. Having the proper combination of circumstances to have this kind of effect on the gene pool is almost unheard of. The condition would have to be autosomal dominant, would have to permit survival long enough for the afflicted persons to reproduce with medical or social support, but not allow them to do so to the same degree without it, and would have to be a condition serious enough to worry about. Moreover, even with all of these conditions met, we would have to take into account the likelihood that the affected person would voluntarily want to curtail his or her own reproduction.

For virtually all circumstances the effect on the gene pool will be so minimal as to be irrelevant for public policy purposes. For most conditions that are genetic the pattern of transmission is autosomal recessive. Producing the undesired condition requires a defective gene from both parents. This is true—for example, for Tay Sachs disease, cystic fibrosis, and sickle cell—for most of the conditions about which we might be concerned. Geneticists tell us that for these conditions it will take many generations, from fifty to one hundred, for there to be even a doubling of the recessive gene frequency in the gene pool as a result of interventions that would sustain the reproductive capacity of afflicted individuals.[19] Given the pace at which medical science is progressing, the development of genetic engineering technologies that could make direct changing of these defective genes possible, along with the long time span it would take to have any serious effect on the gene pool, no one can reasonably argue that we should forego the humane treatment that could be offered to those presently afflicted just to prevent some hypothetical risk to the gene pool fifty or a hundred generations down the road.

The We/They Dichotomy

There is a far more serious implication for the rest of us of this scheme for compensatory egalitarian justice than either the problem of infinite demand or the possible effect on the gene pool. The scheme of providing a "handicap," a compensatory resource commitment to get the retarded back to a starting point where they have as close as possible to a chance for equality of outcome, begins by focusing on a small number of people with severe handicaps. The ethical framework, however, is one that sees us all as a part of a single human community with a claim of justice to be treated as equals and to have a chance for an equal outcome. Reality, however, does not divide the world into a small number of those who are severely afflicted with physical or mental handicaps and the rest of us who already have, based on our natural endowments, a chance for equality of outcome. The natural lottery distributes mental and physical assets in what appears to be a random way with people receiving all manner of assets. Each of us is deficient to some extent in all natural abilities. No one is perfectly intelligent, perfectly strong, perfectly beautiful, or perfectly dispositioned. We are all handicapped. An egalitarian system of justice would provide compensation—medical or educational services—necessary to give us a chance at equality, and it would provide them with priority going to those with the greatest deficits.

The effect of this confession of universal finitude is startling. We are all, in some areas and to some extent, among those who stand to benefit from the theory of compensatory resource allocation. Admittedly, some will benefit more than others and for some the benefits will not come until the future when old age or accident reduces us to a greater level of need. But in one way or another we and those we love stand to receive from the community to some degree.

This means we can no longer dichotomize the world into the others, who will receive the compensatory intervention, and ourselves, who only pay out. The previous discussion of the concerns that the rest of us might have about compensating the retarded—the concerns about infinite demand and about the gene pool—viewed the world as if we were a group of healthy, whole people who would bear the costs of compensating "them." The world was divided into a "we" and a "they" with us paying the costs and them getting the benefits. If, however, we are all handicapped to some degree, this way of viewing the world will not work. We are all in the same boat. To be sure, some will receive on balance more compensation than others. The Eddie Conrads of the world will get more specialized educational intervention than others, but some of the rest of us will benefit (or have our loved ones benefit) in other ways and at times we cannot imagine. More critically, the way we view the world changes if one opts for the egalitarian assumptions including our equality in finitude in comparison with an infinite. The we/they dichotomy collapses. Since we are all handicapped, we are all beneficiaries.

The Implications for an Ethic of Competition

The connection between compensatory justice for the retarded and an ethic of competition for the rest of us may not be obvious, but it is important. We live in a very competitive society, one that rewards talent and ability in many ways, yet the retarded and others with serious disabilities are precisely the ones who can never be rewarded adequately on the basis of talent alone. To be sure, given the theory of disability that has been developed here, not only is everyone deficient in many respects and therefore among the potential recipients of the compensation for these deficiencies, but everyone also has certain strengths and assets that are worthy of praise. Yet some among us—the retarded and the physically handicapped in particular—are in special need of compensation. On balance they will not do well in the free market world of competition for rewards. To the extent that we live in a world that distributes its assets—resources, praise, and glory—on the basis of talent, the handicapped are going to lose. Yet the competitive mentality runs deep in our society. Unless it is challenged or at least made compatible with the goal of equality, the retarded and others with handicaps will never be able to achieve the equality that we strive for. The problem of competition manifests itself in two major areas: sports and games on the one hand and academic competition on the other. These two spheres have traditionally rewarded physical and mental talent, respectively.

SPORTS

Competitive sports and games present the first major challenge to the ethic of equality. Its very essence is the demonstration of inequality and the reveling in the feeling of superiority that accompanies victory in competition. The outrageous, if often quoted, insight of former football coach Vince Lombardi summarizes the ethic of competition well: Winning isn't the most important thing. It's the only thing.

Yet, if we approach the problems of justice from the standpoint of the egalitarian ethic, it becomes more and more difficult to justify rewarding talent. Why should athletes receive praise, glory, and money, the psychological, social, and economic rewards of physical ability? The more carefully one thinks about the way we dole out rewards to athletes, the more irrational it becomes.

The ethic of competition is in many ways the opposite of the ethic that makes resources available to those who have lost in the natural lottery. It is an ethic of individualism. It thrives on a sense of superiority. Its very essence is squeezing satisfaction out of a proof of inequality. At the very least we need to look more carefully at the justifications offered for rewarding physical ability.

Success in sports competition is in some complex way a combination of at least three factors: natural, "god-given" ability, luck, and effort. It is hard to imagine why anyone would believe that people *deserve* to be rewarded for *natural* talent, which, by definition, one did not cultivate oneself. Likewise, it is hard to justify rewarding luck, the random working of statistical odds that favors one team one day, and the other team the next. At most, we might say people deserve to be rewarded for the effort they make to cultivate their natural talent and make marginal improvements on what they have to begin with. Yet that is surely a small, if important, part of success in sport. People seem to be inclined to think of their successes in sports as the result of skill or effort, while their failures are the result of luck. Reason would seem to tell us that that is self-deception.

If people can be said to deserve the rewards of success in sports for, at most, a marginal contribution they make to the result, some try to justify sports rewards by the usefulness of the activity—the enjoyment, sense of accomplishment, and contribution success makes in building a sense of cohesiveness and identification. Yet these more utilitarian justifications are themselves called into question on several grounds. In ancient days it was perhaps useful to be physically talented, so much so that evolutionarily a sense of competition was bred into us. It gave what Konrad Lorenz has called the "killer instinct," a term still used today in competitive sports such as boxing.

Whatever utility there was at some early point in history for rewarding physical talent, that advantage has surely long since outlived its usefulness. There are rare circumstances when it is really useful to a community to reward physical talent. The military might hold a marksmanship contest for selecting those who will be front line gunners to defend the homeland. Fire fighters might hold contests of physical ability as part of the selection process for choosing among new applicants for the fire company. These are highly unusual circumstances. Physical talent is becoming less important in even these areas. The military might want to select on the basis of talent, but it will no longer be brute strength. Fire departments may actually be using tests of physical ability as a way of discriminating against women and men who could perform virtually all of the fire department functions perfectly well. Even if physical ability is occasionally useful to society, the social usefulness of rewarding people on the basis of physical talent in these circumstances can easily be differentiated from sports (even if some similar physical displays are sometimes turned into pure sports contests for competitions between military units or fire companies).

It might also be argued that great talent is useful in another, more subtle way. People are willing to pay great sums to watch superior physical talent. It could be argued that they find it aesthetically pleasing and exhilarating. People with average talent get great satisfaction, so the argument goes, out of watching persons of far superior, finely honed natural talent. If there is such benefit, then do not the talented deserve the incentive they receive in order to stimulate them to provide this aesthetic benefit?

The problem is complex. First, it is not clear that people really pay to see talent rather than the demonstration of superiority. When first-class athletes put on noncompetitive exhibitions, the interest is surely much less than when they were competing—even if in the competition they might purposely not express their full talent (for example, when it is competitively advantageous to withhold some of their ability). The implication is that people are really paying for demonstrations of superiority rather than demonstrations of talent.

Suppose, however, that some people really do find demonstration of talent per se pleasing. Does that not justify rewarding talent just as we reward superior talent for military or public service purposes such as fire fighting? To the extent it does, such rewards must at least be differentiated from rewarding demonstrations of superiority. Beyond that, we need to examine the extent to which socially satisfying talents deserve reward. If one is a utilitarian, especially a preference utilitarian in which the goal is the maximization of satisfaction of personal preferences, then rewarding talent per se would be justified if people in aggregate did get more satisfaction from seeing that talent than anything else they could do with their money. That defense, however, requires a particular kind of utilitarian justification. The entire focus of this book is a case for egalitarian justice, not preference-maximizing utilitarianism. It is possible that a justice-based case can be made for using rewards as an incentive to recruit the most talented military personnel or fire fighters. The least well off will benefit. Moreover, the need that is being satisfied is what we have referred to as "objective." It seems unlikely that the least well off would give such high priority to providing incentives for persons to be great baseball players or jockeys. They would have other ways of spending their marginal resources that would improve their lot even more. In short, the social utility case for rewarding talent as aesthetically pleasing seems to fail. Even if it worked (as the strategy for improving the lot of the least well off), such reward would have to be differentiated from demonstrating superiority per se.

The best argument for sports competition is the often heard claim that rewarding talent builds character and group loyalty. The quality of school life is supposedly improved if there is great school spirit generated by the school's football team. The city's morale is improved if its baseball team has done well in the World Series.

This is at best a feeble defense for rewarding talent. For one thing, sports competition is for the most part a zero sum situation or worse. For every team that revels in the thrill of victory there is at least one (often many) who suffer the agony of defeat. From a strictly utilitarian point of view, the net utility of sports contests would appear to be low. Of course, reality may prove this to be the wrong conclusion. People obviously have reached the conclusion that the risk of losing is worth it, perhaps because their interpretation of victory and loss permits them to take credit for the victory, but write off the defeat. That is not really the point. We are still left with a situation where the benefits of rewarding talent are severely compromised by the disutilities.

The real question at this point is: even if there is great utility in rewarding physical talent, is there any ethical justification for doing so? Even if the net utility is such that the advantages are greater than the disadvantages, it is still a system of rewards that gives people joy only at the expense of others; it rewards people for showing that they are different from, better than, others. To those who live in an egalitarian world and share the egalitarian assumptions about the world, that is not a very good life to live. It takes from those who are most in need of the community's resources and gives it to those who are least in need. If there is a justification, it must be on some grounds other than utility.

The usual defense that is offered at this point is that sports competition is really not, as Vince Lombardi said, primarily for the winning; rather it is for the value to the individual. According to this view, people participate in physical displays in order to build their own character and to improve themselves regardless of how they fare against others. The goal is not to establish that one is different from and better than others; it is to establish that one is really doing one's best.

Many ethical systems hold to a belief in a duty of self-improvement. W. D. Ross, for example, includes it among his list of prima facie duties.[20] The Judeo-Christian tradition is probably part of the basis of such a notion. If so, the duty is not really to oneself but to one's God. That at least avoids the logical confusion of how one can owe something to oneself. This duty of self-improvement probably comes as close as one can to an ethical justification for rewarding physical talent. It seems like there is nothing wrong with individuals competing against themselves to attempt to improve their performance, although improving sheer physical capacity seems to be an odd thing to improve. The weight lifter or jogger who takes joy from improving her previous best weight or time is not benefitting at the expense of someone else (at least if one does not consider alternative uses of time). The time-worn moral lessons of building perseverance, capacity to accept failure, and so on, are all a legitimate part of such competition against oneself. But how easily the weight lifter's struggle against his own best weight or the jogger's pushing to better her own best time turn into a competition against others. Weight lifting and marathon running are both Olympic events and here the objective is to go for the gold. It is considered reasonable to run a tactical race, which often means sacrificing personal records in order to win, to beat others. It is worth reflecting on the ecstasy of gymnast Mary Lou Rettin upon winning the gold medal in the 1984 Olympics. Although her own performance was outstanding, her finishing first and experiencing the overwhelming joy of that position rather than second can be attributed directly to a fall of her nearest competitor from the uneven parallel bars late in the competition. It reveals how much more important beating an opponent is in comparison to the excellence of the individual's performance. Ms. Rettin's identical excellent performance without her opponent's fall would have changed the outcome radically. If we are honest about the ethic of sports, only in a small part is it a competition against oneself. When it comes to an ethic of sports, Lombardi may not have been right, but he was awfully close.

It is striking that in ancient Hebrew and early Christian culture there is virtually no interest in or even mention of athletic contests.[21] At most there are metaphorical references to "running the race" of life and even here the metaphorical uses do not have entirely positive implications for the game. The preacher in Ecclesiastes fatalistically says, "The race is not to the swift, nor the battle to the strong, nor bread to the wise; nor riches to the intelligent, nor favor to the men of skill; but time and chance happen to them all."[22] There is, of course, in the Judeo-Christian theological tradition a positive attitude toward the body. Competing against oneself and striving for self-improvement and self-control are praised. But competing against others for the sake of demonstration of superiority is absent. The one text that might be cited as an example of real competition, in Paul's first letter to the Corinthians, is really nothing more than a metaphor,[23] and even here Paul seems to criticize contests for earthly reward, setting the Christian's race apart from mere secular games:

> Do you not know that in a race all the runners compete, but only one receives the prize? So run that you may obtain it. Every athlete exercises self-control in all things. They do it to receive a perishable wreath, but we are imperishable. Well, I do not run aimlessly, I do not box as one beating the air, but I pommel my body and subdue it, lest after preaching to others I myself should be disqualified.[24]

That is as close as the ancient Hebrew and early Christian culture can come to having something positive to say about competitive games and contests. The contrast with our image of Greco-Roman sports competition is startling. In fact, when we think of contact of the early church with physical contests, the most conspicuous image is one of the unwilling gladiators being forced into the Roman circus competition. That resistance to competing is symbolic of a broader resistance that one would expect of a culture committed to a sense of community and equality rather than an individualism that thrives on a demonstration of differences in ability.

ACADEMIC COMPETITION

If the sports contest is the logical outcome of the anti-egalitarian ethic applied to physical differences among persons, then academic competition is the equivalent of differences in intellectual ability. Here the implications for the retarded as well as the rest of us are especially dramatic. Insofar as academia rewards intellectual ability, the retarded are going to lose and the intellectually gifted are going to win. Once again we face the question, why reward talent, especially when doing so fragments the community and particularly hurts those who are in greatest need, those who to one degree or another lack the ability?

Questioning meritocracy in the academic world is even more threatening than questioning it in sports. It seems obvious that better students deserve better grades and the rewards that accompany them. We are forced back, once again, to parsing the elements that might account for successful academic performance to see if desert is really the proper basis for distributing the rewards. In the case of intellectual ability, more so than in physical contests, the component that can be said to be natural (genetic, biochemical, or otherwise inborn) is extremely controversial. The nature/nurture relationship, linked as it is to some of the most controversial issues of our day, issues of racial and gender stereotype, is endlessly debated. For our purposes, all we need to observe is that to the extent that there is a component of natural endowment, it is hard to see why those so endowed *deserve* to be rewarded for their gifts.

The same can be said with regard to luck. As every student who has guessed correctly on a multiple choice exam knows, there is an element of luck in getting a good grade. But insofar as performance is based on luck, surely it does not deserve reward either. In fact, teachers strive to devise means of eliminating such random chance (by subtracting some fraction score for every wrong answer, for example). Neither natural ability nor luck deserves reward in academia any more than in sports. At most the element that deserves reward is the component that can be attributed to real effort (after discounting for ability and for related uncontrollable characteristics such as natural personality traits, the amount of sleep one needs, and so forth). Effort does seem to justify different rewards for two students who are alike in all other relevant respects. The student who studies longer and with more intensity deserves a better grade. But here, as in sports contests, the component of academic performance that is attributed to voluntary effort is probably greatly overemphasized, especially in accounting for high quality performance.

So far the analysis of academic competition parallels that of sports. The difference arises when we ask whether good consequences justify different rewards. Here, in comparison with sports contests, real issues are at stake about which society has a vital interest. It is important that the brightest, most talented in a particular skill, get jobs that require that skill. We want intellectually talented people serving in roles where their talent is needed to protect the welfare of others, not only in teaching and research, but in a wide range of public and private sector positions. Will not the greater good require developing some system of evaluating academic talent and allocating desired goods like jobs and praise on the basis of that system?

It seems likely that it will. But there must be qualifications. In the first place, at least insofar as we are dealing with the demands of justice, the goal is not to produce the greatest good in aggregate, but to produce greater equality. If we are concerned about justice, that reward system will have to be channeled toward using intellectual ability to benefit those in need, not just to maximizing the good. More critically, the evaluation system, to the extent it is necessary, must be used to identify those who possess special talent that is, in effect, a community resource to be used to produce greater justice. It cannot be used to single out some small, already advantaged group and heap upon them even greater advantage for its own sake. Philosopher Thomas Nagel grasps the pervasiveness of the problem of rewarding intellectual ability:

> The greatest injustice in this society, I believe, is neither racial nor sexual but intellectual. I do not mean that it is unjust that some people are more intelligent than others. Nor do I mean that society rewards people differentially simply on the basis of their intelligence; usually it does not. Nevertheless, it provides on the average much larger rewards for tasks that require superior intelligence than for those that do not. This is simply the way things work out in a technologically advanced society with market economy. It does not reflect a social judgment that smart people *deserve* the opportunity to make more money than dumb people. They may deserve richer educational opportunity, but they do not therefore deserve the material wealth that goes with it. Similar things could be said about society's differential reward of achievements facilitated by other talents or gifts, like beauty, athletic ability, musicality, etc. But intelligence and its development by education provide a particularly significant and pervasive example.[25]

Nagel reaches this conclusion even limiting his attention to the financial rewards of intellectual talent. Were he to include the psychosocial rewards as well, the unfairness would be even more dramatic. He even concedes that intellectual ability may justify richer educational opportunity, a concession that should not pass without challenge. Its only possible justification seems to be one based on good consequences and efficiency, but these are just the criteria about which an egalitarian theory of justice will be suspicious. Unless we add the additional requirements that the consequences must be for the benefit of the least well off and that the differential advantage to the talented must be with the consent of the least well off or their agents, the justification seems to be a purely utilitarian one.

But that is the kind of argument that is most threatening to the egalitarian perspective. The idea that people deserve educational opportunities in proportion to their intellectual ability is directly contrary to the idea that resources in education should be expended with special concentration on those with the greatest deficit so that they can get a handicap that will return them as close as possible to an equal starting point.

The problem of the competitive model of academic evaluation is not just that it rewards people unfairly; the real issues are even more basic. The competitive approach to academics is divisive. It treats people as isolated individuals in tension with all other isolated individuals. It fails to view the community of learners as a more cohesive whole with common objectives. Consider the world of competition in which two students taking a course do very differently, one receiving an A grade and the other a D. In the competitive world, the A student feels elation at the success and the documentation of achievement. It signals opportunities to go on to medical school or a good job. The D student on the other hand feels distress and humiliation. Not only is there the loss of future opportunities, but there is a feeling of inferiority.

In a more cooperative model of education very different feelings would be possible. The poor students might feel relief that someone in the society will be able to fill roles society needs filled. The student who performs well might feel a burden of responsibility in proportion to the documentation of talent.

University of South Carolina Professor Marcia Lynn Whicker was struck by the problems of the competitive model when a bright student approached her complaining that weaker students were given too many opportunities to improve their performances. The student was concerned about demonstrating superiority in order to get into medical school and was distressed that, through the use of make-up examinations and other devices to bring weaker students up to a higher level of understanding, she would not receive adequate recognition of her superiority.[26]

Professor Whicker's response was one of beginning to think about ways of encouraging all students to feel a sense of accomplishment for the success of the group of students as a whole. She has proposed (though apparently she has not yet tried) making a portion of a grade reflect the performance of the group as a whole. This, she argues, would provide a strong incentive to increase the achievement of all the students. She compared it to Japanese companies that use group incentives based on overall collective performance. It is roughly analogous to the joy that a volunteer feels when a retarded youngster first accomplishes a milestone of performance in the Special Olympics. Her intriguing idea would end up rewarding the bright student for helping her fellow classmates rather than feeling she had to compete against them. If our goal is to structure social institutions so as to assist those in greatest need to get the help they need to have a chance at equality, we must encourage experiments of this type, not only among the range of talents in a normal college class, but also among those now singled out for special education. At most, identification of intellectual talent should be seen as a necessary device for providing help to the community by identifying those with gifts and accompanying responsibilities.

OTHER COMPETITION

Athletic and academic competition are two of the most pervasive manifestations of individualism and the anti-egalitarian quest for testimony of superiority in our society, but there are other places where the competitive mentality surfaces as well. Business is one of the most obvious. Here as elsewhere competition is justified by the myth that some invisible eighteenth-century hand will guide individuals so that all works out for the best. Aside from the fact that in a more complex technological and monopolistic society that is obviously a groundless belief, it rests on the ethically suspect and anti-egalitarian conviction that the goal for social policy is to maximize aggregate benefit.

Still another area where we have been able to develop the competitive mode of demonstration of superiority is the aesthetic. Ranging from the most crude forms—the beauty contest—to the more sophisticated—the International Tchaikovsky Piano Competition in Moscow—we have managed to convert aesthetic evaluation into an opportunity to demonstrate inequality. Especially for aesthetic evaluation in the fine arts, it is functional to have some means of evaluating in order to identify the community resources that are held by individuals as gifts. It permits us as a community to enjoy these talents. But superimposed on this use of evaluation to identify gifts is the more aggressive and individualistic urge to demonstrate superiority, thus reducing the beauty of a great pianist's contribution to the banality of a beauty contest or a boxing match.

We need to learn how to differentiate the individualism of the anti-egalitarian contests of superiority from the more social uses of evaluation. In social evaluation, talent is identified as a community resource so that those lacking the particular skill can rejoice that others will be able to provide the community with such skill. It is also identified so that those with the skill can assume the burden of responsibility of channeling that resource to the community and those within it who are of greatest need.

These implications of egalitarianism for athletics, academic life, business, and aesthetics may seem radical, but they are necessary if the retarded and others who are handicapped by lacking basic physical and mental attributes are to receive their fair share. It is simply not possible to give Eddie Conrad the educational services he needs to have a real chance in life and hold on to the idea that educational opportunities should be distributed on the basis of talent. At most, we should use comparative evaluations as a way of identifying the talent that can be used by the community to help it strive for a chance for equality of outcome.

Special Duties and Special Roles

The result of these public policy considerations of the implications of egalitarianism is that different people within the community will play quite different roles in the complex decisions that must be made. The "best and the brightest" will bear responsibility to see that their talents are used constructively to provide the handicap or compensatory adjustment needed to give the deprived a chance at equality. Those who are lacking in some particular skill—and all of us face this deficit in one area or another—can rest comfortably knowing that others in the community are the custodians of the resources needed.

Several special groups of people will be in special roles that need to be identified more concretely in the process of reorienting resources to the handicapped. Parents of the handicapped and other family members, educators, health professionals, and public officials all have special roles to play. As such, even if we agree that there must be some common moral framework that makes community resource allocation decisions either right or wrong, we must recognize special moral duties that attach to special roles for those having impact on the lives of the handicapped.

Parents and Family Members

While in one sense we are all, as a moral community, responsible for giving the Eddie Conrads of the world a chance at equality, his parents are in a special position. Do we want them to have to struggle morally with the question of whether resources in a school system should be diverted from the more normal students' art and music programs to their own son's special speech therapy?

Although there may be limits on the compensatory rechanneling of resources toward the retarded and there may be ethical reasons totally unrelated to justice for retaining some resource commitments for these other programs, it does not follow that the parents and others in a special relationship with the handicapped have a duty to take those reasons into account. It would at least be psychologically difficult for parents to have to weigh the relative claims of their own child and other children in determining how resources should be allocated.

In fact, it can be argued that parents in general have a special obligation to pursue the welfare of their children independent of the needs of others. That would permit parents of relatively well-off children to avoid having to trade off their own child's welfare against that of others. Do parents, for example, when feeding their own child, have to ask themselves whether some other child could benefit more from that food? Do they have to calculate before they spend an evening hour with their child whether some other child could benefit more from that hour's attention? While all of us have some obligation to be concerned about the welfare of the needy, it is limited by special obligations—obligations I have called role-specific duties. They rest on the commitments made when taking on a special role, and they offset to some extent more general duties, such as those of justice.

If that applies to parents in general, how much more it applies to parents of the handicapped where there is a convergence of the role-specific duty of the parent and the more general demands of justice. The parent should feel free to be an unrelenting advocate for the welfare of the child. If limits are to be set at all, as they might be if other children are determined to be in greater need or if other ethical commitments place limits, this must not be the parents' responsibility.

There is a second role that the parent of the retarded should play in addition to advocating for the resources necessary to give the child as close as possible a chance for equal outcome, the parent would normally be the one who is in the position to consent if resources must be diverted to entice elites into offering their services for the welfare of the child. I have argued that inequalities might be justified (even though they are not just) if the inequalities serve the least well off and they (or their agents) consent to the inequality. The retarded often would not be able to consent to such arrangements themselves, but parents acting as their agents can contemplate whether inequalities would be in the interest of the retarded one and give the necessary permission. For the retarded this might be used to justify salaries for special education instructors or payment of lawyers to advocate for the retarded.

In no case, however, should the parents be asked to consent to diverting resources away from the handicapped on the grounds that the general public interest will be served. That is not only unfair to the handicapped; it puts the parent in an untenable psychological position.

Special Educators and Health Professionals

Other groups who may have special role-specific duties are special educators and health professionals. Since these are two groups who will be thought of as having special involvement in providing care for the mentally and physically handicapped, it is important to understand their special responsibilities and the way those special responsibilities have an impact on their role in public policy decision-making.

Health professionals traditionally have felt that they have a special duty to do what they think will benefit their patients. That ethic can be traced back at least as far as the Hippocratic Oath, which originated some twenty-four hundred years ago.[27] Its ethical framework is unique. It focuses on consequences—benefits and harms—but only on consequences to the special individuals with whom the health care professional is interacting. Until very recently, physicians and other health care professionals did not question this ethical stance. Now it is being questioned on several counts. It is now widely recognized that instead of doing what the physician thinks will benefit the patient, some adjustment must be made in the core principle. At least the physician is not justified in acting in a certain way just because he or she *thinks* it will benefit the patient. That would permit all manner of paternalism and even lead to bizarre judgments by some physicians who have unusual value systems. If the physician is going to try to focus exclusively on promoting good consequences, there should be some more independent, reliable standard. Most have gone even further in modifying the Hippocratic formula. They have argued that many other ethical considerations must come into play besides the consequences of the health care professional's actions. They may have to take into account the fact that they have made promises or have a duty to tell the truth. They may have to act so as to protect the autonomy of the patient even if it does not produce the best consequences. If that is correct, then the health professional's duty is to do what is right by the patient, not simply to produce the most benefit for the patient. That is what I have argued at length *A Theory of Medical Ethics.*[28]

That still leaves the health professional with a special duty of concentrating only on the patient, thereby excluding consideration of all others who might be affected by his or her action. Recently, there has been some movement in the direction of insisting that health care and other clinical professionals must abandon this individualism and take into account the more societal dimensions of their actions as well. The American Medical Association, in the latest revision of its Principles of Medical Ethics, not only abandons the exclusive consequentialism of its ethical commitment, it reemphasizes its belief that the physician must be responsible to the community as well as to the individual.[29]

There is, of course, no reason why the society as a whole should accept any particular formulation of a professional's duty just because the professional group says it should be that way. In this case, however, society has actually pushed the profession into many of these recent changes. It was the lay society that stimulated the medical profession into abandoning the blatant paternalism of the Hippocratic Oath. The lay population also pressed for the augmentation of the patient-benefiting principle with concern for respect for the autonomy of the patient and the duty to deal honestly with patients.

The lay population has also exerted some pressure on the health profession to abandon its radical individualism and take into account the welfare of others in the society when making ethical decisions. This has been done in part because lay people have wanted physicians and other health professionals to be more aware of the societal dimensions of what appear to be individual medical decisions. But it is also in part because critical social welfare factors are at stake in clinical decisions. This arises not only in research and in public health, but in consideration of costs and resource allocation dimensions of health care decisions.

There is a high price to be paid in trying to convert the clinical professional into one who focuses more broadly on the social dimensions of decisions. It means abandoning, at least partially, the special duty that the clinical professionals have borne to single-mindedly pursue the welfare of the patient. As a society contemplating the duties we want health professionals to bear, we face two options. We could insist that the health professional abandon the single-minded focus on the welfare of the patient and take into account the interests of others as well. That is the direction in which many are pressing. The consequences, however, would be that physicians and other health professionals should put patients on notice. They should metaphorically post a notice that patients should realize that the physician will pursue the patient's welfare only until the welfare of others gets in the way.

The alternative is to agree as a society that there should continue to be a special obligation for health professionals to focus wholeheartedly on the welfare of the patient. The defense attorney now is given a special duty to pursue the interests of the client. (Even if the defendant's lawyer knows his client is guilty, under normal circumstances it would be unethical and illegal for him to tell the judge.) Likewise, we may want to assign to health professionals the special role-specific duty of serving the interests of their client even if it would do more good for society for the professional to sacrifice the patient. That is, in effect, what we have already concluded with regard to the special duties of parents and other family members.

There may be good psychological reasons as well as ethical reasons for assigning this special duty to health professionals in the clinical relationship. Health professionals who are clinically oriented are committed to serving individuals. Even if it were ethically acceptable to ask them to wear two hats, to serve only the patient's welfare in certain clinical relationships, but partially abandon them when making allocation decisions, it is not clear that it would be humanly possible to do so.

Far better that we permit health care professionals to maintain their traditional orientation of commitment solely to the patient. If we make this ethical move, there may have to be exceptions in extreme circumstances. The physician should be permitted to abandon the immediate welfare of a patient to whom he is giving a physical examination if someone who is not his patient is bleeding to death in the street. The physician must be permitted to stop the physical temporarily to save the nonpatient's life. In extreme cases physicians should take into account the justice of how they allocate their time, even breaking their promise to serve their patients single-mindedly if the need of someone else is overwhelmingly greater. In the more normal circumstance, however, we might want to have an agreement with health professionals that their job is to do what is right by the patient; not to get mixed up in the question of whether they could do more good spending their time and energy doing something else.

If health professionals are given this exemption from the duty of justice—if they have a special role-specific duty to do what is right by the patient—someone else will have to take on the resource allocation tasks. Limits will have to be placed on how professionals can spend their time and how they can spend society's resources. The broader questions of justice, which have been the main focus of this volume, will be the job of someone else—the school board, the planners of insurance coverage, the government at all levels. The result will be that the health professional providing services for the handicapped can be free to be a single-minded advocate for the handicapped, never having to tackle the question of the limits of care except by focusing on what is in the patient's welfare and what will protect the patient's rights.

An ethic for special educators, for those providing Eddie Conrad's speech therapy and other learning services for the handicapped, is much less well developed than the ethic for health professionals, but the problems seem to be exactly parallel. Traditionally, educators have been thought of as professionals with a special set of duties to their "clients." Those duties would include benefitting them as well as honoring their rights. We face the same problem that we did with health professionals. Do we also want them to try to be just in allocating the resources they control between their clients and others who may be in greater need? I have tried to argue that it would be better ethically to exempt them from the duties of justice (except in the most extreme cases) so that they can be free to serve their clients single-mindedly. If they are so exempted, then someone else—an administrator, the school board, or a citizens' group—will have to make allocation decisions.

A corollary of this interpretation of the special duties of special educators is that other educators with special responsibilities for other programs within the school—the teachers responsible for the program for gifted students and those teaching the music, art, and physical education that may be in jeopardy in the decision for the case we are considering—will also have the special duty of advocating for the students in their programs. They will also be biased if they are to participate in the resource allocation decisions. Anyone who has a special set of obligations that would conflict with their responsible allocation of resources should be exempt from that task.

Administrators, Public Officials, and School Board Members

If parents, health care professionals, special educators, and other teachers who have special agenda are exempted from the duties of justice so that they can advocate for their clients, then who should be making the resource allocation decisions and on what basis? These are fundamentally public policy questions to be based on the ethical, religious, and philosophical commitments of the society as a whole. Unless we take the view that the nature of that set of beliefs and values is arbitrary, relative, or unknowable—a position I have been arguing against—then it is crucial that the public operate on the proper set of beliefs and values. That, in effect, is the objective of this volume: to build the case for the egalitarian interpretation of the principle of justice based on the basic assumptions—the faith commitments—derived from the Judeo-Christian tradition.

The task, however, belongs to the public and to its agents. Rationally, we will discount the contributions of those who have special duties that create a conflict of interest—whether they be parents, educators, or health professionals. Nevertheless, we will have to listen to their pleas along with those of others pleading special causes based on their special obligations. Once all this is sorted out, the task of the administrators of the school (hospital or other institution), the representatives of the public on the school board (legislature or other official decision-making body), and the councils drawn together to assist in the decision-making process is to allocate the resources in the right way, taking into account the principle of justice as well as the other ethical principles at stake.

With regard to the specific decision to provide special speech therapy needed to bring Eddie Conrad back closer to a fair starting point to give him a chance to be as equal in outcome as possible to others, the presumption has to be in favor of the resources going to him. I have suggested possible limits that keep this demand from being infinite. The just claims of others would have to be taken into account if allocations to speech therapy would drive someone else's opportunity for well-being down to an even lower level; the consent of the retarded or their agents would justify inequalities provided they were designed to contribute to the welfare of the least well off; other inherent right-making principles (the deontological principles) might provide counterveiling considerations; or, finally, depending on one's ethical theory, overwhelming social welfare might justify placing some limits on the speech therapy. I have argued, however, that this last consideration is unacceptable and that the administrators, public officials, or other decision-making body should not take the speech instruction away from Eddie Conrad simply because more good would be done on balance if the money were spent elsewhere. The mere fact that more happiness or more well-being would be produced if the money were spent on music or art or physical education does not count. If, and only if, the good to be done by spending the money elsewhere would help students who are even worse off than Eddie would the decision-making body be justified in diverting the resources from the speech therapy. If others even more poorly off were not benefitted from the diversion then it could not ethically take place unless Eddie or his agents consented to it for his own good or there were other deontological considerations that were introduced and considered overriding. In the case of the speech therapy, it is hard to imagine how any of these resource-limiting principles could be relevant. The decision-makers should opt for the therapy.

Notes

1. Aristotle, *Nichomachean Ethics* V, Chapter 3, 1131a.
2. K. Charlie Lakin, Robert H. Bruininks, David Doth, et al., *Sourcebook on Long-Term Care for Developmentally Disabled People.* (Minneapolis: University of Minnesota, Department of Educational Psychology, 1982), p. 85.

3. David Braddock, Richard Hemp, and Ruth Howes, *Public Expenditures for Mental Retardation and Developmental Disabilities in the United States: Analytical Summary (A Working Paper)* (Chicago: Expenditure Analysis Project; Evaluation and Public Policy Program; Institute for the Study of Developmental Disabilities, University of Illinois at Chicago, March, 1985), pp. 14–15.

4. *Ibid.*, pp. 15, 17.

5. Lakin, et al., *Sourcebook on Long-Term Care,* p. 72.

6. Braddock, Hemp, and Howes, *Public Expenditures for Mental Retardation,* pp. 18, 19.

7. *Ibid.*, pp. 21, 79.

8. *Ibid.*, p. 40.

9. Lakin, et al., *Sourcebook on Long-Term Care,* p. 55.

10. *Ibid.*, p. 74.

11. Braddock, Hemp, and Howes, *Public Expenditures for Mental Retardation,* p. 54.

12. *Ibid.*, p. 72.

13. Robert Dworkin, "What is Equality? Part 2: Equality of Resources," *Philosophy and Public Affairs* 10 (1981):286 ff.

14. *Ibid.*, pp. 297–98.

15. Thomas Schelling, "The Life You Save May Be Your Own," *Problems in Public Expenditure Analysis,* ed. Samuel B. Chase (Washington, D.C.: The Brookings Institution, 1968), pp. 127–76.

16. Jan Acton, "Measuring the Monetary Value of Lifesaving Programs," *Valuing Lives,* special issue of *Law and Contemporary Problems* 60 (Autumn 1976):46–72.

17. Norman Daniels, "Health Care Needs and Distributive Justice," *Philosophy and Public Affairs* 10 (No. 2, Spring 1981):146–79. Daniels also argues that the infinite demand problem (or "bottomless pit" as he calls it) can be avoided by recognizing (1) that not every treatment one can receive can be considered a need; [this point is offered against Charles Fried, who argues that equal access to health care could be disastrously expensive ("imagine some elaborate way to retard the effects of normal aging") Charles Fried, *Right and Wrong.* (Cambridge: Harvard University Press, 1978), p. 128] and (2) that expenditures can be limited by using a four-tiered system of health services, the different levels representing types of care with different degrees of moral urgency. The first tier, the most important, would be invested in before the second, and so on, such that a society could know how to spend within its limits of financial resources.

18. Marc Lappe, "Humanizing the Genetic Enterprise," *Hastings Center Report* 9 (December 1979):10–14.

19. James F. Crow, "Population Perspective," *Ethical Issues in Human Genetics,* ed. Bruce Hilton, Daniel Callahan, et al. (New York: Plenum Press, 1973), pp. 73–80.

20. W. D. Ross, *The Right and the Good* (Oxford: Oxford University Press, 1939), p. 19.

21. See "Games" in *The International Standard Bible Encyclopedia* (Chicago: The Howard-Severence Company, 1915), pp. 1168–73.

22. Ecclesiastes 9:11.

23. For other obvious metaphorical references to sports contests, see II Timothy 4:7 and Hebrews 12:1.

24. I Corinthians 9:24–27; see also Charles Hodge, *Commentary on the First Epistle to the Corinthians* (Grand Rapids, Mich.: William B. Eerdmans Publishing Co., 1953), p. 167.

25. Thomas Nagel, ''Equal Treatment and Compensatory Discrimination,'' *Philosophy and Public Affairs* 2 (Summer 1973):357.

26. Marcia Lynn Whicker, ''A New Way of Grading Students: The Achievement of the Whole Class Should Count,'' in *The Washington Post* (July 24, 1983), p. C5.

27. Ludwig Edelstein, ''The Hippocratic Oath: Text, Translation and Interpretation,'' *Ancient Medicine: Selected Papers of Ludwig Edelstein,* ed. Owsei Temkin and C. Lilian Temkin (Baltimore: The Johns Hopkins University Press, 1967), pp. 3–64.

28. Robert M. Veatch, *A Theory of Medical Ethics* (New York: Basic Books, 1981).

29. American Medical Association, *Current Opinions of the Judicial Council of the American Medical Association* (Chicago: American Medical Association, 1981), p. ix.

7

Equality and the Problem of Stigma

The egalitarian principle of justice produces a very strong case for intensive speech therapy for the retarded and for similar interventions to improve the lot of the more disadvantaged among us. The demands the principle places on society are not infinite, but the responsibility is great. Certain among us are charged with special responsibility to be advocates for these citizens of special need, but all of us—the community as a whole—have resources available to respond and an ethical responsibility to respond in our public policy deliberations.

One remaining problem with this conclusion must be addressed. There is a paradox posed by egalitarianism. The principles for which I have argued require identifying those among us who are of greatest need and determining what would be required to do what we can to give them as much of a chance as possible for equality. That, in turn, requires some sort of calculus such as Dworkin's hypothetical "equal auction" to determine the relative amounts of compensation that would be needed. Once the society has gone through some such exercise, the amounts owed to the retarded and others with severe handicaps would be known. The results of that exercise, however, would be a kind of handicap score that could be used against the handicapped, signalling the degree of stigma they are to bear. A commitment to equality taken seriously may actually identify those to be stigmatized and even provide a kind of point total (measured in dollars or services to be provided to each) that could mark the extent of the stigma. The result could actually be a greater, more identifiable, discrimination against the handicapped.

We are left with a paradox that defenders of the egalitarian solution to Eddie Conrad's speech therapy must confront. The egalitarian interpretation of the principle of justice built on three core assumptions of the Judeo-Christian tradition and its secular surrogates leads us to a commitment to do what we can to give the retarded and others who are handicapped an opportunity for a level of well-being over a lifetime equal to that of other persons. That presses us to provide compensatory resource commitments to strive toward equality. But the very fact that we are singling out people for compensation for their handicaps stigmatizes them as being different, and almost inevitably that difference is interpreted as inferiority. Thus striving for equality produces stigma and stigma produces feelings of inferiority and therefore inequality. Equality may be self-defeating.

The Problem of Stigma

Stigma is a problem not only for the retarded, but for all who are or could be identified as bearing some handicapping condition. Irving Goffman is professor of anthropology and sociology at the University of Pennsylvania and author of *Stigma: Note on the Management of Spoiled Identity,* which is the classical statement of the sociology of stigma. He defines stigma as "the situation of the individual who is disqualified from full social acceptance."[1]

The Idea of Stigma

The notion of stigma comes from the Greeks. It originally referred to bodily signs that exposed something unusual or bad about an individual, but now it more often refers to the disgrace itself rather than the bodily evidence of it.[2] According to Goffman, three types of stigma can be identified: those involving physical deformities, those signalling what Goffman calls "blemishes of individual character" (such as weak will, dishonesty, alcoholism, etc.), and those involving tribal stigma of race, nation, or religion transmitted through lineages.[3]

We can make several striking observations about Goffman's classification. First, he makes certain judgments about empirical facts—that alcoholism is a blemish of character rather than a physical disorder, for example. More critically, while Goffman does not deal directly with mental retardation, he classifies mental disorder as a character blemish rather than a physical deformity. We will see in a minute why this could be very important for one concerned, as Goffman generally is not, with the moral and public policy dimensions of stigma.

Finally, we should observe that stigma necessarily involves an evaluation, a value judgment. Goffman variously refers to a stigma as a deformity, a blemish, or something "unusual and *bad*." All of these terms are inherently negative. It is impossible to have a good stigmatizing condition. Handicap is a similar term. It is impossible to refer to a "good" handicap (except in a relative or indirect way). To label a condition as a handicap is to say simultaneously that it is a condition we would rather not have.

ITS EVALUATIVE CHARACTER
Goffman and many other sociologists of stigma acknowledge this evaluative character of stigma, but they often see themselves engaged in a value-free, scientific, sociological study of the stigma and the stigmatizing process. Goffman sees his task as primarily descriptive, thus avoiding the questions that are essential for those concerned about the ethical and public policy dimensions of stigma. For the most part, he avoids asking whether we *ought* to disvalue the stigmatizing condition. In fact, he takes it as a given of the society he is describing that the world is divided into a "we" and a "they" and that the stigmatizing characteristics are disvalued by the society.[4]

At the same time that stigma is taken as a given, labeling theorists since Lemert[5] and Becker[6] have recognized that the creation of the label to which stigma is attached is a social process.[7]

This view of labeling and the generation of stigma creates a pair of problems. The stigma is viewed as inevitable, yet the values that feed into the labeling are viewed as "merely social." This means that the disadvantage suffered by the stigmatized has no objective basis and, in turn, there is no objective basis for deciding how the stigmatized could be compensated for their disadvantage.

There is a sense in which all reality is "socially constructed." We have known that at least since the work of Peter Berger and Thomas Luckmann.[8] The concept of the atom is a product of social imagination.

Religious belief systems are the product of social imagination. The language and symbols we use to represent our beliefs—about the basic physical structure of the universe or our concept of what is ultimately valued—are necessarily products of our social system. They are the best that mere finite humans can do to represent ultimate reality. So, likewise, the values upon which we label stigmatizing conditions are surely social products. This, of course, leaves open the question of whether there is some objective reality that can be said to underlie our concept of the atom or of religious belief systems or of the value judgments that are part of the assigning of stigma.

In ethics, if not in old-fashioned descriptive sociology that is attempting to be value-free, it is critical to press beyond this observation that all labeling involves a social process. In analyzing the values upon which stigma judgments are based, we have to distinguish between those we want to treat as objective and those we treat as subjective.

Stigma attached to race (and probably age and gender as well) incorporates value judgments that we are inclined to treat as merely subjective. Any "bad" that attaches to being a member of a certain race, we are wont to say, is *only* in the eye of the observer. It is subjective in this sense. For subjectively grounded stigmatization, our ethically appropriate response is to attack the value judgment, to argue that there is really nothing significant, especially nothing *wrong,* with being a member of a certain racial group.

On the other hand, some value judgments that are incorporated into stigma assignments appear to be quite different. Stigmas involving serious physical handicaps are examples. Among those Goffman views as being stigmatized by serious physical deformities are the blind, the paraplegic, and the seriously burn-scarred. While it is true that a social group must construct its image of these handicaps and generate a concept of what life is like with these conditions, it is a mistake to try to deny their inherent negative quality the way we might do with race or gender. We can, during our social construction of a social concept of blindness or paraplegia, envision the negative evaluation as having more of a basis in reality. It is as if the disvalue were somehow objective, that is, rooted in external reality. That means if someone said, without confusion and without considering some indirect benefits such as insurance or welfare, that he considered it valuable to be blind or paraplegic, we would consider him not merely strange, but wrong. We would say of him that he has made a mistake. Blindness and paraplegia are what we might call objective disvalues. We can, in our social construction of reality, think of these conditions as if they were really and objectively bad. This does not mean that people with these conditions cannot lead good, productive, and enjoyable lives. It is just that no one in his right mind would actually prefer these conditions. We can, without stretching our use of the language, refer to these conditions as objectively disvalued.

If that is the case, the critical classification, at least for ethics and public policy, is not Goffman's (physical deformity, blemished character, and tribal stigma), but, rather, whether the evaluation is merely subjective (as with race) or more objective (as with blindness). For subjectively grounded stigma, our social task is to force a reassessment of the disvalue of the apparently stigmatizing condition. On the other hand, for someone with an objectively disvalued condition our task is to accept the evaluation and determine if compensation is in order to provide for a chance at being equal on balance with others. In turn, if one is concerned about a *chance* at being equal, the judgment about compensation will depend upon whether the objectively disvalued, stigmatizing condition is the result of voluntary behavior of the individual or whether it is a disvalued condition that the individual acquired through no choice of his own. We are more likely to favor compensatory support to restore the individual to an equal starting point in cases where the disvalued condition is nonvoluntary. If a stigmatizing condition is viewed as objectively disvalued *and* nonvoluntary, social intervention is called for.

Consider, for example, alcoholism. I take it for granted that it is what I have called objectively disvalued. No one really argues seriously that it is a good thing. If we take it as a fact that it is a genetically caused disability not involving any voluntary choice, we are more likely to favor medical and social support than if it is viewed as a voluntary condition resulting from choices freely available.

VISIBLE AND INVISIBLE STIGMA

In spite of the fact that the classical value-free sociologists' discussion of stigma does not lend itself to the kind of analysis needed in ethics and public policy discussion for the care of the retarded, there are additional elements of their conception of stigma that are important in our assessment of the retarded. Goffman, for example, distinguishes between the potentially stigmatizable individual and the one who is actually stigmatized. He introduces the unfortunate terms of the "discreditable" and the "discredited" to distinguish those who have some hidden stigmatizing condition permitting them to escape the stigma in certain groups (such as being homosexual or a former prisoner) and those who are in fact stigmatized. Goffman uses the terms to refer to nothing more than whether the societally judged disvalued condition is actually recognized. They could, however, imply considerably more. To be discreditable can imply that, to use my language, one has an objectively disvalued condition whereas being discredited might imply only subjective disvalue.[9] Moreover, it may imply that one is personally and voluntarily responsible for the condition as if avoiding the "blemish" were to one's credit and failing to avoid it were similarly to one's discredit.

Goffman, as I understand him, means none of this, but rather he is simply distinguishing whether the disvalued condition (objective or subjective) is actually perceived by others or merely there hidden from their awareness. The fact that some can "pass for normal" when their stigmatizing condition is hideable is important when a community decides whether to adopt public policy (such as classifying and compensating) that will increase visibility. It has been observed by labeling theorists that the development of classification schemes and even the mere naming of a particular condition can increase its visibility and therefore make it more difficult for the stigmatizable person to pass as normal.

THE WE/THEY DICHOTOMY

This emphasis on "passing for normal" makes clear a final important element of stigma theory as presented by the descriptive sociologists. The entire theory of stigmatization rests on the purported fact that social groups necessarily create we/they dichotomies. Goffman's study is organized around the problems of the relation of a "we" and a "they," the "normal" and the "stigmatized."[10] Some of the normals are "wise"; they recognize that the stigmatized are not everything that most normal normals take them to be. They recognize, for example, that the stigmatized may not be morally culpable for their abnormality even though ordinary normals may treat them as if they were. Still, it is inconceivable that the distinction between the normal and the stigmatized could be challenged.

When one's attention shifts to the ethics and public policy dimensions of stigma, this we/they dichotomy will be critical. Some policies will have a tendency to create two identifiable classes as when school children in subsidized lunch programs can be identified by having to present vouchers for their meals or when Medicaid patients are processed differently from private patients. Some policies may increase the visibility of the we/they dichotomy and thus make the burdens of stigma worse.

Stigma and the Retarded

The sociologists of stigma and labeling theory have normally not dealt at length with the stigma of retardation. The problem is a serious one, however. Retardation is a condition that lends itself to analysis in the terms we have been discussing. In fact, several scholars concerned with the ethical dimensions of retardation have focused on the problem of labeling.[11]

Ralph Potter notes the dual result of labeling in the mentally retarded—that is, qualifying the retarded for special assistance while simultaneously associating them with a socially disfavored group.[12] Thus, while he feels labels must be assigned to provide special care equitably, they must be accurately and justly applied so as to benefit those labeled without reducing their opportunities for development. He suggests that the boundaries of a label's definition must be narrow enough to guard against a "contagion of statuses" so that a specific weakness such as that of mental deficiency need not be taken as grounds for discrimination in areas not affected by the handicap. Similarly, we must guard against injustice in the application of labels by recognizing that the label of mental retardation as "a predictor of future capacity" may result in a self-fulfilling prophecy.

Arthur Dyck points to certain injustices associated with the label "mental retardation" as compared with other, less questionable, diagnostic labels. Dyck says that the mentally retarded unfairly tend to be labeled for life even if they achieve an independent living status, whereas a patient with appendicitis is only temporarily labeled with little or no associated stigmas.[13] He asserts that while a patient with appendicitis can routinely expect therapy for his illness, the mentally retarded individual often is deprived of the special care he requires to help overcome his incapacities. Furthermore, while the appendicitis victim retains his basic rights, the retarded are often deprived of some or all such rights solely because of the label they bear. Finally, Dyck maintains that someone suffering from an illness such as appendicitis is given special deference—sick leave—while someone labeled ''mentally retarded'' risks losing his status as a person or at best being viewed as a second class citizen. He concludes ''that it is not just to label persons mentally retarded if the use of the label does not serve to provide them with help, and if the label is not erased even though the condition that justified its use has been improved to the point where help is no longer needed.[14]

Laurence McCullough similarly acknowledges the dual effect of labeling the mentally retarded and argues that the benefits need not be gained at the expense of the individual's full moral status.[15] He identifies both intrinsic and extrinsic value dimensions of a handicap label corresponding to objectively and subjectively grounded stigma. On the intrinsic side, McCullough rejects a ''fixed state'' view implying that the retarded person is broadly incompetent, and therefore has diminished moral status in the same way for all individuals.

By focusing only on the intrinsic aspects of the label, McCullough tries to eliminate the arbitrary losses of moral status while retaining the special assistance to which they are entitled.

When one focuses specifically on mental retardation, one begins to see the dangers of Goffman's classification. In particular, it is hard to determine whether retardation should be a physical deformity or a character disorder. More important, it is not clear what difference it makes unless those categories are surrogates for something else, say, the distinction between voluntary and nonvoluntary conditions. We often view physical conditions such as blindness as nonvoluntary whereas some character disorders, such as being a former prisoner, seem to be more voluntary. That is, however, at best a crude way to distinguish between voluntary and nonvoluntary conditions. Certain physical deformities may be voluntary in the sense that the individual consciously chose to take the risk of sustaining the injury. An amputation or burn suffered by an explosives expert might be an example.

On the other hand, although most of the so-called character disorders Goffman lists seem to have a substantial voluntary component (holding radical political beliefs and being dishonest, for example), not all of them are. Mental disorders are particularly ambiguous here. While, historically, many have viewed mental problems as partially voluntary, contemporary views treat them as much more nonvoluntary. Certainly, mental retardation fits almost perfectly into the nonvoluntary component. We need not even address the question of whether it is a physical condition. If so, it may not make any difference whether it is a physical or character disorder.

Using the terms we have developed, it is easier to characterize mental retardation and to identify some of the implications of adopting an egalitarian position. Mental retardation of the sort seen in Eddie Conrad and others like him is surely not a voluntary condition. It is, however, a serious condition, one that any reasonable person would rather not have. In our terms, the disvalue is objective. This means that we cannot cope with the problem of stigma simply by trying to re-educate people into thinking that the condition is not inherently bad. Retardation is not like race or gender stigma. Even the most dedicated and sympathetic advocate for the retarded acknowledges that it is a serious problem. That is why both private and governmental agencies make substantial commitments to research to attempt to minimize it. Certainly, education of the so-called normal can do much to eliminate misunderstandings that have led to inhumane treatment of the retarded. But the problems of Eddie Conrad would not go away completely if those in his community were completely reoriented to a more accurate and sympathetic understanding of his situation. He still would have, among other things, a speech problem and need help in coping with it. That problem is real. It is so clearly a bad thing to have that we can act as if it were objectively a bad condition.

It should now be clear why the case of speech therapy for the retarded is an ideal case for examining the problems of equitable treatment for the handicapped. It is a pure case of a nonvoluntary, objectively disvalued condition, a condition that produces the clearest demand for compensatory support in an effort to give a better chance at equality. It brackets the problem of the individual who brought on the handicap through some free choice of a risky life-style. It brackets the problem of subjective evaluations posed by less clearly disvalued conditions. If, and only if, we can get clear on how to treat the retarded can we move on the more complex cases posed by less serious and less obviously disvalued conditions. If we cannot form a clear response to the moral claims of the retarded, then all of us who are less than perfect are in jeopardy.

This discussion of stigma also makes clear the problem created for the egalitarian who is advocating a compensatory scheme based on consideration of equality. Retardation is what might be referred to as a partially visible condition. Many retarded individuals, especially mildly and moderately retarded individuals, can mask their handicap and pass for normal at least for some of life's tasks. They can, as is now well known, travel, shop, hold a job, and enjoy life, often without others even knowing that they have a handicap. Any policy innovation that increases visibility in the face of recognition that the condition really is a bad one poses additional threat of stigmatization. Merely naming and classifying do so. Formalization of testing and the invention of a numerical IQ scoring appear to objectify the stigmatizing condition. If, on top of that, a process is developed to determine how much compensation is appropriate for each handicap, then the stigma, by becoming more visible, can be made more severe.

Solutions to the Stigma Problem

This leaves us in a terrible situation. We must acknowledge that retardation really is an undesirable condition both in order to be honest and in order to justify compensatory resource commitments to give the retarded a more equal starting point. Yet, compensation will surely increase visibility and, if we are not careful, increase stigmatization as well.

The problem is one that should not be simply denied. In fact, we may have to acknowledge that, short of the key starting assumptions of the egalitarian perspective, there is no possible solution. The three key premises or starting assumptions—our faith moves—may end up not only creating our moral dilemma, put providing a basis for solving it. They create the dilemma because without them we would have no sense of obligation to the handicapped in the first place and no resources at our disposal to respond. With those same premises, however, we have the beginnings of a way out of the egalitarian's stigma paradox.

The Communitarian Perspective

The three basic premises of the Judeo-Christian tradition and its secular surrogates reorient us toward viewing individuals as equals in comparison to an infinite value. In many manifestations of that tradition, this had led to a sense of solidarity, to a feeling that, to use the traditional metaphor, we are all brothers and sisters sharing the same father. This provides a sense of community that is otherwise lacking. The second and third major premises, likewise, drive us toward what might be called a communitarian perspective. When there is no such thing as unowned resources out there to be appropriated, some alternative view of the ownership of resources is adopted. In the religious traditions they are originally God's and are entrusted to the community for proper use. In the secular surrogates they are viewed as belonging to the community as a whole. When some version of a sense of responsibility for the task of restoring equality is accepted—that is, some doctrine of stewardship—each individual is seen as bearing an obligation of justice to see that the commonly held resources are used within the community to help the handicapped and give them a more equal starting point. In all three starting premises we find corollaries with strong communitarian overtones.

This means that we can begin to perceive retardation not as someone else's problem, not as Eddie Conrad's worry or that of his parents, but as *our* problem. There is something wrong with us because there is something wrong with our community. It is out of sync because there is not equality, and that is a flaw in us because it is a flaw in our community. There is no sense of satisfaction in demonstrating superiority over others intellectually, physically, or any other way. To the contrary, as we have seen in the discussion of athletics and academics, an ethic of competition collapses. It is replaced with an ethic of cooperation. Stigma results in a sense of satisfaction that derives from dividing the world into a ''we'' and a ''they'' and judging rightly or wrongly that the characteristic that the ''we'' possess is superior to the one that the ''they'' possess. The stigma is, as we have seen, even more invidious when the value judgment about the superiority of the characteristic that the ''we'' possess is a correct one—that is, when it is valued ''objectively.'' The communitarian perspective implied in the premises underlying the Judeo-Christian and secular egalitarian tradition does not attack the value judgment. Instead, it attacks the process of dichotomizing, of separating the world into the ''we'' and the ''they.''

Destroying the We/They Dichotomy

The destruction of the we/they dichotomy is essential if the retarded and others who are handicapped are going to be given a chance at something closer to a more equal starting point without creating our paradoxical stigmatization. If our reference point for deciding who among us is handicapped is an infinite value—a god or some functionally similar secular surrogate—then all of us are handicapped. Moreover, there are many different abilities that each of us values. There is mental ability (or more reasonably many different mental abilities), physical skill, beauty, aesthetic sensitivities, and virtuous character traits that each of us possesses or lacks in varying degrees. In comparison to an infinite, however, we are deficient in each. Moreover, we are deficient in varying degrees. We are all handicapped, and in some area or another we are likely to be seriously handicapped. To be sure, some of us are going to be more handicapped than others and in aggregate some are going to be relatively talented in a great number of areas. That poses a fascinating problem of how we interpret—to ourselves and others—the fact that some are so richly blessed with many seemingly unrelated talents. (But that is a subject for another volume.) What is important for now is that the differences that assuredly are present are merely differences in degree of deficiency. In comparison to an infinite standard of reference, all finites are equal. We are all handicapped.

According to the egalitarian perspective developed here, all who are deficient in these objectively valued skills that are critical for living are entitled to compensation so that they can be restored as closely as possible to a chance for equality. But, since all are handicapped, all, in principle, are entitled to compensation—or at least they would be were there resources available to meet all the just demands. In the real world of limited resources, not all of the just demands of all members of the community are likely to be met. In fact, we went to some lengths in Chapters 5 and 6 to construct a set of limits to escape the infinite demand problem. What is important, though, is that everyone is, in principle, in the same condition. We all have handicaps that would entitle us to compensation if only the resources were adequate. Since all are in this situation, all are in one class. Everyone is handicapped; no one is part of the group we call "they," no one should be stigmatized.

It might be argued that even though all are handicapped (in the sense of being less than perfect), not everyone will, in fact, receive compensation. Some person (possibly some group) will on balance be best off and that person or group would have no claim. Moreover, to imply that all persons have claims to compensation based on handicap could seriously dilute and weaken the claims of the more seriously afflicted. Isn't the precise point of the equality principle to bring some persons closer to an admittedly somewhat mythical but still culturally and morally indispensable "average" level of well-being?

Two responses to this provocative objection to egalitarianism are in order. First, the goal is not simply to get the less well off up to a mythical average. The goal is to identify the worst off and bring them up to the next group then bring that (now larger) group up seriatim so that the floor continually rises. That means that everyone (except perhaps one hypothetical best-off person) is eventually on the agenda. That in no way dilutes the priority for those nearer the bottom.

Second, even those who are relatively well off might, in fact, be among the worst off if they did not receive the benefits of certain universally available social benefits such as immunizations. Thus everyone is potentially in the category of those to be compensated. In fact, it may be extremely important that at one time or another throughout one's life everyone actually receives some compensation from the community's resources.

In discussing the problem of infinite demand, I argued that one of the limits on distribution to the retarded is posed by the principle of justice itself. We should transfer resources to the retarded only to the point where the diversion would make some other group even worse off than the retarded. In fact, without some basic medical and social service programs—prenatal care, immunizations, and basic primary and secondary education, for example—ordinary citizens may actually be worse off than some more obviously handicapped citizens. We argued that on these grounds, justice would require buying something like a mass public immunization campaign for everyone (of course, including the retarded). If so, everyone is, in fact, a recipient of at least limited distribution of commonly held resources. This does not detract from the high priority egalitarians give to the least well off.

Similarly, social security to protect us in old age is offered to everyone. It is offered for many reasons, but at least one of them is that any one of us could easily be among the least well off if some guarantee of minimal support were not available for us in our old age. It is clear from the experience with social security that it is psychologically very important that everyone (or nearly everyone) be part of the program whether poor or wealthy. Many is the time that reasonably well-off persons have complained bitterly about social security withholding throughout middle age only to recant during their retirement when Medicare or other benefits provided literally life-saving support.

As part of an egalitarian theory designed to give the retarded and others who are among the least well off an opportunity for a start in life that is as nearly equal as possible, it is critical to symbolize our common membership in the community of the finite by making everyone a recipient of at least token support from commonly held funds. It is in the long run in Eddie Conrad's interest as well as that of the rest of us that we acknowledge our deficiencies and our claim on the community that grows out of our finitude. The welfare of the retarded and others with handicaps is served in the long run by acknowledging that we are all in some sense equal in our finitude, that resources are available to meet needs as they arise in order to give people a chance to live out that equality, and that as a community we all share a responsibility for bringing about that restoration.

Notes

1. Erving Goffman, *Stigma: Notes on the Management of Spoiled Identity.* (Englewood Cliffs, N. J.: Prentice-Hall, 1963), p. [i].

2. *Ibid.,* pp. 1–2.

3. *Ibid.,* p. 4

4. *Ibid.,* pp. 12–13, 115.

5. E. M. Lemert, *Social Psychology* (New York: McGraw-Hill, 1951).

6. Howard S. Becker *Outsiders: Studies in the Sociology of Deviance* (New York: The Free Press, 1963).

7. See also Rosalyn Benjamin Darling, *Families Against Society: A Study of Reactions to Children with Birth Defects* (Beverly Hills: Sage Publications, 1979), pp. 30–34; Michale S. Sorgen, "The Classification Process and Its Consequences," *The Mentally Retarded Citizen and the Law, ed. Michael Kindred, et al. (New York: Free Press, 1976), pp. 215–44.*

8. Peter Berger and Thomas Luckmann, *The Social Construction of Reality* (Garden City, N.Y.: Doubleday, 1966).

9. This use of the language parallels the axiologist's distinction between the desired and the desirable where something is desirable if it is rationally or "correctly" desired. John Stuart Mill as well as contemporary axiologists such as Clyde Kluckhohn make this distinction. Clyde Kluckhohn, et al., "Values and Value-Orientations in the Theory of Action: An Exploration in Definition and Classification," *Toward A General Theory of Action,* ed. Talcott Parsons and Edward A. Shils, (New York: Harper & Row, 1951), p. 394.

10. Goffman, *Stigma,* pp. 12, 115.

11. *Ibid.,* pp. 19–31.

12. Ralph B. Potter, "Labeling the Mentally Retarded: The Just Allocation of Therapy," *Ethics in Medicine: Historical Perspectives and Contemporary Concerns,* ed. Stanley Reiser, Arthur Dyck, and William Curran (Cambridge, Mass.: MIT Press, 1977), pp. 626–30.

13. Dyck, Arthur J. "Mental Retardation as a Label: A Problem in Justice," *Linacre Quarterly* 45 (May 1978):111–15.

14. *Ibid.,* pp. 113–14.

15. Laurence B. McCullough, "The World Gained and the World Lost: Labeling the Mentally Retarded," *Ethics and Mental Retardation,* ed. Loretta Kopelman and John C. Moskop (Dordrecht, Holland: D. Reidel Publishing Co., 1984), pp. 99–118.

Index